Topics in Down Syndrome

TEACHING READING to CHILDREN with DOWN SYNDROME

A Guide for Parents and Teachers

Patricia Logan Oelwein

Lotto

happy · sad

angry · afraid

The fat cat sat.

My Schedule			
Period	Time	Subject	Room
1			
2			
3			
4			
5			
6			
7			

WOODBINE HOUSE **1995**

Published by Woodbine House, 6510 Bells Mill Road, Bethesda, MD 20817. 1-800-843-7323.

Copyright © 1995 Patricia Logan Oelwein

Cover illustration & design: Lili Robins

Interior illustrations: Alison Oelwein

Photos on pages iv, 7, 30, 61, 128, 144, 165, 188, 198, 200, 209, and 218 courtesy of CDMRC Media Services

Library of Congress Cataloging-in-Publication Data

Oelwein, Patricia L.
    Teaching reading to children with Down syndrome : a guide for parents and teachers / Patricia Logan Oelwein.
        p.   cm. — (Topics in Down syndrome)
    Includes bibliographical references and index.
    ISBN 0-933149-55-7 (paper) : $16.95
    1. Mentally handicapped children—Education—Reading. 2. Down's syndrome. 3. Reading—Parent participation. I. Title.
II. Series.
LC4620.036 1995
371.92'8—dc20   94-37979
                                CIP

Manufactured in the United States of America

10 9 8 7 6 5

DEDICATION

This book is dedicated to my first class of readers, who taught me how to teach, and taught all of us that children with Down syndrome can, indeed, read. I proudly list you by name, and rest assured that you will proudly read it: Jeff Benson, Christy Byron, Lupita Cano, Patrick Evezich, Glenn Farmer, Aaron Gallant, Scott Gatto, Lori Hawthorn, Bronwyn Joy (B.J.) Hill, Martha Hinojosa, Dennis Holton, and Kari Sellars.

Table of Contents

PREFACE

Twenty-two years ago, when I first started teaching children with Down syndrome, the person with Down syndrome who could read was considered the exception. Today, my experience is that the person with Down syndrome who does *not* read (at least to some degree) is the exception. Most children with Down syndrome are capable of learning to read and should have the opportunity to learn to read (and all other skills that are important, meaningful, functional, and enriching) in programs that are designed to ensure their individual success.

If a child* has been unsuccessful in a reading program, it does not necessarily mean that he is an unsuccessful reader. It may mean that he was unsuccessful in that program; it was not programmed to meet his needs. There are many programs and methods used to teach reading. All of these programs are successful with some children, and some children will be successful in any number of reading programs that are used with them. Indeed, it is not necessary to use the program described in this book for children who do not need special programming and are successful in other programs designed to teach all the intricacies of reading. I do not wish to tamper with success. It's failure that needs fixing.

This book is designed to give parents and teachers of children with Down syndrome and other developmental delays an alternative reading program that offers strategies for success. The basic program described here was developed in the Program for Children with Down Syndrome and Other Developmental Delays in the Model Preschool Center at the Experimental Education Unit, Child Development and Mental Retardation Center, University of Washington, 1971–78. This model program was one of the original programs of the Handicapped Children's Early Education Programs (HCEEP), and was funded for outreach until 1987. During this period the techniques developed were expanded and adapted for use in various educational settings and for all age groups.

This original model program was an early intervention project that served children from birth to six years of age. The goals of the program were to provide innovative early intervention for the children and their families, and to develop educational techniques and strategies that would enhance the child's development and help the family adjust to their child. Because of the children's ages, teaching reading was not one of the original goals of the program. The reading program was developed as a tool for the development of language and was only a small part of the overall program.

I was classroom teacher in the project, and the coordinator was Valentine Dmitriev. I was relating to her how Dennis, who was four years old and did not say words, took a toy dinosaur to a book about dinosaurs and pointed from the toy to the book, communicating that they were the same. We were discussing how remarkable his discrimination skills were, yet how delayed his language was. Dr. Dmitriev said, "Give him a means of communication. Teach him to read."

Being a new teacher and anxious to follow the boss's orders, I set out to teach Dennis to read, using the techniques for teaching discrimination that Dr. Dmitriev had taught me. Dennis soon learned to read his name, Mommy, Daddy, and his brother's name. I heard the first clear word from him when he was reading. Reading became his favorite activity. With the suggestion of the speech clinician, we taught him to sign the words he read. When reading, he verbalized some words, signed some, and for animals, he responded to the

---

* This book focuses on individuals with Down syndrome; unless specified otherwise, the child, adolescent, adult, or student to whom I am referring has Down syndrome. To avoid the clumsy use of "his/her," "she/he," and the like I will alternate the use of each gender by chapter.

Figure P.1. Dennis, four years old, pondering a flash card.

written words with the sound each animal made. His mother wrote in a letter of support for the program that 90 percent of his vocalizations were the words he read and alphabet letters. (See figure P.1.)

Encouraged, and quite excited about Dennis's progress in reading, we started teaching reading to other children in the class, using the same method. We discovered that some children were talented readers and most children in our program could learn to read. Also, we learned that reading could be used to enhance spoken language. We found that most children with Down syndrome were visual learners, and that, in some cases, they could learn a visual language before a spoken language. When the pupils developed discrimination skills to the point that they could discriminate words, we introduced reading—teaching them to read meaningful, functional, words.

Although I receive requests for information about this reading program from teachers, most of the requests I receive are from parents. Parents are usually the most consistent educators in their child's life and face the challenges of meeting their child's educational needs throughout his lifetime. It is parents, in most cases, who provide continuity as the only consistent members of the IEP team, year to year. Their involvement is ongoing, whereas individual teachers have relatively limited time with the child. (If the child did not learn to read this year, then it is someone else's problem next year.) Therefore, I have elected to write this primarily for parents, although there should be a high level of parent-professional collaboration in implementing this or any reading program. Parents and teachers are expected to team together in developing the reading goals and objectives for the child and to provide continuity between home and school to maximize the child's progress in reading. The techniques and strategies presented here can be adapted, at school and at home, to reinforce and supplement other reading programs, if another reading program is chosen for the child, and he needs the additional practice. Most likely, many teachers will already be applying these basic special education principles and are adapting these techniques to supplement the basic curriculum.

In some cases, this program will be used as a "starter" program, to build the child's confidence and to "turn him on" to reading. This early success and comfort with reading will give some children a "jump start." They will learn what reading is about, the value of reading—the practical use and power of the written word and the pleasures it brings. And most important, they will learn that they are capable of solving the "mystery" of the written word. For some of these children, this program will offer a successful beginning that will enable them to move on into a basal reading program. This is especially true for some children who are included in regular classroom instruction. The teacher (or parent) can use some of the techniques in this program to supplement these basal programs, if needed.

In other cases, this program may be the only program in which the child experiences success in reading. When some children move into basal reading programs, the stories they are asked to read (and in some cases the reading concepts presented) do not have meaning to them; these children may not have some of the basic concepts necessary to understand the story, or they are not interested in the story—it is not relevant to them. They often feel defeated and disinterested, and see little value in reading the material; in addition, they do very poorly on comprehension questions. This often leads teachers to say, as I have heard many times, "Well, they can call words, but they do not understand what they read." For these children, incorporating reading as a means of teaching concepts that are useful and meaningful to them will certainly be more valuable than using reading to demonstrate their deficits. This program is an individualized program that is meant to be adapted to meet individual needs and learning styles. Teaching reading using these strategies may be the most appropriate program for these children throughout their education (a lifetime activity for all of us).

There will be a very few children with Down syndrome for whom reading is not a meaningful and useful skill, and for whom it is not feasible. These are usually children who have severe mental retardation and often have other impairments that interfere with learning. They have difficulty understanding language and the use of symbols. They are often unable to relate to others and objects in a meaningful way. If your child fits this description, it would be futile and a waste of his time and yours to pursue reading, for it gives him another area in which to fail.

Our experience has been that we were able to teach most children with Down syndrome to read using the techniques presented in this book. Not all children learned at the same rate, and not all children reached the same reading levels, but all children whose progress we have tracked made progress in reading. In addition, some children had a special "talent" for reading and made rather remarkable progress. In Chapter 1, I summarize some data about the reading abilities of children who have learned to read using this program.

This functional, language-experience approach *adapted* for children with Down syndrome is designed to meet the special needs of children who have difficulty learning to read using traditional programs. (See Appendix A-1 for a description of the basic language experience approach.) It gives these children the option of *learning* to read. It gives them a valuable and powerful tool that leads to their independent functioning. It makes written words concrete tools that facilitate learning, enabling them to organize information, to have access to printed information, and to practice and rehearse material. It helps to compensate for deficits in auditory memory and verbal skills. It can help articulation. It can lead to recreational reading, further enriching their lives. In the long term, it increases employment options. And, success in reading does much to build self-esteem, one of the most critical aspects in the development of any child.

FOREWORD

This book is an important piece of writing. Parents and teachers should welcome it as a significant contribution towards understanding how children with Down syndrome learn, and, especially, how they can be taught to read. The ability to read is crucial to survival in the modern world. We are surrounded by written words. Words direct, instruct, inform, admonish, and entertain. For the person with Down syndrome, even the most rudimentary reading skills can be the lifeline to gainful employment and independence.

In the past it was believed that children with Down syndrome or other mental impairments did not acquire academic skills such as reading because they were not motivated to learn. It was also believed that it was impossible to "motivate" anyone who did not already possess an inherent "inner motivational drive." Assuming, therefore, that a lack of motivation was an irreversible condition associated with mental retardation, it was generally concluded that any attempt to teach children with Down syndrome to read would be a futile endeavor. Fortunately, research has shown that this is not the case.

Given the proper opportunity, every human being, regardless of the degree of mental or physical disability, can learn, at least something. The individual with Down syndrome is no exception. In an educational setting that is geared to meet individual needs, interests, and abilities through a program of systematic, individualized instruction which focuses on performance and not on abstract concepts of motivation, children with Down syndrome do, indeed, learn. In many instances their progress surpasses our most sanguine expectations.

Teaching Reading to Children with Down Syndrome: A Guide for Parents and Teachers tells the reader exactly how to develop and implement such a program. Patricia Oelwein, author and originator of the reading program at the Experimental Education Unit, Child Development and Mental Retardation Center, University of Washington, is an extremely gifted and creative teacher who has spent more than twenty years teaching children with Down syndrome to read. She is also an excellent communicator and instructor of parents and teachers. She writes with clarity, compassion, humor, and enthusiasm.

In Part 1 of her book, Ms. Oelwein describes how children with Down syndrome learn and process information. She explains how one can maximize these children's learning experiences, how to capitalize on their strengths, and how to compensate for deficiencies. Case histories and anecdotes illustrate what the author has to say. This part—an introduction to what follows, the actual reading program—should be read with care. It offers valuable insight that will be most useful to the reader.

Part 2 and Part 3 describe the reading program. It is a detailed, comprehensive presentation of a unique, highly imaginative, and successful individualized reading program. The beauty of the program lies in the versatility: the ease with which instruction can be modified or adapted to meet the specific learning needs and abilities of each pupil.

It has been said that when a pupil fails to learn it is not the fault of the child. It is not the fault of the parent, nor is it the fault of the teacher. Rather, it is the fault of instructional methodology and the program. As a guide to parents and teachers, this book may very well be the key to a successful and pleasant learning experience for parent, teacher, and child.

Valentine Dmitriev, Ph.D.

ACKNOWLEDGMENTS

To acknowledge those who contributed to this book, I must start with the people from the University of Washington who made it possible for me to serve children with Down syndrome, their parents, and their educators: Dr. Valentine Dmitriev, who first gave me the opportunity to teach children with Down syndrome, and whose "tricks of the trade" are well utilized in this book; Dr. Alice Hayden, Dr. Rebecca Fewell, and Dr. Michael Guralnick, project directors who provided the support that enabled me to provide continuous service to this population over a 22–year span.

Special acknowledgments go to: Dr. Harolyn Hatley, Director of Special Education, Dr. Joan Griggs, Instructional Supervisor, and Ms. Grace Dickerson, Special Education Teacher, Desoto County Schools, Hernando, Mississippi, for contributing Appendix A–1: Reading Approaches, Programs, and Materials; Charlotte Bell, Cherie Poyner, Mary Kapter Maher, Ericka Sabaan, Linda Michael, and Marita Hopmann for sharing information and stories; Patrick Evezich, Becca Winger, Reed Hahne, Dan Mitchell, and Glenn Farmer for allowing me to use their writing; all the children, parents, and teachers whose stories have enriched this book; Susan Stokes and the staff at Woodbine House for their encouragement, assistance, and perseverance; my daughter, Alison, for the illustrations for this book—and for creating many of the illustrations in the "original" books, when she was a child; my son, Walter C., for assisting with the photographs, for literary consultation, and for being a wonderful model for "field testing" my ideas during his childhood; and my husband, Walter R., who provided the technical support by keeping things in order and by "picking up the slack" for me, as well as by providing the much needed emotional support throughout this project.

PART 1

Before You Start: Background Information

The focus of this book is on teaching children with Down syndrome to read. Before getting into the specific techniques, instructions, and procedures (Part 2 and Part 3), it is important for you to have a basic understanding of the learning process in general and learners with Down syndrome in particular. The chapters in this section of the book therefore provide background information helpful to know when teaching children with Down syndrome.

Chapter 1

HISTORICAL PERSPECTIVE

Before the late 1960s, research on reading for students with moderate mental retardation was virtually nonexistent (Conners, 1992). The general belief was that children with moderate retardation were only "trainable" and unable to learn academics. They were, therefore, most often placed in classes labeled "trainable." Children with Down syndrome were routinely given this label and placed in these "trainable" classes (in places where these classes were available), based on the diagnosis of Down syndrome, rather than on their abilities. Not only was research on reading for these children virtually nonexistent, but opportunities for them to learn to read were virtually nonexistent as well.

The Exception Was the Reader

When I first started working with children with Down syndrome in 1972, there was little documentation of persons with Down syndrome who could read. The glimmer of hope was the book, *The World of Nigel Hunt.* Nigel Hunt was a young Englishman who had Down syndrome. He wrote an autobiography, supplemented by explanations by his father. His mother taught him to read and his father taught him to type. He was considered the "exception" to the rule that persons with Down syndrome could not learn to read. I respect and admire Mr. Hunt for his accomplishments and feel very grateful to him for his great contribution. (Val Dmitriev used his book as a reference when she wrote the proposal for the original Down Syndrome Program at the University of Washington.) However, I must confess, I do not believe that Nigel Hunt was the exceptional one: his parents were the exception. They gave him the opportunity to learn to read and type.

In the early 1970s, I read another book, *Yesterday Was Tuesday, All Day and All Night,* about a person with Down syndrome who could read. Since that time, I have had the opportunity to know and learn about several adults with Down syndrome, who grew up before the 1970s, who could read and write. Some learned at school, some at home. For the most part, most of these adults' academic accomplishments went unnoticed because their data were not published in professional journals, nor were books published about them. David Dawson was one of these people, unknown to most of us, until he and Jean Edwards told his story in *My Friend, David* (Edwards and Dawson, 1983). These persons with Down syndrome were fortunate enough to have teachers, parents, and others who believed in them and taught them how to read and write.

In 1969, L. Rhodes et al described how reading was used to teach language to children in a state instruction. A "star" of the project was Janet, a little girl who had Down syndrome. They made a movie about Janet, named for a sentence she learned to read, "Janet is a little girl." I saw the movie in an education class, sometime after we had started teaching the children in the preschool to read. It was very encouraging to me to know that others had documented their success at teaching reading to young children with Down syndrome and found it useful in enhancing speech skills.

They taught me to read. When you can read you can go anywhere and do anything.

A young man with Down syndrome spoke to a University class during the 1970s. One student asked him, "What did your parents do for you that you appreciate the most?" His answer was, "They taught me to read. When you can read, you can go anywhere and do anything."

Prejudice

Perhaps the greatest single reason that so few children were taught to read in past decades was simple prejudice. Reading, among educators and the educated, is rather holy and noble, for the "intelligent" and the "accomplished." When individuals with Down syndrome demonstrated that they could read, the consensus was that they had learned to just "call words" and it was sometimes referred to as "just a parlor trick." Because many people with Down syndrome typically have difficulty answering comprehension questions, the conclusion was that they did not understand what they read. Reading was, therefore, a useless skill for them; a waste of time for these students and their teachers. It was considered a disservice to these children for their parents to have such high, "unrealistic" expectations of them.

She could read a medical book, but she did not understand a thing she read.

I read an article that told of a remarkable young woman with Down syndrome who could read a medical book. As I recall, her parents had taken her to the doctor (who wrote the article). When they told him that she was an accomplished reader, the doctor handed her a medical book, and sure enough she could read it. But when he asked her what she had read, she could not tell him. He then wrote the article stating that reading was a useless skill to teach persons with Down syndrome, because they did not understand what they read.

(I, personally, feel very fortunate that no one has made a judgment as to the value of my reading ability, based on how I handled a medical book. I fear that I would have flunked the reading as well as the comprehension test.)

I was so ignorant that I did not know that children with Down syndrome could not read.

One teacher told me that, years ago, when she first started teaching, she had two students with Down syndrome in her special education class. She took them in her "reading group" and taught them to read. These boys lived on farms, and she focused on teaching them to read the names of stock feed (chicken, hog, cow, etc.), so they could help out by feeding the livestock. It changed their lives and their roles within their families. They, and their parents, were thrilled with their accomplishments, as was the teacher. The teacher said that she did not learn until later, when she attended an in-service class, that it was considered inappropriate to teach individuals with Down syndrome to read. She told me, a little misty eyed, "I was so ignorant, I just didn't know better."

(And here I am, years later, still writing rationale for teaching children with Down syndrome to read. I still feel obligated to defend it.)

Some parents may feel incensed when reading the above. I am relating these stories as an example of the general thinking and educational policies before the 1970s. The educators who followed these policies were faithful to the beliefs they were taught, or to the policy of the school. As I stated earlier, reading is not a viable option for all students with Down syndrome (although it is for most). I think that it is important for parents to not dwell on the past and negative experiences they and others have had. Those things cannot be changed; we can only act on the present and future.

What is wrong with those teachers, anyway?

Sherry was 18 years old when she and her mother first came to see me. Her mother was upset because Sherry had not learned to read at school. After a short lesson, Sherry was reading several words, on flash cards and in sentences (she was reading what she wanted to read—about herself and her boy friend). After observing Sherry read, her mother said angrily, "What is wrong with those teachers, anyway? Why didn't *they* do this?"

I advised the mother to forgive the teachers for not having the information they needed, or the wrong information; for not attending the "right" conferences; for not reading the "right" books and journals; for not having the "right" professors; for being too busy or feeling too harassed and overworked to take the time to teach reading; and for anything else that may have made them less than perfect. After all, the mother did not have this information previously either.

I believe that all of us—parents and teachers—do the best we can, with who we are, with what we know at the time. We deserve forgiveness and support. The children deserve the advantage of having teachers and parents who are able to work together in a constructive manner to enhance their education.

The Exception Is the Non-Reader

Now, in the 1990s, I think that it is the non-reader with Down syndrome who is more apt to be the exception. This conclusion is subjective, based on my personal experience with and knowledge of many young adults, adolescents, and children that I know who have had the opportunity to learn to read. When I refer to the "non-reader" I am referring to the person who does not use reading to *function* in his environment; I am not using the usual criteria of literacy, which is at the fifth/sixth grade level (although I know some young people who qualify). I do believe that today, with more enlightened attitudes and inclusive education, most children with Down syndrome are given the opportunity to learn to read, and most are taking advantage of that opportunity. They are learning to read well enough to help them get around in the world, to work, to shop, to follow written directions, to order food, etc., and many read for recreation as well. (A 21-year-old woman with Down syndrome told me that she had read Chris Burke's book, *A Special Kind of Hero,* six times, and she had started reading it again.)

To date, there have been very few formal studies of the reading abilities and achievements of persons with Down syndrome. In 1992, however, F. A. Conners reviewed and analyzed the research on reading instruction for students with moderate mental retardation (only IQ's are given with no reference as to specific disabilities, such as Down syndrome). This article compares sight-word instruction, word-analysis instruction, and oral reading error-correction. Thirty-five studies were analyzed. The reading levels reported in these studies ranged from "nonreaders" and "some sight words" for students whose mean ages ranged from 33 to 7 years, to reading levels as high as 7th grade (3 students, 13-15 years). Conners concludes that sight-word instruction and word analysis instruction for student with moderate mental retardation is feasible and appropriate. She also points out that due to individual differences, no one instructional approach is best for every person with moderate retardation. The exciting news is that these data support teaching children with moderate retardation to read.

One of the few studies in which reading skills of children with Down syndrome in particular were analyzed appeared in *New Perspectives on Down Syndrome*. Reading scores were reported from a randomly selected sample of students with Down syndrome in school districts in Oregon (Fredericks, et al., 1987). Of the nine students, 7 to 13 years of age, seven had some reading ability. The range of level by grade was 1.2 for the 7-year-old to 3.8 for the 13-year-old. These authors point out that a much larger sample is needed to determine if these data are representative of children with Down syndrome. They conclude, however, that reading instruction should at least be *tried* with all students with Down syndrome and that they should be provided with as much reading instruction as needed.

Information is also available on reading skills achieved by students with Down syndrome who learned to read using the program described in this book. In 1981, information on the reading skills of children in an Australian project modeled on the original University of Washington program (Macquarie University Project) was reported. (Pieterse and Treloar). Follow-up data on eight "graduates" of the preschool program showed that their mean reading age was 7.2 (2.2 grade level), with a range of 6 years (1.0 grade level), to 9.4 years (4.4 grade level). At the time, these children had a mean chronological age of 8 years.

Thirteen children (7 girls and 6 boys) who first learned to read in the University of Washington program have been followed formally and informally since they entered the program in the early 1970s. In the spring quarter of 1973, data were first reported for these children. They had a mean age of 4 years, 5 months and had been in the program a mean of 2.5 quarters (approximately 8 weeks of instruction per quarter). The mean number of sight words these children had mastered was 29, with a range of 103 to 10.

The following spring, data were again obtained for the five children (mean age, 5 years, 7 months) from the original group who were still in the sight reading program. The mean number of words these children had now mastered was 53, with a range of 62 to 40. Data were also obtained for four children who had moved on to the phonics program, described in Chapter 10 of this book. (When the children had 50 to 100 words in their sight vocabulary, and could recognize the letters of the alphabet, they were taught phonics.) Three of the children (mean age 5 years, 6 months) had mastered 21 consonant sounds, and one had mastered 19. They were reading preschool readers, such as those in the Dr. Seuss Reading for the Beginning Reader series (Random House). They had mastered (read with 80 percent proficiency) a mean of 3.25 of these books.

In spring 1977, five of the original 13 children were tested on the reading section of the Wide Range Achievement Test (WRAT), which measures word recognition. Their mean reading grade level was 2.5, with a range of 4.5 to 1.9. This was about one year below their mean chronological age of 8 years, 7 months. (The super reader in the group, the youngest pupil, was reading about two years above his chronological age—this skews the mean scores.) In 1983, 6 of the original 13 children were again given the WRAT. This time, their mean grade level was 3.6, with a range of 6.9 to 2.2.

Finally, in 1988, I informally collected data on three more of the original children who had not been tested in 1983. Clara, who was 17 years old at the time, scored on the sixth-grade level in reading on the *Brigance Diagnostic Inventory of Early Development* (1978). Peter, at 18 years old, on the *Woodcock Reading Mastery Test,* Form A (1973), received scores at the seventh grade, sixth month level on word identification and fourth grade, third month on passage comprehension. Sam, who was 17 at the time, was reading at the third-grade level (according to his teacher).

The young people in this original study are now in their mid-twenties. They are working in the community at a variety of jobs where they use their reading skills daily—regardless of the grade level they reached. They use their reading skills constantly: to read the weather report in the paper to determine what to wear; to follow bus schedules and travel independently in the community; to read and write letters, invitations, notes, and speeches; to follow recipes and laundry directions; to find out what is playing at the movies and on TV; to check out and read books from the library; and one young woman is planning to write a book.

Unfortunately, a whole generation of children with Down syndrome have now gone from early intervention to vocational training, and we have only a vague idea of what the providers of education have accomplished for these children during their school years (Zadig, 1987). The data are scarce, but we know, beyond a doubt, that many children with Down syndrome can learn to read when given the chance. In addition, it is the belief of educators and researchers who have taught reading to children with Down syndrome, that: (1) these children should be given the opportunity to learn to read; (2) for those who can learn to read, reading should be a part of their education throughout their school years (and in some cases after); and (3) reading is a valuable skill to them, regardless of how meager it may seem.

Lupita made me cry again!

In the summer before Lupita's fifth birthday, her mother took her to Peru. Her mission, in addition to visiting with relatives, was to inform parents and professionals about the abilities of people with Down syndrome and to raise their expectations and educational opportunities. Lupita was her example of what even young children with Down syndrome could accomplish. When Lupita demonstrated her reading and language abilities, her mother was told by some Peruvian professionals there that there had been a mistake in her diagnosis; children with Down syndrome could not do those things. Her mother continued her campaign to parents. On one occasion, Lupita was reading aloud from her book, *All about Me,* which had been made just for her. As she read each page, she looked up at the parent who was her audience. The woman was not responding to her reading with the usual praise that Lupita had learned to expect. Lupita soon figured out the problem. The woman could not understand English, so she started translating each page into Spanish.

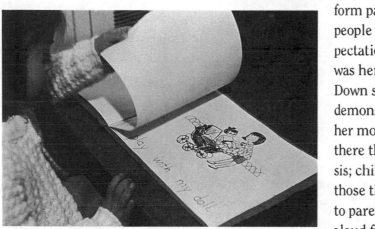

Figure 1.1 Lupita reading the book she translated.

Her mother was so moved by Lupita's perception, she cried, from happiness, of course. How could Lupita translate text written in English into Spanish if she could not comprehend its meaning? It is incomprehensible to me that some people are still saying that people with Down syndrome cannot comprehend what they read! (See Figure 1.1.)

(I recently had a similar experience in Venezuela; a beautiful fifteen-year-old woman with Down syndrome translated a menu into English from Spanish, for me.)

Chapter 2

LEARNING DIFFERENCES AMONG PERSONS WITH DOWN SYNDROME

As Alike as Peas in a Pod?

The more children with Down syndrome you know, the more it is apparent that not all children with Down syndrome are alike. The fewer you know, the more apt you are to generalize that they are all alike, and that their potential is the same. Children with Down syndrome are not all born with identical learning problems, health problems, appearance, and potential, nor are they born in the same environment. All children with Down syndrome have some characteristics (physical, health, appearance, cognitive, and personality) in common with some other (but not all) children with Down syndrome. Some of the variables that contribute to differences are: (1) genetic differences; (2) untreated, uncorrected, or undiagnosed secondary conditions associated with Down syndrome (heart, vision, hearing, thyroid dysfunction, etc.); (3) the occasional presence of additional disabling conditions not associated with Down syndrome (autism, brain damage, attention deficit disorder, fetal alcohol syndrome, etc.); and (4) environmental factors.

Genetic Differences

Genetic mapping is enabling researchers to identify specific genes on the 21st chromosome that cause various differences in persons with Down syndrome. The "dosage" of genetic material that each child receives may determine: if the child has a heart defect, intestinal blockages, vision problems; the degree of mental retardation; immune deficits; risk of leukemia; the link to Alzheimer disease; and other conditions associated with the syndrome (Korenberg et al, 1992). Therefore, two children with Down syndrome who have the same parents, grow up in the same environment, and have the same educational opportunities can be very different individuals with very different potential. One mother I met had two children with Down syndrome: the older child has mild disabilities; the younger child, severe mental and physical impairments. Of course, other factors may be involved, but I think that the major differences in these two children was caused by genetic differences in the "expression" of genes on the 21st chromosome.

I'm half American, half Japanese, and half Down syndrome.

Andrew has a father of Japanese descent and a Caucasian mother. He came to school wearing a T-shirt with USA printed on the front. His teacher asked him what USA meant. He responded, "America." She then asked, "Are you an American?" He said, "Yes, I am an American." He then hesitated, waved his hands to signal, "erase that," and said, "No, wait, wait! I'm half American and half Japanese." He paused, then again, waved his hands, "erasing," and said, "No, no, wait, wait! I'm half American, half Japanese, and half Down syndrome."

Andrew knew that, in addition to what he had inherited from each parent, he had something extra. On that 21st chromosome, he had 150 percent. He had "normal" genes, with "normal" genetic information. He just had too much genetic information on that 21st pair. This extra amount expresses itself differently in different individuals.

Secondary Conditions Associated with the Syndrome

As mentioned above, there is a higher incidence of heart defects, ear/hearing problems, vision problems, thyroid dysfunction, chronic upper respiratory infection, and other conditions that, untreated, can interfere with learning. Most children receive aggressive medical care, and these conditions are successfully treated or corrected. In some cases, however, these problems go untreated, or are unsuccessfully treated, further impairing the child. Sometimes there may be vision problems that are not corrected; ear infections that are not treated; hearing loss not augmented; constant upper respiratory infections or heart defects that sap the child of energy and interest in learning; attention deficit disorder, undiagnosed and untreated; and thyroid dysfunction that goes untreated. These problems, left untreated, can greatly impair *anyone's* learning.

I just don't want him to be placed in special education classes, as I was.

The mother of a child with Down syndrome told me the horrors of her elementary school years in special education. She was placed in special education because she was diagnosed as mentally retarded and emotionally disturbed. It was not until she was 10 years old that someone discovered that she did *not* have mental retardation or an emotional disturbance, but a severe hearing impairment. In her case a simple operation solved her hearing problem, but in the meantime she lost much of her childhood and a great deal of self-esteem. This parent was fearful that her child would be faced with the same inappropriate special education she had received. We must do all that we can to be sure that we are, indeed, treating the real impairment, and that the education is, indeed, special.

The wax build-up in his ears was so great that I don't know how he stood the pain.

When Andrew (by coincidence the same child mentioned above) was four years old, he became aggressive at times and would bite, hit, and kick others. His parents transferred him from his local program to the University of Washington program, hoping for better behavior management expertise. After careful observation of Andrew, the teacher observed that just before his attacks on other people, his face contorted as if he were in pain. She recommended that his parents take him for a complete check-up. The doctor found wax impacted in his ears. He said that there was so much, he did not know how Andrew had withstood the pain. After the removal of the wax, Andrew's "recovery" from his aggression was remarkable. Attacking others was the way he was dealing with his pain.

It is important to determine whether learning and behavior problems are caused by physical conditions that can be treated, and to see to it that your child receives the proper treatment. The best of teaching and behavior management techniques are ineffective in correcting these problems if the cause of the problem is not eliminated.

Additional Disabling Conditions Not Associated with Down Syndrome

In addition to the aforementioned problems associated with Down syndrome, it is possible for children with Down syndrome to have the same prenatal, perinatal, and postnatal injuries that cause mental disabilities and other delays in children who are born with 46 chromosomes. Having Down syndrome does not immunize a child from having these other disabling conditions.

He is the lowest functioning child with Down syndrome I have ever known.

A professor who was consulting with a school district to help develop a program for Charles, an adolescent who had been in the University of Washington program, asked me for my input on the teenager. In explaining the situation, he said, "He is the lowest functioning person with Down syndrome I have ever known." I knew, however, that Charles had been diagnosed as having autism in addition to Down syndrome. It was as inaccurate to put this child in "range of functioning" of children with Down syndrome as it would be to put children with 46 chromosomes who have autism in the range of functioning of children with 46 chromosomes, or typical children. This young person is in a category of his own.

(Charles has dedicated parents who have, throughout his life, provided every advantage available. In spite of the early intervention, special tutoring, special programs, and dedicated follow-through on the part of the parents and educators, his gains have been very minimal.)

The most "severely involved" children—those who do not learn basic self-care skills (feeding, toileting, bathing, and dressing) and do not interact and communicate with others in a meaningful way—often have these additional problems. Some of these children have had meningitis or encephalitis; have epilepsy; have been poisoned with toxins such as lead, alcohol, or drugs; have received head injuries; have had brain tumors; or have experienced other injuries before, during, or after birth.

There are also children with Down syndrome who are not as severely involved, but still have more difficulty than usual learning, attending, and behaving in a socially acceptable manner. These children may have additional handicapping conditions such as attention deficit disorder (ADD), obsessive compulsive disorder, or depression.

Environmental Factors

It is well known that the environment has an important impact on the development of any child. All development stems from interaction between the individual's genetic makeup and her psychological and physical environment. The first two years of life are normally the most active period in brain development. The brain reaches 80 percent of adult size, tripling in bulk as it develops by constructing the complex networks of interconnections needed for learning advanced behaviors (Wishart, 1988). Deprived environments put all children at risk for developmental delays, and would certainly compound the delays that are often seen in children with Down syndrome. Children growing up in deprived environments are often the same children who do not receive the needed medical care mentioned above. A nurturing and enriching environment that fosters the child's development and puts her "in tune" with the world and others certainly enhances the child's development and ability to learn.

Interaction is the basis for all learning. A child cannot learn the basics necessary for learning if her environment does not facilitate interaction—that is, if her efforts to communicate are not "read" and responded to, and if she does not "read" and respond to the communications of others. If positive interactions with others (verbal or nonverbal) are not well established, the child needs to learn this before she can be expected to learn more complex communication systems such as reading. Therefore, if your child is not interactive, it is important to establish this interaction before expecting her to learn how to function in her world. You may want to work on the techniques of "turn taking" described on the left to help establish this interaction.

Early intervention programs have been instrumental in providing support, information, and techniques that parents often need to feel confident and competent in parenting their child with Down syndrome and in meeting her special needs. These programs deserve much credit for their impact on the children and their families; they have been instrumental in changing attitudes about Down syndrome and demonstrating the potential of children with Down syndrome.

Turn Taking

"Turn taking" is a set of procedures in which the more skilled communicator (the adult) observes the child carefully and follows her lead, letting her initiate the "topic" and level of interaction. The adult responds to the child by imitating her, then waiting for her to take the next turn, and after she has, the adult again takes his turn. When this interaction is established, the child and adult are taking turns, as in a tennis match, with the ball going back and forth. The adult can then, on his turn, expand on what the child does (or says) and take it farther by modeling a higher level of response or play.

For example, if the child throws a block, the adult imitates her by throwing a block, then waits to see what the child does on her next turn. (This usually gets the child's attention, and she becomes very interested in the fact that *she* has the power to influence what an adult does. I have found that children often "test" their power by doing some very interesting things, just to see if the adult will, indeed, follow her lead.) The adult repeats what the child does on her second turn, and so on, until the turn taking is going smoothly (the tennis match is going well with the ball going back and forth). Once the child is engaged in the activity, the adult, on his turn, may drop a block in a container (a higher level skill). Then the child does what she wants to on her turn. Often, the child will respond by imitating the adult. If not, the adult may want to go back to the child's level, to be sure they are still "communicating" and on the same topic ("block throwing"). (If the adult continues to put her blocks in a container on his turn and the child continues to throw, they are not on the same "topic." The adult, the more skilled communicator, needs to make the adjustment and try "dropping" later.)

On his turn, the parent can also add a sound, or expand on a sound the child makes. For example, if the child says "ba," the adult repeats it and waits, with an expectant expression, for another response from the child. (The adult does not keep saying it over and over, taking all the turns, as in a dart game.) If the child repeats "ba" and the interaction partners start saying "ba" back and forth, then the adult may say "block" (or ball, or bubbles, or whatever the child is interacting with or seems to be trying to say), and then wait for the child to take her turn. If waiting is too difficult, the adult may prompt the child to take a turn by watching closely with an expectant expression. If this doesn't work, he may then cue the child and say, "Your turn." Likewise, if the child starts taking all the turns, the adult may cue her and say, "My turn."

For more information on teaching turn taking, see either Susan Sandall's video *My Turn, Your Turn* (available from CDMRC Media, University of Washington, Seattle, WA 98195) or Dr. Libby Kumin's book *Communication Skills in Children with Down Syndrome* (available from Woodbine House, 6510 Bells Mill Rd., Bethesda, MD 20817/800-843-7323).

Not just early, continuous.

Although early intervention *is* important, on its own, it is not enough. Continuous intervention is needed throughout your child's education. Very few of us would expect an outstanding preschool for our typical children to have so great an impact that we need not be concerned about the quality of their elementary, secondary, vocational, or college education. Learning is a lifetime experience, and most children with Down syndrome will need support to help them learn throughout their lifetime. Therefore, an enriching environment conducive to learning is important during all stages of life. High quality, challenging, early, and continuous education bridges the gap between potential and performance for *all* children throughout their lives. There are actual physical differences in brains that are stimulated and kept active—we must use it or lose it.

Studies conducted all over the world have shown that the more education someone has, the less likely that person will suffer from memory-robbing disorders such as Alzheimer's disease. For example, Marilyn Albert, a Harvard neuropsychologist, studied 4,000 elderly Bostonians from 1988 to 1991. She noted that the risk of developing Alzheimer's disease declined 20 percent for every additional year of formal education these people had had. This may be because the *synapses*—the connections that allow one brain cell to communicate with another—are influenced by a person's experiences. Synapses that are used in learning new information grow stronger, while those that are not used grow weaker. The brain physically changes, acquiring more synapses as the person has more experiences.

All brains are limited by genetic endowment. Due to the impact of the extra genetic information on the 21st chromosome, the brains of people with Down syndrome are more limited than usual. Clearly, this makes it doubly important that children with Down syndrome keep their brain working and active. We want them to keep making new synapses and not lose any old ones. I believe that reading gives a means to exercise the brain, to make new synapses.

I am a strong advocate for early and continuous intervention. It has been the focus of my professional life for the past 20 years. But I must caution parents not to make judgments about their child's potential and ability to learn based on a deprived environment. The first child with Down syndrome that my colleague, Val Dmitriev, taught to read was a seven-year-old girl who was institutionalized.

There have been many people with Down syndrome who grew up in institutions and were able to make the transition into the mainstream. I know of a woman who learned to drive a car, follow complex directions given over the phone, and take care of and serve as interpreter for a woman with cerebral palsy (whose articulation was such that only this young woman with Down syndrome could understand her).

And when he crawled across the floor there was not a dry eye in the room.

Years ago, James, a four-year-old with Down syndrome, entered the program at the University of Washington. He had been placed in a foster home that provided him with only custodial care. He was what was referred to as a "crib baby," as that is where he had spent the first four years of his life. He could not sit independently, and his head dropped when he was held in a sitting position. He had been only bottle-fed and refused solid foods. He did not make eye contact with people and objects, and he seemed interested only in engaging in self-stimulating behavior. He was a good example of what a deprived environment can do to a child. I never met his first foster parents, but they most likely thought that because he had Down syndrome, he would not be able to do anything anyway, and needed nothing more than custodial care. When he came to the University of Washington program, he had been placed in a different foster home (these new foster parents later adopted him). With intensive help (we were able to provide one-to-one instruction for him and his family) and a nurturing, "inspired" family, he made remarkable gains. In time, he learned to walk, feed and dress himself, play, make friends, talk, and, yes, read.

Perhaps the most moving moment in the program occurred one day when James was sitting on the floor across the room from the door when his special teacher, Chuck, walked in. James looked up at him, smiled, and crawled to Chuck as fast as he could. We all knew that this was a most significant moment. He had bonded to his teacher and recognized him as an individual. And he had the skill to reach him. James was going to make it. He was going to be an active participant in his world. And there was not a dry eye in the room.

Of course, we must acknowledge that the children in these examples would have achieved much more sooner, and most likely would have achieved more later, and they would definitely have lived a higher quality of life, had they not experienced these deprived environments. Also, in the case of James, we do not know if there would have been a point in his life where he would have experienced so much damage, that he could not learn basic skills. The point is: because a child comes from a deprived environment does not mean that she is not an able learner. Her deprived environment (or even the lack of early intervention) has not taken away *all* of her potential. It is inhumane and immoral to neglect and deprive a child of basic needs and opportunities to develop, but if this has happened, *all* is not *always* lost.

If only she had had early intervention.

I am making this point because I do not want parents to think that they have put their child's ability to learn in jeopardy because she was not in an early intervention program (or the *right* early intervention program). And I do not want teachers to think that a child with Down syndrome cannot learn because she has not received "readiness" skills in early intervention programs. Each child's Individualized Education Program (IEP) should be based on individual needs, not on generalized or preconceived ideas as to the child's potential based on her diagnosed disability and her previous education. We are not going to worry about what should have been done in the past, or what was not done. We cannot change the past; we *can* change, or "act on," the present and future.

I did the best I could, with who I was, with what I knew at the time.

Some parents have expressed remorse to me about decisions they have made concerning their child's early experiences, education, or behavior management. They feel responsible for all their child's problems and think that if only they had known better and had done things differently, their child would not be having the problems she has now; they think their child would be like another child they know (or saw in a video tape, or read about) who also has Down syndrome, but has accomplished much more. Chances are very good that these parents have actually done a good job parenting their child. Remember that environment is not the only variable. I do believe that most parents (and teachers) do the best they can, with who they are, with what they know at the time. For parents (and teachers) I recommend the self-forgiveness affirmation that I learned from our local mental health advisor, Jennifer James: "I did the best I could, with who I was, with what I knew at the time." Forgive yourself for any mistakes that you think you may have made in the past. Forgive teachers and other professionals for being less than perfect as well. Put your energy in today and tomorrow. You have another chance.

Chapter 3

TEACHING CHILDREN WITH DOWN SYNDROME

How Do You Teach a Child with Down Syndrome?

As stated earlier, children with Down syndrome are not all like two peas in a pod. They do not all have the same potential, as with the population in general, and not all children with Down syndrome learn the same way or have the same learning impairments. That is why we have Individualized Education Programs (IEPs), to meet these special needs. I receive many calls from parents and educators asking me how to teach children with Down syndrome, or how to manage their behaviors. There is no such thing as a *Down Syndrome Education Plan* or *Down Syndrome Behavior Management Plan*. We need to work on applying basic educational and behavioral principles to individuals, based on individual needs and learning characteristics. The child's success is the key. If the child is successful in learning what we are teaching, then we know we are on the right track. If the child is experiencing little or no success, then we know that we need to examine the curriculum (IEP) and determine if the skills and concepts being taught are meaningful and useful to the child, and/or if our instructional techniques and programming are designed to meet the individual learning differences of the student.

It is important to remember that the curriculum for regular education students is determined by the school district. The curriculum for the special education students is determined by the *student*. This curriculum is the IEP. That is why special education is *special*. We *can* plan a program to meet individual and unique needs. If this individualized program is not successful, then we must figure out why not and make changes so that it is. If the child fails in a program developed just for him, then something is wrong with the program. Special education is a *service,* not a *placement.* A child should receive the support of the special education services wherever he is placed, and the IEP should be designed to help him to belong and grow in all his environments. Teachers should not be expected to teach the child without support and a plan, the IEP. Objectives should be written for each period of the school day. The teacher needs a plan so she will know what objectives will be met during each period, and what is expected of her and the learner throughout the day: Just what is the learner going to learn in each period? (Is he going to have the same objectives as his classmates and receive the same instruction as his classmates—get it the "regular way"? Will he have the same objectives, but need adaptations? Will he be working on different objectives than his classmates during some periods? During what periods will he need the support of an aide? Of peers? Of volunteers?

If, for example, one of the child's goals is to increase his reading skills, an objective may be: Jeremy will receive 15 minutes of systematic instruction from his aide during the reading period; he will practice reading words and comprehension by playing reading games with peers and alone on the computer during the activities period; at each transition, he will consult a schedule with written words and symbols and tell the teacher what is going to happen next; he will complete a "yes" and "no" journal during journal period and consult the calendar and circle the day of the week on the journal page. Depending on his progress, the IEP will be updated to include, perhaps: During Morning Exercises, Jeremy will call roll and read the school menu once a week (not on the same day); he will follow a written schedule without symbols; during social studies, he will assemble materials for the class using a written list.

Now you know how we felt when we first had her.

During a team meeting about a child who was to be included in a kindergarten class, the kindergarten teacher said, "Frankly I am scared. I don't know how to teach this child, what to expect of her, or how to deal with her behaviors." A father of another girl with Down syndrome who was also at the meeting responded, "Now you know how we felt when we first had her. We were scared too. We did not know how to parent her, what to expect from her, or how to deal with her behaviors, but we learned. You will learn too."

This father had the support of an early intervention program and the child's team. The "regular" classroom teacher should have the support of the child's team—the special education service and the parents—to help her learn how to meet the child's needs as well. Parents often forget how devastated they were when they first learned that their child had Down syndrome, and that the "regular" education teacher is much like they were, unprepared for this child with special needs. Special education teachers are comparable to parents who adopt children with Down syndrome; these parents and teachers made a decision to care for and serve these children—it was their choice. The birth parents are comparable to "regular" education teachers; caring for and serving these children was not what they were prepared to do—it was not their original choice—it was something they needed to learn about, after the fact. Parents and "regular" education teachers learn that the child is a child first, a unique individual to cherish and nurture through the learning and growing process. Understanding and caring about *children* is the key. Basic developmental, behavioral, and educational principles apply to children with special needs as well. We need to learn to individualize, to make adaptations, and to apply special techniques and strategies to meet special learning needs.

We must all be able and willing learners, if we are going to be effective in teaching the child with special needs. We must learn to learn from the child: to learn to respond to and adapt to his cues (rather than expecting the child to always respond and adapt to ours); to learn how the child learns best—through visual or auditory stimuli—and develop materials and techniques to maximize his learning; to learn to teach him how to compensate for his impairments, (rather than to try to fix them or ignore them); to learn to recognize when our instruction is ineffective or inappropriate for the child, and be willing to change our approaches; to learn what we can teach the child that will be most useful and meaningful to him, and be willing to change his curriculum to meet his needs; and to learn how to apply basic learning and behavioral principles to the individual, given his differences. We can grow and learn with the child and learn to meet his special needs. We are most afraid of what we know the least about. Become a expert on your child or students. Celebrate his differences and meet the challenge of educating him with confidence. Remove the fear. When the teacher is successful, the student is successful. When the student is successful, the teacher is successful. They are both learners, and there is great joy in learning.

But Don't They Usually Plateau?

I think he has plateaued, like they usually do.
She didn't plateau, like they usually do.
We will change her placement next year, because she will plateau and no longer benefit from the inclusive classroom.

I received a phone call from a teacher asking for help with a child named Brandon. When I asked her what the problem was, she said, "Well, he has had the same IEP goals for three years. I think he has plateaued, like they usually do." On another occasion, when I was gathering follow-up-data, I called the teacher of a former student, Kate, who was 15 years old. This teacher answered enthusiastically, "She is reading at the sixth-grade level, writing stories, and learning division. She didn't plateau like they usually do." Recently, a mother called me and inquired about the plateauing. The special education director had recommended that her daughter, Beth, be transferred from the inclusive classroom, where she was making good progress, to a self-contained classroom, because she was ten years old and "would be plateauing and no longer benefit from the inclusive classroom."

I can understand why teachers and special education directors expect the plateauing. There have been studies over the years that have documented that many children with Down syndrome plateau—that is, they display a pattern of advances and declines in their rate of development in specific areas. One study reported that grammatical development plateaued between the ages of 7.5 and 10.5 years (Fowler, 1988). Another study found alternating advances and declines in the rate of cognitive development from approximately 8 to 11 years and slowing again during adolescence (Gibson, 1966). Recently, researchers have reported data that indicate that the relationship between chronological age and adaptive age is stronger during the early years and weaker during the middle childhood years, with a general plateau between 7 and 11 years. (Dykens, et al., 1994). That is, skills are generally more age appropriate in younger children than in older children. These researchers stressed, however, that not every child plateaued during the middle years, indicating different developmental patterns among individuals with Down syndrome.

Other researchers have found that children with Down syndrome show relatively stable development during portions of their childhood and adolescent years (Loveland and Kelly, 1988, 1991 and Carr, 1988). John A. Connolly (1978) suggested that a lack of extended educational opportunities (placement in vocational-training environments) may account for the decrease in intellectual function in individuals with Down syndrome during the adolescent years. He stated that the "evidence of decreasing ability with increasing age has been misinterpreted in the literature."

I agree with Mr. Connolly. I believe that much of the plateauing, or decline in the rate of development, is due to educational programs that do not continue to meet the educational needs of individual students. I also believe that the data have been misinterpreted, as in the case of Beth, whose special education director wanted to change her placement because she *expected* her to plateau because she had Down syndrome. The data from children in some studies should not be used to make programming and placement decisions for other children who also happen to have Down syndrome. ***Each child's IEP should be developed based on his own demonstrated present performance, not on the assumed long-term potential of other children who have been in studies.***

We should not assume that Brandon "plateaued" because he was destined to because he has Down syndrome; that Kate failed to because she was an exception to the plateau rule; or that Beth is going to because of her age. However, I will acknowledge that the "plateauing" does happen with not just a few children with Down syndrome. (I know that "Denial ain't just a river in Egypt" [Franken, 1992], and it will not help you for me to be there.) As always, we need to be alert and observe the child, and when the child is not making progress, we should do our best to try to figure out why and do what we can to help him. The problem could be programmatic or medical. I think there is even a *possibility* that some children get a "dosage" of a gene that causes them to "plateau," just as some get the "dosage" that causes a heart defect, etc. (wild speculation, only). I *wish* that I knew the reason; however, I do not. But I believe that we should explore the possibilities of a child's lack of progress before we sit back, fold our hands, and say, "Well, he's plateaued, just as expected. There is nothing we can do but wait for him to pull out of it." We need to check out the possibilities that we can do something about.

Programmatic Problems

Perhaps the difference in Brandon and Kate was that the curriculum (IEP) presented to Kate was useful and meaningful to her, and the techniques the teacher used were appropriate for Kate's learning abilities and style. If Kate's teacher had taught another student with Down syndrome, and he "plateaued," this student may have found the curriculum (skills being taught, IEP objectives) not meaningful, useful, or developmentally appropriate. Or the techniques and methods used may not have been appropriate for his learning abilities.

It is not unusual for parents (and sometimes teachers) to report that a student has not reached an IEP goal for three years. We need to learn to make educational decisions based on the child's responses to our instruction and to the cues he gives us. Three years is a long time to wait to explore the possible causes and do something about it. Chances are, the student has learned more than the educators have over the three years, although this learning is not reflected in his IEP. The problem is, the student has not learned what the educators intended to teach him.

What has the student learned during these three years with the same IEP? Most likely he has learned something that is very useful to him. Students often learn how to avoid failure by finding a means to escape from lessons that are not meaningful and useful to them, and/or are not appropriate for their learning capacity and style (or just too hard for them, or too boring). In this case, it is obvious that he has *not* spent three years working hard on the IEP goals and objectives that were developed and planned for his success, or that the educators responsible for his education learned from the student and changed the program to better meet his needs. The IEP is an on-going process of assessment, setting goals and objectives, planning and implementing programs to meet these goals and objectives, evaluating the student's progress toward meeting these goals and objectives, and developing new goals and objectives based on the evaluation (student progress, or lack of progress).

Avoidance Behaviors and Learned Helplessness

Some children with Down syndrome learn behaviors that are effective for avoiding learning situations where the tasks are too difficult, too easy, or too much trouble for them. They frequently develop these strategies at an early age and continue to use them throughout their lives, if these behaviors continue to be effective in getting them out of the lesson or task. This avoidance behavior is sometimes referred to as "learned helplessness." Distract the teacher, refuse to cooperate, or find another agenda, and you don't have to do it (and you avoid failure). Likewise, find ways to avoid getting dressed and ready for school in the morning, and Mom or Dad will do it for you. The child has learned how to be helpless. And it works, but he does not learn the skills that will be most beneficial to him and allow him to develop independence.

(Of course, he may not see it that way; he may like having a servant and has found a way to have one without learning how to make the money to pay for one. In addition, he can maintain an intimate relationship and interaction (one-on-one attention) during this time. Group home staff members have told me that some of their adult residents with Down syndrome still require someone to dry and dress them. Now who is the smart one here? How many of us can afford a personal maid? These adults are living like someone who is independently wealthy. All their needs are met with little effort on their part. They don't even have to worry about "keeping the help." When I suggested a program for teaching an adult with Down syndrome to dry and dress himself to a group home staff member, his response was, "That's too much trouble; I'd rather just dress him." This staff member did not want to bother learning and implementing a program. He was avoiding learning as well, and chose the option that took the least effort on his part. In the short term, it may be more cost effective to dry and dress the resident, because it takes less time; in the long term, it will be more cost effective to teach him to dress independently, because he should become independent and require no help at all.)

An Edinburgh study found that preschool children with Down syndrome learned to avoid attending to cognitive tasks that were too difficult or too easy for them by developing compensatory social behaviors (Wishart, 1989). The typical "switching out" behaviors the children in this study used to divert the adult's attention were: catching the eye of the adult and staring or smiling fixedly at her; clapping their hands; blowing raspberries; or performing other "party tricks." Such behaviors not only interfere with learning but also make obtaining accurate test scores difficult or impossible. Children using such strategies will sometimes be found "untestable" or show declines or no gains in learning. Their true potential, skills, and knowledge remain unknown. This misuse of these "social skills" increases a child's handicaps, and, of course, can be interpreted as plateauing. The child has plateaued. What he has learned (avoidance behaviors) has interfered with his development, and he is not moving forward by learning new developmental tasks.

These "social skills" may continue to work for some children as they get older. I have worked with and observed elementary-age and teenage students who still use these strategies quite successfully. However, these strategies sometimes stop working for older students when they are in more "group learning" situations. In order to avoid the lesson, or to get the teacher's attention, they may need to learn to use more powerful, noticeable behaviors. These behaviors can be very undesirable.

Examples of typical adaptive behaviors used to escape lessons or to get attention are: refusing to attend and respond (general non-compliance and withdrawing); "acting out" (shouting, running around the room, destroying materials); escaping (running out of the room) and hiding; lying or sitting on the floor and refusing to move; and behaving aggressively. Students who use these behaviors have learned a lot. We just don't like what they have learned, and we can't check it off on the IEP. So, when changes are made in the IEP, they are usually changes that state the "inappropriate" behaviors, and the objectives are to eliminate these behaviors. These are the very behaviors that work for the student, however, and that the educators have inadvertently taught by reinforcing them. By using these behaviors, the student *did* get out of the lesson (running around the room and doing school work are incompatible), and/or the teacher came *right away* (he received her undivided attention, even though it was not necessarily pleasant). If the behavior that works for him is eliminated, and no acceptable substitute behavior is taught, he will most likely learn another behavior to replace the old one, and it may be even more undesirable than the old one. (Perhaps he will learn that hitting the child next to him works as well as running around the room.)

If undesirable behaviors are a problem, the IEP should be changed to state the "substitute" behaviors that the child will learn to use in order to meet the needs that the undesirable behaviors now meet. First, however, you need to determine what these needs are—attention getting or escape behaviors. (These two broad classes of behavior—attention-seeking, controlled and maintained by positive reinforcement, and escape behavior, maintained and controlled by negative reinforcement—are the most common causes for disruptive and undesirable behaviors).

When writing the IEP, the substitute behavior should be stated in the objectives. For example, an objective may state, "John will call the teacher by name, when he wants her to come to him." Or, "John will say, 'Am I doing okay?' when he wants teacher approval or attention." Or, "John will say, 'Help me,' when the task is too hard." Or, if John is nonverbal, "John will ring a bell, when he wants teacher attention." Or, "John will ring the bell for teacher attention, then sign 'help me,' when he needs help." Of course, the teacher needs to be committed to encouraging these behaviors by responding to them as immediately as she responded to the undesirable behaviors. During the period of learning these new behaviors, they need to work *better* than the old behaviors. Delays ("I'll be with you in just a minute") can be added after the student has learned the replacement behavior and found it effective. The student now has to learn to wait (and that can be written in his IEP as well).

In summary, the program may be to blame for a child's apparent plateauing. How the child is functioning in this program needs to be observed and evaluated carefully. Next, program changes should be made based on these observations and evaluations, as well as the child's performance, learning style, and interests. The information and skills taught should be *appropriate, useful, and meaningful to the student*.

Medical Problems

There may be medical causes for the "plateauing" instead of, or in addition to, the programmatic reasons. As mentioned before, there are many possible medical problems that may cause changes in a student's rate of progress: hearing loss; vision problems; chronic illnesses; hypothyroidism; depression; and attention deficit disorder are possibilities. These causes (and other rarer causes, such as brain tumors) should be ruled out. And, of course, diagnosed, treatable problems should be treated.

A plateau may be a place that some children with Down syndrome will visit, but don't expect and encourage them to live there. Learning is a lifetime experience for people who have Down syndrome, just as it is for those who do not.

Chapter 4

THE LEARNER WITH DOWN SYNDROME

The Learning Process

Several steps go into the learning process. First there is the *input* of sensory information—information gathered by seeing, hearing, touching, tasting, or smelling. Then there is *perception*—the processes of organizing and interpreting sensory information, enabling us to give meaning to objects and events. Next is the *storage* of our perception of the sensory input in our memory. Last, there is *output* (response)—retrieving and using the information we have stored.

At any given time, we could be seeing, hearing, touching, smelling, and tasting—or doing any combination of these things. Usually, we are able to filter out the information that is not important and focus on the events and objects in our environment that are most important to us at the moment. We rely on our "filtering system" to help us determine just what is important to enter and store in our memory. Some of this information is entered automatically; other information needs rehearsal before it is stored. As the information is entered into our memory, it needs to be organized (related to other information on the subject) and stored, so we can retrieve it when we need it.

This system is often compared to a computer, and it is very much like a computer, except it's better. Someone has to tell a computer exactly what to remember, but much of the information stored in our memory is put there automatically. In addition, a computer has a limited number of bytes (memory) and has to be told what to remember and delete, whereas we can learn and remember a limitless amount. We are able to automatically forget the things that we no longer need to remember, to make room for new, needed information. (Can you imagine how cluttered your brain would be if you remembered everything you had for dinner each day of your life, what you wore each day, the songs you heard each day, news events of each day, etc.?) To retrieve information from a computer, we must enter precisely correct requests before it will give the information back to us; our files can be recovered by any number of commands—we are much more flexible.

A child with Down syndrome may have difficulty with each of the processes described above. Her sensory input may not be acute (due to poor eye sight or hearing, or taste and smelling dulled by bad colds, etc.). She may have perception problems. That is, much of what she sees, hears, touches, smells, and tastes may have little or no meaning to her. (She may lack concepts of objects and events, or may not have the vocabulary to label them). Her filtering system may not be automatic—she may not instinctively know what information in the environment is important to attend to at any given time. She may not have the time she needs—or adequate information—to organize events and objects and store them, making retrieval impossible or very difficult. Information not retrieved cannot be used.

A computer or a bucket?

I will share with you an analogy that Robbie Blaha gave during a 1988 lecture on common learning differences among children who are deaf and blind (and often mentally retarded as well) often experience. She explained that we have this wonderful file that enables us to store and retrieve information about any subject that we have a file on. She gave the example of the subject of "Halloween." Just seeing (or hearing) the word very likely stimulates you to retrieve from your Halloween file all sorts of information about Halloween and experiences that you and others you know, have had on Halloween. Within this Halloween file, there are sub-files: Halloween decorations and colors; parties you have attended and traditional Halloween party activities; traditional foods and beverages served on Halloween; costumes; customs and history concerning Halloween celebrations; "trick or treating," etc.

Ms. Blaha said that the children that she works with most often do not have files: they have buckets. This graphic analogy helped me to understand some of the differences that many children with Down syndrome have. For example, if you ask a child with Down syndrome to tell you what she did on Halloween, she may not find Halloween in her file, with all the exciting things she did stored there under Halloween for easy retrieval. She may have stored her memories without a category (such as Halloween), without any organization, like grains of sand in a bucket, making retrieval difficult or impossible for her. She may remember that she went "trick or treating" when asked, "Did you go trick or treating?" Or that she was a black cat, when asked, "Were you a black cat?" However, she may not remember that the day was called Halloween, or that the two events (wearing the costume and going trick or treating) were related to each other or Halloween, or that what she wore was called a costume. If asked, "What costume did you wear?" she may not have a costume file, and would not be able to retrieve this information.

Some children with Down syndrome do not have the concepts to understand the meaning of events or information. In addition, they may not have the vocabulary to assign file names to information for retrieval, or they are unable to consolidate new information with old, storing it away in a category, or file, so it can be retrieved. We need to focus on helping these children learn to organize information so that they can effectively file, store, and retrieve it. (This is why I use so many lotto and bingo games to teach reading and have the lessons in this book organized in units by category.)

Re-learning previously learned concepts?

In 1988, Jennifer Wishart reported that some children with Down syndrome who were three to five years old could not initially do certain cognitive tasks that other children with Down syndrome could do by age three years. With practice, however, these three- to five-year-olds learned to do the tasks in just *two months*. This was a remarkably short period of time, considering that it takes normally developing children (at a younger age) *two years* to unfold the mysteries of these tasks. Ms. Wishart speculates that these children were actually *re-tuning* earlier learning that had not been adequately consolidated when first acquired. With practice, they remembered, or re-learned the task. Perhaps this is because it took them a while to find that file and retrieve the previously learned information. They obviously had not used it enough to have consolidated it well and have it readily available for retrieval to apply to new learning situations.

It was Teacher Pat!

Some parents have told me that their children with Down syndrome have remarkable long-term memories. Most likely the information remembered was practiced, filed, used, and stored well. I, too, have experienced these good memories in children with Down syndrome.

Christy, a student in a preschool class I taught, learned to read and had a number of sight words in her reading vocabulary. When she turned five years old, she returned to her local school district to attend school. A year and a half later, her mother called me, concerned, because Christy's current teacher had very low expectations for her. This teacher was delighted that Christy could paste a circle, square, and triangle on a piece of paper, a skill that Christy had learned three years earlier. At my suggestion, her mother brought Christy to see me, so I

Figure 4.1. Christy, on the right, and her friend Debbie, in preschool. Recently, these young women served on a panel at a conference where they told of their jobs in the community.

could teach her how to continue with Christy's reading program at home.

When Christy came in she was shy, and her responses to conversation were minimal and soft. After a short review, however, she was able to read all the words I had taught her over a year and a half before (they had been consolidated). When she was leaving, she walked around the hall corner, out of my sight, and exclaimed loudly to her mother, with great joy, "It was Teacher Pat!"

Oh, those wonderful joys of teaching! She not only remembered the words, but she remembered me as well. Today, as a young adult, she still likes to share her successes with me. Newspaper clippings of her achievements decorate my office door. (See figure 4.1.)

Tell Laura what you are really looking forward to doing when you get older.

A researcher, Laura, called to thank me for a wonderful Saturday. She told me that she had seen several young people with Down syndrome I had referred to her, and that they were all delightful. She told me this story:

Eliot, who was 14 years old, came in with his mother. His mother was encouraging him to engage in a conversation with Laura. She said, "Tell Laura what you are looking forward to doing." Eliot thought, searching his "things-I-want-to-do file," and looked blankly at his mother for another category or retrieval cue. She said, "What are you *really* looking forward to doing when you get *older?*" Then, he reached into his "what-I-am-looking-forward-to-doing-when-I'm-*older* file," and he responded with great confidence, "Oh ya', I want to have sex!"

His mother wanted him to tell his plans for learning to drive a car. Next time, I am sure, she will use some more precise file retrieval cues (maybe jingle her keys). Eliot gave an honest response, one that most boys his age would have "filtered" out as something that his mother would not want him to say to a researcher. But then, it is these surprises and honest responses that make being with young people with Down syndrome so delightful and refreshing.

The ferry boat left a quarter under my pillow.

When seven-year-old Ben related his experience of placing his tooth under his pillow and finding a quarter there the next morning, he said that the ferry boat had left it. Ben lived on an island, and he made frequent trips on the ferry. Therefore, he very likely had an extensive "ferry boat" file, but his "tooth fairy" or "fairy" file was limited, or nonexistent. When his mother told him the tooth fairy would leave him money for his tooth, his filtering system picked up "ferry," and he put the information in his ferry boat file, where he found it when he related the experience. Ben is a smart boy and has a good filing and retrieval system. He just did not have enough information to file it properly (it was given to him verbally). If he had seen a picture of a tooth fairy, he would have had some addition sensory input. His perception of a tooth fairy very likely would have had more meaning and he would have started a new file. (I am sure that his mother took care of this little matter, once she realized what happened.)

Operant Learning

Learning that takes place as a result of the influences of the environment is referred to as "operant learning." This learning is measured by a change in behavior. (A behavior is anything we do that can be observed and measured.) When we can see a change in behavior and can measure this change, then we know that learning has taken place. Baby John could not hold his head up, but now he holds it up 45 degrees for two minutes at a time. Milly would say only nonsense sounds, but now she says 12 words. Steve could not walk, but now he runs all over the place. Vicki could not read, but now she reads over 200 sight words. In all of these cases, operant learning took place. All of these children learned new behaviors because of their experiences with the environment. The environment provided both the *opportunity* and the *motivation* for the children to learn new behaviors.

Opportunities to learn are usually provided through materials and instruction. Motivation is provided by "rewarding events" (praise, food, desirable objects, fun) that make the learner *want* to do the task. A rewarding event that encourages a learner to do a specific behavior, and that is *contingent* on the performance of this behavior, is referred to as *reinforcement*. For example, a child might be given her favorite dessert of chocolate peppermint ice cream whenever she stays in her seat during dinnertime instead of getting up and running around. The reinforcement is getting the ice cream for behaving as her parents wish.

It is important to understand that if an event does not maintain or increase the desired behavior, then it is not reinforcing to the learner. Something that may be very reinforcing for one individual may not be reinforcing for another. Some children may *hate* chocolate peppermint ice cream. Likewise, one child may work hard for praise, while another may be indifferent to it. (Or she may find praise meaningless because she gets it all the time, whether she is really trying or not.)

The principles of operant learning are very effective teaching tools. Children who receive controlled and consistent reinforcement contingent on certain behaviors are more likely to learn those behaviors. If their behavior is reinforced inconsistently, however, they may learn more slowly, or may even learn undesirable behaviors. The section called "Scenarios in Operant Learning," below, offers examples of how operant learning can lead to both desirable and undesirable learning.

According to Jennifer Wishart (1989), typical infants can detect a contingency for a specific behavior by two months of age. Children with Down syndrome, however, may have more trouble learning from contingencies. One reason, according to Wishart, is that desirable behaviors of children with Down syndrome may not be reinforced as consistently. This, in turn, may be because children with Down syndrome have more trouble producing behaviors that lead to a desired effect on their environment. For example, a child may want her mother to come. When she attempts to call her mother, however, she may not "call" loudly enough for her mother to hear her, or her mother may not read it as a "call," but think it is just babbling. Her polite "calling" behavior will decrease, because it is not reinforced by the arrival of her mother. If this child is very motivated to get her mother to come, she will try another way until she gets the desired effect. She may find that screaming brings her mother. Because it gets the desired effect, her screaming increases, and she learns to call her mother by screaming. The environment has taught her to scream to get her needs met. Another inconsistency that could confuse a child is learning that sometimes she doesn't have to do *anything* for the desired effect to happen. For example, her mother may come to her even when she makes no attempt to call her. She may learn that if she just waits, sooner or later her mother will come.

Another reason children with Down syndrome may have difficulty learning from contingencies is that they may not find them as motivating as other children do. They may not be willing to work for the same "rewarding event" that typical children will work for—perhaps they do not have the cognitive concepts to appreciate and understand the event well enough to find it interesting, or because they have vision or hearing problems that interfere with their enjoyment of the event. In any case, the "reinforcer" that is contingent on a specific behavior may not be actually reinforcing for the child.

A study conducted in Edinburgh by Jennifer Wishart (1989) points out some differences in the way "typical" children and children with Down syndrome respond to reinforcement. The study compared learning behaviors of babies and young children with and without Down syndrome ages three months to two years, who were tested at three-month intervals. The children were placed comfortably in a baby chair in a semi-dark room in front of a translucent screen. Any leg movement would cause an infra-red beam to trigger a one-second movement of a brightly colored mobile that was projected onto the screen. Leg movements were rewarded according to different schedules during the study: sometimes 100 percent of leg movements were reinforced (every leg movement caused the mobile to move); sometimes the mobile moved for 80 percent of the leg movements; and sometimes the mobile moved 10 percent of the time, whether or not the legs moved.

Both the babies and young children who did not have Down syndrome were more highly motivated during all schedules of reinforcement. They explored different timings of response, sustained their attention longer, and seemed intrigued by the occurrence of the reward when they did not move their legs (the 10 percent of the time when the mobile moved anyway) and by the absence of the reward when they did move their legs (the other 20 percent of the 80 percent schedule). *Babies* with Down syndrome, too (9 months average age) responded well during all three conditions, although it took them longer, on average, to detect the reward. However, *young children* with Down syndrome (21 months in sample data) seemed to make little attempt to explore and master the conditions. In both conditions (100 percent and 80 percent), they settled happily for the small percentage (10 percent) of "free" reward, even though a much higher rate of "reward" was available, if they exerted their own control over the situation.

One question raised by this study (and the cognitive tasks study described in Chapter 2) is why babies with Down syndrome seem to learn more efficiently than children with Down syndrome. Do children with

Down syndrome actually *learn* these counter-productive learning patterns as they grow older? Or are these learning difficulties inherent to children with Down syndrome? Ms. Wishart theorizes that the former may be true. Children with Down syndrome may learn to avoid difficult learning situations and settle for low success rates, because they learn in infancy that they are more likely to make mistakes and fail if they try. Wishart thinks that it may be possible to minimize this learned helplessness with "appropriately timed and carefully structured intervention" (p. 258). She also thinks that children with Down syndrome may make poor use of earlier learning, losing instead of building upon newly acquired learning.

The Edinburgh studies show important differences in the way children with Down syndrome learn, compared to children who do not have Down syndrome. To facilitate learning for children with Down syndrome, we must therefore be aware of these differences and make appropriate adaptations in our instruction and procedures. These adaptations include: (1) programming for success (breaking tasks down into small steps that make it likely the child will succeed, not fail); (2) consistent, contingent reinforcement for correct responses, and avoidance of rewards for incorrect responses; and (3) opportunities to practice and consolidate newly learned material and to transfer and generalize new learning to different situations. The procedures and techniques presented in this book demonstrate the use of these adaptations to teach children with Down syndrome to read.

Scenarios in Operant Learning

Amy, Jon, David, Molly, and Peter are crawling and approaching the "pull to stand" stage in their development. These particular children with Down syndrome are "earth bound"—have low tone and little strength, and have not learned good techniques to get to standing. They are therefore unlikely to make much progress in learning to stand if the environment does not provide them with the motivation and opportunity to do so.

To help these children learn to stand, the environment must first provide the equipment that makes pulling up possible (furniture of the appropriate height that they can pull themselves up on). Second, there must be a reason—a motivation—that makes them want to do the required work. Third, they must receive instruction and help, making the behavior possible for them to perform. And last, once they have pulled themselves up, they must receive reinforcement so they will want to do it again and again, building strength, practicing technique, and getting better at it so they can pull to stand independently.

Following are some examples of what can happen when children, who are at about the same developmental level, are working on this "pull to stand" objective. All of these environments have the same coffee table, suitable for a child to learn to pull to stand (this coffee table is so perfect, it is padded). Imperfections in the environment are described in all but one scenario (the very supportive one). They point out that the principles of operant learning are always working, whether or not you are in control of them.

The "Very Supportive Environment" Scenario

Amy was playing on the floor when she noticed an attractive toy duck on the coffee table several feet away. Her mother had put it there for motivation (bait, waiting for Amy to bite). She knew that Amy would work harder if she were allowed to *initiate* the activity—if it was *her* great discovery and *her* goal to obtain it. Amy crawled to the coffee table, reached up, grasped the edge, and tried to pull herself up. The task was very difficult for her. Her mother read her cues. (Amy wanted to reach that object on the coffee table and was trying to pull herself up to get it—she was going for the bait.) Her mother responded by positioning Amy's legs properly and then giving her minimal assistance to stand (just as the physical therapist had showed her, letting Amy do most of the work). Once Amy was standing, leaning on the coffee table for support, her mother made sure that the toy she had worked so hard for was within easy reach (Amy's efforts were reinforced), so she would try again next time.

Obtaining the toy was contingent on Amy's working on pulling herself to stand (with help, as she was *learning* to stand). After obtaining the toy, if Amy sat down and took the toy duck with her, she was allowed to continue playing with it. (Standing was not a contingency for playing with the toy.) When Amy abandoned the toy, her mother placed it back on the coffee table, so it would be there to motivate Amy to pull herself up again. This should also help Amy's memory by providing a consistent place for the toy. Mother can ask Amy, "Where's the duck?" when she wants her to work on pulling to stand again. Playing with the duck will be contingent on her working on pulling herself to stand. If Amy tires of the duck, her mother will find something else more exciting. Amy will most likely learn to pull to stand before this happens, however. She is going to learn fast because she understands the contingencies.

The "I-Want-To-Teach-Him-What-No-Means" Scenario

Jon's grandmother was visiting. She advised Jon's mother to leave all her "objets d'art" around so that Jon would learn what "no" means and grow up to be an obedient, well-behaved child. She had done it with her children, and look how well they turned out.

Jon spotted a beautiful object on the coffee table and decided that he must have it. (He was *very* motivated.) He crawled to it, and was trying to pull himself up so he could reach it. His mother, anxious to show her mother-in-law what a good mother she was, said, "No, no, Jon!" Jon persisted, hanging onto the table, fussing a little, begging for help. His mother took him away from the coffee table, telling him "No!" again. When Jon returned to the coffee table to try again, she spanked his hands and sternly told him "No!" Then she took the crying baby away and put him in his playpen. Jon's grandmother praised his mother for not being ruled by a crying baby. She sure showed him who was boss and was a firm disciplinarian.

This praise reinforced Jon's mother and increased her behaviors of leaving everything down low, telling Jon "no," and punishing him when he did not respond to "no." She "worked" on his pulling to stand tasks by trying to get him to pull himself up on the bars of his playpen. Jon cried and refused to cooperate with his mother. When she was able to prop him up in the standing position for a few seconds, she praised him (the therapist had told her to "reinforce" him). But Jon did not hear her praise, because he was crying too loudly. (It would not have meant anything to him, anyway. He did not earn it.)

In the meantime, Jon was not learning good positive interaction with his mother. (This is basic for all learning—the reinforcement that is so essential to learning.) She was not responding to his attempts to communicate that he did not *want* to stand holding onto the playpen—there was no motivation and no reinforcement, it was hard, and he was afraid he was going to be put in the playpen.

Jon's mother has concluded that reinforcement does not work on Jon. (Her "praise" was not reinforcing to Jon—in no way did it increase his pull-to-stand behavior.) She is also worried that he can't learn what "no" means because of his mental retardation and stubbornness. He continues to crawl to the coffee table and try to obtain the art object, every time his mother's back is turned. (He's smart. He knows when the coast is clear. He just may teach himself to stand and get his hands on that beautiful thing.) He has started hitting her back when she spanks his hands and shouts "No" (this is what she has modeled). She worries because Jon crawls the other way when she calls him. He does not cooperate when she is trying to get him dressed, and he frequently used the only word he can say—"no."

This mother tries so hard and sees so few results. She is convinced that behavior principles just don't work for her son. The problem is, they work too well. She just does not know how to make them work for her and Jon. With just a little more (and better) advice, there would be a lot of hope for this mother and her son. . . .

The "Bait-and-Switch" Scenario

David's mother, who also kept her beautiful art objects displayed on her coffee table, was told by her therapist how to teach him to pull to stand. The therapist told her about motivation and that children generally work harder if they initiate the activity. David showed a lot of interest in a particular art object and was trying to pull up on the coffee table. His mother picked up the object and tapped it on the table, making it even more attractive to him, and said, "Come on, David, you can do it. Come and get it." Then she gave him the help he needed to pull to stand. However, when David was standing and reached for the object, she took it away and gave him a toy instead. David did not get what he worked for. The real "reinforcement" he was working for was not available to him. If his mother continues to use this bait-and-switch "reinforcement," David will learn not to trust her and will very likely stop working for rewards he does not receive.

The "Phone-Rang" Scenario

Molly's mother saw her approach the coffee table and try to pull herself up to obtain a toy. Molly's mother started to go help her, just as Amy's mother had done, but the phone rang. She left Molly and answered the phone. While on the phone, she heard Molly "fussing" softly, but did not respond to her. Molly started to cry loudly enough so that it interfered with her mother's conversation. Her mother left the phone to find out what was wrong. Molly was obviously crying for the toy she could not reach, so her mother gave it to her. Molly stopped crying, and her mother returned to the phone.

Her mother was reinforced by Molly's quietness. Her "giving-the-desired-object-when-Molly-cries" behavior increased. Molly learned that crying loudly is an effective way to get what she wants, especially if her mother is on the phone. Now she cries when her mother tries to get her to pull to stand. She does not want to do the hard work. She is learning to be helpless and get her needs met by crying.

Both Molly and her mother understood the contingencies. Molly cries, she gets the reward; her mother gives her the reward, Molly stops crying.

The "I'm-Confused-about-the-Advice" Scenario

Peter's father had just come from a session with the speech therapist. The speech therapist had told him to reward Peter by responding to all his efforts to communicate. Peter's father was inspired and watched Peter carefully for any gesture he could reinforce. He saw Peter trying to pull himself up to the coffee table, obviously trying to obtain a very desirable toy that had been left there. He rushed over to Peter and said, "Duck? You want the duck?" Peter pointed at the duck and nodded his head. His father gave him the duck, pleased that he had responded to Peter's efforts to communicate. However, he was a little worried because he knew that his wife had placed the duck there to motivate Peter to pull to stand. She had wanted Peter's getting the duck to be contingent on his pulling himself up. But he had used it to reward Peter's gesture that he wanted the duck. He wondered if he had done the right thing, but was afraid not to give Peter the duck when he indicated that he wanted it, because it might hamper his communication development.

Peter learned that he did not have to stand to get the duck; he just had to let his father know he wanted it. That took less work. The contingency had changed.

These goals (communication and motor) did not need to conflict with each other. Peter's father could have responded to his son's gesture, reinforcing the communication, and helped him learn to stand. When he said, "Duck? You want the duck?" and Peter pointed and nodded, he could have then asked, "Want help?" He could next have helped Peter pull up, responding to what Peter was doing by saying, "Up, up, up," when Peter was pulling up. Then he could have said, "Wow, you made it!" when Peter was standing, and "You got it!" when he obtained the duck.

Although no parent can keep complete control over their child's environment, we have to do the best we can to meet our own needs and those of our child. Understanding and applying the principles of operant learning should make meeting these needs easier. And we should be less likely to inadvertently reinforce undesirable behaviors that interfere with learning desirable behaviors. "Behavior problems" are perhaps the greatest obstacles we face when teaching children with Down syndrome. But when there are no (or few—no one is perfect) "behavior problems," there are seldom learning problems.

Typical Learning Differences

I hear, I forget
I see, I remember
I do, I understand
(Chinese proverb)

Given the uniqueness of each child, there are learning differences that are typical of many children with Down syndrome (though not all). Keep in mind as you read this that not all children with Down syndrome will have all of these differences, but most of them will have some. Observe your child (or your student) and try to determine which of these differences she may have. Also, note that some of these problems overlap and are related to each other. These are discussed separately for clarity.

Memory: The Magic Seven, Plus or Minus 2

Channel capacity is determined by the number of new items, or bits of information, that an individual can retain briefly in their short-term memory. Having an understanding of channel capacity and an awareness of the channel capacity of your child can be a key to programming for her success and is very helpful in avoiding mistakes that may set her up for failure.

The average number of memory channels the population in general has is seven. Some people may have nine, others five, but the average is seven. That is why phone numbers have seven digits. To make phone numbers easier to remember, the numbers are "chunked," three numbers/four numbers, 453-7832. Some of us "chunk" it again, four fifty-three, seventy-eight, thirty-two. When we look up a phone number, we can usually remember it long enough to dial it. However, if before we dial it, someone distracts us, by talking or giving new information, our channels become filled with the new information, and we lose the number and have to look it up again. Psychologists often refer to this as the "the Magic Number Seven, plus or minus two" (Miller, 1956).

We retain information in the short-term memory long enough to put it to immediate use. Once used, we drop it and fill our channels with new information that is useful for our next activities. If we are aware that this information will be of future use to us, we either write it down and file it away so we can retrieve it, or we store it in our long-term memory, filing it away so we can retrieve it from our memory file. In order to do this memory filing we need to "ponder." We think about it. We think of ways to remember it using associations and mnemonics. We rehearse it, and place it in the appropriate "file" in our mind, where we have other information in that category stored, ready to retrieve when needed. This information must be used and rehearsed, if it is to stay available in the long-term memory, otherwise it will be dropped to make room for more.

A simple example would be the telephone number. If it is a number that we do not anticipate needing in the future, we may not write it down and keep it, and we certainly would not bother to store it in our long-term memory. If it is our own new number, or if the new number belongs to a friend we call often, we will be sure to write it down, and, in time, with use, practice, and pondering, we will store it in our long-term memory. Once there, it will stay there as long as we use it and have a need to remember it.

Fewer than the Magic Seven, plus or minus 2.

Many people with Down syndrome have fewer memory channels than the Magic Seven, plus or minus 2. Although children in general usually have fewer memory channels, children with Down syndrome are apt to have fewer than their peers at any age. When we expect someone with Down syndrome to perform as if she has seven channels, when, in fact, she may have only one or two, performance falters. The child is unsuccessful and becomes confused and disinterested.

When I am introducing new sight words to a student, I start with one word, providing opportunities for her to ponder, practice, and use the word. Then I introduce a second word the same way, and then, perhaps, a third, fourth, and fifth, depending on the student's channel capacity. When the child starts making errors, I know that, most likely, I have exceeded her channel capacity. I need to return to the success level and provide more opportunities for the child to practice and use those first words until they are stored and filed in her long-term memory. This accomplished, I can introduce the new word(s), building on the words previously introduced and providing continuous practice with all words taught.

The typical test for channel capacity is to ask the child to repeat numbers or non-related words after you, such as: 5, 2; 8, 1, 6; 7, 2, 4, 9; 6, 8, 3, 2, 4; etc. The number of numbers she can repeat usually suggests her channel capacity. Of course, this tests *auditory* (echoic) memory, and learners with Down syndrome often have better *visual* (iconic) memory than auditory. To test visual memory, pictures, written words, or written numbers are useful. For example, one picture is shown to the child and then removed, and she is then asked, "What did you see?" The number of pictures shown gradually increases. The number that the child remembers suggests her channel capacity.

Testing may give you an idea of your child's channel capacity. However, day-to-day instruction decisions should be based on her daily performance. On-going evaluation is the key to making thoughtful and constructive decisions about programming, teaching techniques, and strategies.

Auditory Memory

Auditory memory refers to the ability to hear and understand words and sounds long enough to process and respond to them. This process includes hearing the auditory information, understanding its meaning, relating this information to other information stored on the subject (finding it in the "file"), retrieving it, and responding (demonstrating that it is remembered). Children with Down syndrome generally (there are always exceptions) have difficulty with this process.

Perhaps the major reason children with Down syndrome have problems with verbal language in general, and understanding and processing auditory information in particular, is the frequent occurrence of ear infections, or *otitis media*. Even in children without Down syndrome, recurrent ear infections at an early age can lead to later language learning problems. In one study, "normal" third-graders with a history of ear infections did significantly worse on tests measuring auditory sequential memory, selective auditory attention, and sound blending than children who did not have these symptoms during their first three years (Kessler and Randolph, 1979).

Children with Down syndrome also have a high incidence of *serous otitis media*—a non-infected accumulation of fluid in the middle ear with no observable symptoms that is often missed by parents and physicians. This puts children with Down syndrome at risk for yet another syndrome: minimal auditory deficiency syndrome. It occurs when there have been recurrent bouts with otitis media beginning in the first year of life and continuing during the periods of crucial language development. Those at risk for this syndrome are infants and young children who have had more than three bouts with otitis media during a six-month period, during the first two years of life, or have had a hearing loss of 15dB or more for more than half of the time during a six-month period. The continuation of this condition, untreated, increases the probability of later auditory language learning problems (Downs and Balkany, 1988).

Besides having conductive hearing losses related to fluid in the ear, children with Down syndrome are also more likely to have sensorineural losses. (A conductive loss occurs when the transmission of sound waves is impeded somewhere in the ear canal or middle ear; a sensorineural loss results from damage to the inner ear, auditory nerve, or both.) In one study of 107 individuals with Down syndrome, 78 percent were found to have at least a mild hearing loss (more than 15dB) in at least one ear, and 65 percent had significant hearing losses in both ears. Fifty-four percent had conductive hearing losses; 16 percent sensorineural; and 8 percent, a combination of conductive and sensorineural (mixed losses) (Downs and Balkany, 1988).

Patricia Kuhl, who has researched the very early foundation for language development in infants, found that infants are born as "universal linguists"—that is, they are able to hear the differences among the sounds used in all languages. As early as six months of age, however, infants learn a filtering process that allows them to distinguish sounds in their native language, but not in a foreign language. By adulthood, our repertoire of speech perception has narrowed so that we are unable to discriminate sounds that are not a part of our native language. For example, adults whose native language is Japanese have great difficulty discriminating between words containing the English sounds of "r" and "l," because these sounds belong to the same underlying category in Japanese. This research emphasizes the importance of early exposure to language and suggests that there may be a "critical period of language development." Dr. Kuhl says this explains why infants who have recurrent bouts of otitis media have been found to have language problems later in childhood (McCreary, 1992).

If I've told her once, I've told her a thousand times.

Often, difficulty with auditory memory is interpreted as a behavior problem (as are so many other learning problems). Typical complaints parents have are often: "If I tell her once, I tell her a thousand times. She understands everything that I say, but she pretends not to, or she does the opposite. She is so stubborn." It could be that during the time the parent was talking, the child did understand what she was saying, but by the time her mother stopped talking, she had forgotten most or all of it, or remembered only part of it, most likely the last thing her mother said. For example, if her mother said, "Put the dirty glasses in the sink and stack the newspapers," she may have remembered, "stack the newspapers" or "stack the glasses." If her mother added other information, such as "And see to it that it is done before your daddy gets home, and when you finish you can watch TV," the child may have retained only that last bit of information: "Daddy is coming home" or "watch TV."

Consider your child's channel capacity. With so much information coming so fast, it may be unrealistic to expect your child to remember all of it. The spoken word exist only an instant. Your child may also have a longer than expected *latency*— that is, the lapse of time between the cue (your request) and your child's response. It may take her longer to process the information and follow through. While she is still "pondering," you may have decided that she is stubborn and not willing to do it. She may simply need shorter instructions, given more slowly, and uncluttered with unnecessary information. She may need the instructions written down or illustrated in order to remember them. (After all, that's what *we* do when we need to remember things.)

When she is given unnecessary and excessive information, your child must go through yet another process she may not be equipped to handle. In addition to hearing, understanding, storing, retrieving, and responding, she has to filter out the information that is not important, and remember the important information. Typically, children with Down syndrome have trouble with this "filtering" process as well. I would expect the above hypothetical child's filter to pick up on "Daddy's coming home," or "Watch TV," and forget all the rest that was so important to her mother.

It's a test, not a curriculum.

A typical test item on receptive communication assessments tests the child's ability to follow verbal directions (object-action commands). For example, when six items, such as a cup, spoon, doll, paper, blanket, and pencil are placed before the child, the examiner gives novel commands, starting out with a one-object, one-action command, "Put the spoon on the paper." Then on to two-object, two-action commands, "Place the pencil in the cup and the paper over the doll." These commands get more complex for higher developmental ages, one object, three actions, three actions, three objects, etc. The point is that this is one way to test auditory memory and to determine how many elements the child can remember. Children with Down syndrome usually have difficulty with these items. There was a time, when I did not know better, that I tried to teach children to follow these nonsense commands, because they were "developmental" skills. Now I know better. If children are to follow directions in a sequence, these directions should have meaning and purpose, and should make sense to the child. Now, to teach a sequence, I use illustrations. (See the box on the next page).

Teaching Children to Follow a Sequence

A typical sequence of instructions given by the teacher at school may be: "It's time to get ready for a snack. Wash your hands, find your place mat, put it on the table, pass out the napkins, and sit down at your place." If we are serious about children learning to follow these directions, each step (task) in the sequence should be illustrated and/or written (depending on the skills of the children) and posted so that the children can learn to follow the sequence independently. Sometimes, the teacher (and the parent) constantly cue a child each step of the way, and the child does not have to think or remember the sequence (more learned helplessness). The teacher may announce snack time, and some children will go and sit at the table. Then she reminds them to wash their hands, and they get up and wash their hands (or she drags them to the sink). After handwashing, some children may come back to the table and some may wander around the room. The teacher then cues them to get their place mats, then she may tell one to get the napkins, or to sit down and wait for the snack. After snack, she may tell them, one by one, as they finish, to put their dishes in the sink, to wipe off their place mat, put it away, then wash their hands (and go to the toilet, if they need to), and to choose a toy or book to entertain themselves while the other children finish up. It is usually a hectic time, and the teacher complains, "These children really have trouble with transitions."

If the sequence of tasks is clearly illustrated (and I like to number each sequence to get the math concepts in as well), and posted at the child's level, the child can learn to follow the sequence independently. The teacher can cue her to consult the chart to decide what to do next. When using the chart, she learns to think, to follow illustrated directions, to follow the sequence on her own, and to build her independence. Rather than depending on the teacher to tell her what to do next, the *child* tells the *teacher* (or points to the task on the chart). If the child is running around the room, the teacher can cue her, "Look at the chart and see what you need to do next." Or, if she does not go independently, the teacher may take her to the chart and ask her what she has done, and what she needs to do next. The teacher can expand the lesson and make "sequence" cards using the illustrations, and the children can learn to put the cards in order, practicing the sequence. (She could also make lotto games. See Chapter 18: Schedule lotto.)

I encourage parents to do the same for trouble areas at home, such as getting the child ready for school in the morning. So often, parents struggle, constantly reminding the child what to do next, and always taking responsibility for getting her out of the door on time. I recommend making a chart, having your child set a timer for each task, and rewarding her for "beating the clock" (perhaps by putting marbles in a jar—and each marble will buy a certain amount of video time after school). It is important to make your child responsible and to build her independence, and this needs to be taught systematically, taking into account her learning style.

I know it is often easier for parents to do a task for their child than to teach her to do it. After all, you have a lot to do in the morning. But remember the article cited in Chapter 3 that found that the rate of learning adaptive behaviors slowed in many children with Down syndrome ages seven to eleven? Can it be that the decline in the rate of learning these skills is due to lack of systematic, effective instruction?

When in doubt, say it louder.

We often adapt our speech to our audience. When we are speaking to someone who is not proficient in English, we speak more slowly and clearly and use a lot of gestures; to someone who is hard of hearing, we speak louder and clearer (and also use gestures). We are making adaptations in our delivery. Sometimes we get confused and use the wrong adaptation. We speak to those who are not proficient in English as though they are hard of hearing, and the adaptation is ineffective and often insulting to the listener as well as embarrassing to us. We often try this adaptation for children with special needs as well. If they don't respond to us when we are using our usual voice, we get louder. Louder does not usually help, unless the child has a hearing impairment. We need to find appropriate adaptations that work for each individual.

We typically and naturally (it's second nature to us) speak to babies in "motherese," an exaggerated, melodic, high-pitched, slower-paced speech with clear vowels (Grieser and Kuhl, 1988). Babies have taught us, by the way they respond, to speak "motherese." As the child learns the language and becomes proficient, our pace increases, and we rely less on making our voice interesting and more on content to maintain our interactions.

When interacting with and teaching children with Down syndrome, we often fail to learn by their responses, or lack of responses, and to make adaptations accordingly. We move into our faster-paced speech, repeat it over and over, or say it louder, hoping to get our point across. Considering the short existence of the spoken word, and the abstract, symbolic nature of language, the spoken word can be very elusive to many children with Down syndrome. In addition to having trouble grasping the word(s), the child may have intermittent (or constant) hearing loss due to ear infections, differences in auditory perception, fewer memory channels, a longer latency, and a poor "filtering" system. We need to find another way.

Visual Learners

A picture is worth a thousand words: I have found another way.

Most children with Down syndrome I have known are visual learners. Visual stimuli are generally very effective in helping children with Down syndrome to learn and to compensate for fewer memory channels and difficulty with auditory memory. I have found illustrations, symbols, pictures, and reading to be powerful tools for learning. Unlike the spoken word that vanishes so fast, the written word, pictures, drawings, and objects can remain for as long as a child needs them.

Given this strength—the ability to learn through visual stimuli—*some* children with Down syndrome can learn to read words before they can say them; they are able to use visual language (recognizing and understanding the written word) before they can use the verbal language (saying the words). This is unlike the way we teach typical children, who usually master a verbal language before even attempting a visual language. Visual learners can use the visual language to facilitate learning the spoken language and other concepts they need to learn. This book focuses on using the child's visual discrimination skills to teach reading, and using reading to teach other concepts and skills. Detailed instructions are given in later chapters.

Why Some Children with Down Syndrome Don't Learn to Read

There is no simple answer as to why some children, despite all efforts of parents and teachers, do not learn to read, or refuse to try. Each child and each situation is unique, and I do not pretend to know the reason in all situations. Some cases will remain a mystery forever.

Here are some *possible* reasons, given that the child has had the opportunity to learn to read:

(1) Failure or the fear of failure: When an instructor (parent, teacher, sibling, etc.) tried to teach the child to read, the program or method they used was not one that was appropriate for the child's interest or abilities. It was not programmed for this individual child's success. She did not understand the concept being taught. The words, letters, and/or concept had no meaning or use to the child. The child became confused and did not understand the value or purpose of the tasks asked of her. The "reading lesson" became a negative and unpleasant experience. The child learned to avoid failure by escaping from the reading lesson by refusing to attend and respond, or by "acting out" in other ways, when asked to participate in reading tasks. This behavior communicates that, "It is too hard for me. It is an aversive activity that I must escape, regardless of the cost." (If I have to go to time out, if I have to go to the principal's office, if I have to stay in at recess, if I have to give up tokens, I don't care. I must escape this confusing stuff. I must gain control. Anything is better than failure. I am unhappy and upset.) The instructor, thinking that trying to teach the child to read is futile, gives up. (See Avoidance Behaviors and Learned Helplessness in Chapter 3.)

An instructor-made mental block?

A well-known educator estimated that 90 percent of learning disabilities were teacher-made. He stated that, "Perhaps 90 percent or more of the children who are labeled "learning disabled" exhibit a disability not because of anything wrong with their perception, synapses, or memory, but because they have been seriously mistaught. Learning disabilities are made, not born" (Engelmann, 1977).

We know that children with Down syndrome generally do have biological differences that interfere with their ability to learn the way children who do not have Down syndrome learn. However, most of these children likely have the ability to learn to read (to some degree), but have shown little or no progress in learning. Perhaps they have been "mistaught" with methods and techniques designed for "typical" students, or for special education students who do not have the same learning differences. The child failed, at some point, became intimidated, afraid of the subject, and developed a "mental block" for the subject and was unable to focus or concentrate. Her mind "shuts down" when presented with reading tasks.

We don't think he can learn to read.

Tom, a ten-year-old boy with Down syndrome, had been in an inclusive class with the same group of children since kindergarten. He coped very well in the classroom, participated in most classroom activities, spoke well, interacted with peers, and had a delightful sense of humor, but he refused to try to read. His teachers had tried many times with different approaches, but he refused to cooperate. The teacher told me, "We don't think he can learn to read." They had exhausted all their strategies. Meanwhile, a girl with Down syndrome, who was his age, and had been in the same class for the same length of time and had the same teachers, was reading very well.

I was invited to Tom's school to consult about his reading. He told me that his birthday was coming up November 2nd. I suggested that we play the "Birthday Game," and, in a game-like format (using the matching, selecting, and naming procedure to be described later), he learned to read *happy, birthday,* and *November* in just a few minutes. He could read the words on flash cards and in the sentences ("Happy Birthday, Tom, November 2." and "November 2, Happy Birthday, Tom.") I started with "Tom," to assure success. He could recognize his name.

We all had a good time that day. It was the beginning of the making of a reader. He learned that he could read, he had experienced success, and was able to read the important words on his birthday cards. Seven months later, his teacher told me that he had 40 words in his reading vocabulary.

(2) The child may not understand the concept of reading: Some children just don't understand what it is all about; what it is that you want them to do. They don't have the concept that printed words are symbols that represent specific words that represent specific people, places, objects, actions, feelings, and ideas. The child may pick up a book, talk about the pictures, and say that she is "reading." She is "reading" the picture symbols, rather than the written symbols, and she may think that that is what others do when they "read." When the instructor presents words or letters, she does not understand what it is all about; she may fail to attend, just guess at the words, or show disinterest. She does not understand what is expected of her, and again fails to meet the expectations of her teacher. It is a very uncomfortable situation for the child—one that she wishes to escape.

I swimmed! I swimmed!

A mother called me concerning the problems the instructors were having teaching her ten-year-old son to swim. She told me that he would not follow his teachers' instructions; he just flapped his hands and kicked his feet and ignored their attempts to instruct him. Then she told me of an incident that identified the problem. He had fearlessly jumped in the deep end and had to be rescued. When the rescuers brought him up, he came up smiling, shouting, "I *swimmed!* I *swimmed!*"

He did not understand what "swimming" was. He did not realize that there was a difference between "playing in" or "being in" the water and swimming, and to him, the deeper the water, the greater the "swim." He did not understand what they were trying to teach him— that he was expected to stay "on top" of the water, and that there were specific techniques and skills involved. He thought that he was already an accomplished swimmer! After all, he had tried the deep end.

It is easy to understand how children can be confused. They often take things very literally and sometimes do not pick up on subtle things, incidentally, as we often assume that they do. His parents, as all of us do, most likely called it "swimming" anytime they took him to play in the water—in a swimming pool, wading pool, lake, or ocean. Also, they may have pointed to fish in an aquarium and told him they were *swimming,* and he could have concluded that swimming takes place *under* water. Likewise, we tell children to "read" books, long before they are able to read. And when we "read" to them, they may not understand that we are using the symbols rather than the pictures to tell the story (and for young children we are often just interpreting the picture for them —the best way to "read" to maintain their attention and interest, adapting it to their level).

Some children who have learned letter sounds (i.e., they can respond to printed letters by saying the sound of the letter) do not understand how these sounds go together to make words. When asked to read a word, they will say the sound of each letter, but not the word. They are "stimulus bound," responding only with isolated sounds as they have been taught. They simply do not understand the relationship these letters have to forming words and are unable to transfer their knowledge of letter sounds to actual words. These children do not understand the concept of reading.

(In my limited experience with children who say letter sounds rather than words, I have not been successful in teaching them to read words. This is one reason why I like to start with sight words.)

(3) The child is not motivated to read: For some children, the material in reading books has little or no meaning. They are not interested in, nor can they relate to, the story or the characters. They may not understand what is happening in the story and find "calling" the words meaningless. In addition, they do not understand the long-term value of learning to read. They become bored and disinterested, and lose all motivation. They had much rather do other things, and, again, will do all they can to escape their reading lessons.

(4) The child's attention span is not long enough: Some children have difficulty settling down and concentrating. Their attention span is such that they are unable to focus on the words and comprehend their meaning and actively participate in reading games and activities. In some cases, these children have an attention deficit disorder (ADD). If your child cannot settle down long enough to become actively engaged in learning activities (she is inattentive, impulsive, and hyperactive), it may be worthwhile to check out the possibility of ADD. If ADD is the problem, it can often be treated with medication and/or behavior management strategies. This can be a determining factor in whether or not the child learns to read (and could make a big difference in how she behaves and learns other things as well).

(5) There may be vision, hearing, or thyroid problems: About half of all people with Down syndrome have vision problems; approximately 65 to 80 percent have some conductive hearing loss. Hypothyroidism (an underactive thyroid gland) is also more common than usual. These health problems, untreated, greatly affect a child's ability to read.

If your child is not seeing well enough to discriminate the words, trying to teach her to read would be futile. Have her vision checked, and, if needed, provide her with corrective lenses. Sometimes children with poor vision need adaptations in materials. The words and letters may need to be big and bold, or magnified in other ways.

If your child has a conductive hearing loss, a hearing aid will usually improve her hearing. Using sign language in addition to spoken words, as suggested throughout this book, can also help.

If your child has hypothyroidism, it can cause sluggishness, weight gain, and dry skin, and also further impair your child mentally. It is therefore important that this condition, as all health problems in children with Down syndrome, be treated aggressively. Medication can bring hypothyroidism under control.

(6) The child may not have the ability to learn to read: As mentioned earlier, children with Down syndrome have a range of abilities. For some children, though I expect the number to be small, reading is not feasible. They do not have the tools to understand the symbolic relationships necessary for reading. Using picture symbols will be a more efficient means to relay information to them on paper, and perhaps for them to communicate with other people.

In summary, I believe that most failures of children with Down syndrome in learning to read are due to the use of inappropriate programs for the child, and/or poor instruction that allows the child to fail and to develop a fear of and a dislike for reading. Sometimes, the child may have an impairment that interferes with learning to read. In any case, reading becomes aversive, an activity from which the child tries to escape, rather than the joyful experience it should be.

Chapter 5

SUCCESS IS THE KEY

Setting the Stage for Success

We all want to succeed in everything we do. The tasks in which we succeed are those we generally enjoy doing, and want to do again and again. Success inspires us to go on and experience more success. Failure often defeats us, and we try to avoid situations in which we expect to fail. Learning a skill that is as complex and difficult as reading can be a real challenge and lends itself to a lot of opportunities to fail. If a child does not understand what it is all about, can't remember the letter sounds or words, and makes a lot of mistakes, then reading becomes aversive, and he will try to escape the aversive situation. Knowing this, and knowing that many children with Down syndrome might not understand the long-term benefits of reading and may not have the perseverance to continue and work harder, in spite of failures, we must program reading so that the child is successful every step of the way.

I hope you name it "Success Is the Key."

Recently, I was talking with the mother of one of the original early readers in the University of Washington program. I told her that I was working on this book. Her response was, "Well, I hope you call it 'Success Is the Key.' We often seek the key to success. When teaching our children to read, success is the key. It was wonderful how the program was designed to assure success each step of the way, and *all* the children had the opportunity to learn—not just the brightest. Teaching the children to read was the program's most significant and important contribution to their education."

How to Help Your Child Succeed

Make Learning an Almost Errorless Process

To help children succeed in anything, the positive approach is the most effective. We need to teach them the joy of learning. The task itself becomes rewarding, and children feel intrinsic pleasure in their own accomplishments. Learning should not be unpleasant, but fun and rewarding. Strategies, methods, and techniques are described later in the book. However, here are a few guidelines to keep in mind—to assure your child's success each step of the way.

Your child is going to make mistakes. It is all right to make mistakes, and your child should know that. There is no shame in an error, but we need to correct our errors and learn from our mistakes. To keep the lesson on a positive, pleasurable track, and make the tasks motivating and fun for your child, he needs to make at least 8 correct responses out of 10. We learn best when we are practicing the correct responses and becoming fluent using the skill. Mistakes interfere with the flow and the feeling of success. Therefore, we need to break the task of reading down into small, simple tasks so the child can succeed. We want to be sure that he has the ability to do the tasks and understands the tasks before we ask him to do them.

If your child's rate of correct responses is less than 80 percent, try to determine why he is making mistakes. Here are some possible reasons and some suggestions of what to do.

(1) He does not understand the task, it is not meaningful, or it is too difficult for him.

In this case, you can model for him (demonstrate what you want him to do), go back to a simpler level and provide practice at that level, and/or change the reading material (so the words presented are meaningful and useful). If he still does not understand or is uninterested, put it away for a few weeks or months and start fresh later. Perhaps he is not ready, or the program is not broken down into small enough steps. Do not allow him to continue to fail; you will accomplish nothing but a power struggle and a dislike for reading if you insist that he continue when he is not succeeding.

(2) It is too easy, lacks challenge, or is just plain boring.

Your child may find the program too easy and boring. It could be that you are not moving fast enough to keep it challenging and interesting. (This is another reason for keeping track of correct/incorrect responses; it helps you to know when to move on.) Try to keep the program moving and interesting with the various activities suggested in this book. For example, if he is bored with matching, selecting, and naming flash cards and picture cards, skip this part and play lotto and other games with him. If he does not like the alphabet book, put it aside and play Alphabet Bingo. If he is bored with the subject matter, try another unit that offers a different "subject" and activities. (The "Household Words" unit is good for children who are tired of "desk" work.) Or, if he is ready for a greater challenge, you may move on to phonics, or you may try another reading program.

(3) The reading sessions are getting too long and tedious; he is more interested in something else at the present; he is tired of reading; or he is just plain tired.

Reading should be a wonderful, positive experience. If your child's attention starts to wander, and he is not attending and making mistakes, chances are he is not learning much. You can try to "beef it up" to make it more interesting, add a reward, but if your child is tired or more interested in something else that is going on in his environment, your efforts may be futile. Teach him to let you know when he has had enough reading, using another means of communication besides making mistakes. Teach him to be in control in a positive way by telling you that it is too hard, that he needs a break, or he is through (all done!). Often, when children learn that they do have a choice, that they are in control, they will choose to read with you. You don't want your child to learn to escape lessons by not attending and making errors. It's establishing bad habits and rewarding poor means of communication.

(4) He is teasing you. It is more fun for him to make an incorrect response than a correct response—you know he knows the word, but he is responding incorrectly on purpose.

Often children like to play games and tease. It is a part of being a child and a good sign that he is creative and wants to make things more interesting. However, allowing him to play games by giving the wrong response is not constructive. If you know that he knows the words and is making incorrect responses on purpose, teach him a more constructive game. Give him a "pay off" for correct responses and a penalty for incorrect responses. State the rules and keep score. For example, drop a marble in a jar labeled with his name each time he makes a correct response (he scored); drop a marble in a jar labeled with your name on it when he makes incorrect responses (you scored). On incorrect responses say, "I tricked you; I score." (Preface this by saying, perhaps, "I'll bet you are going to get this one wrong. I'll bet I can trick you this time." Pretend that it's to *your* advantage for him to make an incorrect response when matching, selecting, or naming). If he corrects himself after you "score," say, "I was wrong—I can't trick you. You score!" and move the marble from your jar to his.

I like to give a "second chance" to try to maintain a child's interest in the game. (If you are doing all the scoring, and he has no other chance, he may not want to play—the rules are too hard for him). If, however, he consistently makes an incorrect response on the first try, and he is enjoying the "game" of going through the procedure of making an error and correcting it, change the rules and make the first response "count." This usually works when children are making mistakes on purpose. We want it to be more fun for them to give the correct response.

(5) He is not motivated; he has learned helplessness.

When a teacher or parent tells me that a particular child "cannot be motivated by anything," I know that we have a hard case on our hands. It is motivation that makes us want to do everything we do, and gets us up doing and growing. If we lack motivation, very little gets done, and in potential learning situations, very little or no constructive learning takes place.

The program described in this book is designed to be motivating to children with Down syndrome. One reason that family photos and family names are used in teaching younger children is that children are generally motivated to read these words and look at the photos (they are very meaningful to them). If your child shows little or no interest in these photos and words, and your praise and excitement do not motivate him to do these simple tasks, perhaps your child has the learned helplessness discussed in Chapter 3. Receiving your attention randomly when he is not reading, and receiving your attention when he tries to avert your attention from the task, may be enough reinforcement for him. As with the "teasing," which can be an avoidance behavior (trying to distract your attention from the task at hand), you can try adding a more tangible reinforcement that is specifically contingent on correct responses. The marbles or coins in the jar (that can be traded in for video rentals, trips to favorite fast food restaurants, etc.) can be used for children who understand the concept of "earn now and spend later."

If your child does not understand the earn now - cash in later concept, you may need to use a more tangible, immediate reinforcement, such as a favorite food, to get his attention and to get him to *try* to do the task, so he will learn that he can indeed do it. If food is used for these very hard-to-motivate learners (nothing else works for them), here are a few guidelines:

(1) Be sure that the food is, indeed, reinforcing. Your child is willing to work for it, and it does increase correct responses. If it does not increase correct responses, given that the task is something

your child can do, and he understands the contingency (match the cards, then you get the treat), then this food is *not* reinforcing to him (or not at that moment anyway— maybe he's just had a big meal, or has tummy pains). By definition of reinforcement, if it does not increase your child's correct responses, then it is not "reinforcing" to him. (If, however, your child knows that he will get it later, "free" with no work, he may choose to wait, even though it is reinforcing.)

(2) Do not use foods that are harmful to him. It goes without saying that you would never give a diabetic candy, although he may really work hard for it. But there are some "gray" areas that may require some good judgment and careful consideration on your part. For example, if your child is overweight, and *the only thing he will work for is ice cream,* it might be a counter productive choice to use ice cream. The "trade off" may not be worth it. However, if he gets ice cream anyway and does not have to read, work, or cooperate in any way to get it, then ice cream might be considered for a reinforcement. In this case, he would be eating no more ice cream than he usually eats, except now he is working for it; it is contingent on his cooperation in doing reading tasks. (He should, of course, be weaned to non-fat ice cream or yogurt. When he learns to read, he can learn to read labels and select foods that are healthy for him to eat.)

(3) Use a very small quantity for each response you reinforce. If your child becomes satiated, he has no reason to work (the treat will not be reinforcing), and he may even try to escape the task because the food has lost its appeal.

(4) Phase out the food when your child is willing to work without it. For this difficult-to-motivate learner, you may, initially, have to reinforce after each response. Very soon, however, if the tasks are really appropriate for your child, he should find the reading itself and your praise (always paired with the food) reinforcing enough.

The M&M era.

The '70s is sometimes referred to as the "M&M era" in special education. We routinely used food reinforcement, and M&M's® were frequently used because most children were willing to work for them. Behavior modification—operant learning—gave us valuable "new tools." Most special education students could be motivated by food, and used properly, it generally brought fast results.

In our program, for a time we made instant pudding every school day and took a small amount with us when we worked with the children individually. It did work well. We got children's attention and interest, and they worked well. However, it was soon evident that we did not need to continue to use food in most cases. The activities themselves became reinforcing. I can remember taking the pudding to individualized sessions and noticing that it was unused by the end of the session. I "forgot" to use it, and obviously the student no longer needed it. I think that the food was often more of a crutch for the teacher than for the child; we could fall back on it when we lost the child's attention, interest, and/or motivation. Today, I have found that most children do not need food reinforcement. The interesting materials and activities at their ability level are motivating enough for most children.

If your child is, indeed, using his "learned helplessness" to avoid reading, food reinforcement may be necessary. *Everyone* is willing to work for *something*. If it is food, at least food is deliverable and we can control it, unlike some things, such as "a woman" that older males may find reinforcing. If using food makes the difference between a child's learning to read and not even trying, I, personally, would use the food reinforcement. I think that it is better to be overweight and literate than overweight and illiterate. If weight is a problem, I seriously doubt that not using food for a reinforcer will have an impact on the weight problem. Other measures will have to be taken to make a difference in the individual's overall eating habits.

Well, he just loves potato chips.

A single mother brought her seven-year-old son in for a consultation. The boy was overweight and a major behavior problem. His mother could not physically handle him anymore and had placed him on the waiting list for a state institution. Although he was "oppositional" and uncooperative in general, her major problem was that he was not toilet trained. I asked her what he liked to eat. She said, "Well, he just loves potato chips." I told her to make his receiving potato chips contingent on positive "toilet behaviors." He was to receive just one chip for each time he verbalized that he needed to use the toilet, one for each time he went to the toilet on his own, and one for each time he used the toilet. Within one week, toileting was no longer a problem. He was still overweight, but he used the toilet, and he was never put in the institution. If we had not used the potato chips, he would have still been overweight, *not* toilet trained, *and* institutionalized.

(This child also came to the university for tutoring in reading and math. He learned that it was more fun and satisfying to cooperate and do the tasks, and that he *could* do them. He learned how to learn and discovered that he was a successful learner. I saw his mother a couple of years later. She said, "I wish you could see him now. He is *nice* to be with, a *real pleasure.*")

Use your common sense. Food reinforcement, contingent on the desired behavior, may be a breakthrough for the learned helplessness. Some people are afraid to use tangible reinforcements and refer to the use of them, especially food, as "bribes." Keep in mind that a bribe is a contingency for a corrupt behavior; a reward (reinforcement) is a contingency for a worthy behavior. People who are critical of food reinforcement very likely were never faced with these very difficult cases. It is heartbreaking to see children "do themselves in" by not cooperating with those who care for them. Food reinforcement is just another possible tool, and it just may work.

To maintain motivation in reading, provide opportunities for successful, interesting, and meaningful practice: Make bingo, lotto, and active games using the words and/or letter sounds. Provide opportunities for your child to play these games, and make them fun. Make books for him using the words he knows. Plan opportunities for him to actually use his skills in everyday activities. (I will give lots of ideas later.)

Discriminate Teaching from Testing

Teaching differs from testing in that when testing, the teacher is seeking knowledge—measuring the student's proficiency in order to determine what the student knows or can do; when teaching, the teacher is imparting knowledge, facilitating learning.

So often we think we are teaching, when actually we are testing. "What is this letter? What sound does it make? What is this word? What does it start with?" Asking questions such as these is testing. We are putting the child on the spot, asking him to come up with the answers—very few of us enjoy lessons when we are constantly quizzed. Asking questions is *obtaining* information, not *imparting* it. There are times when you will want to test, to evaluate and see just what your child has learned and understands—and how effective your teaching has been, and when it is time to move on to the next step. But do not confuse testing with teaching and make your *teaching* sessions *testing* sessions. In one research study, teachers were asked how much of the reading time they spent on teaching comprehension. They reported that it was 20 percent. When researchers went into the classroom and measured how much of the reading time these teachers actually spent on teaching comprehension, they discovered that the teachers were spending 20 percent of the reading time *testing* comprehension. They were asking comprehension questions, not teaching comprehension.

Whenever we ask a question that we *know the answer to,* we are *testing* the other person. We are not asking the question for information, but rather to see if the other person knows the answer. This can make the other person very uncomfortable, and, I am afraid, it happens often to children with Down syndrome. They soon learn to distract the adult, or to just not answer. If they make a mistake, the adult is sure to correct them, and expose their ignorance. For example, an adult may say something to a child such as, "What color is your coat?" The child may say, "Red." The adult then may say, "No, it's not red. Now tell me what color is it?" and keep quizzing her until she either guesses or stops responding. Or the adult says, "No it's not red, it's blue." Either way, the child has been exposed. She learns that it is safer for her to remain helpless than to risk failure.

Rather than constantly testing your child, why not improve your conversation skills? We often ask these questions because of our own limitations in knowing how to carry on a conversation with a child. Try to let your child take the lead in determining the topic of the conversation.

When we are teaching, we are facilitating learning by providing the student with learning opportunities—opportunities to think, to acquire new skills and information, to practice skills, to problem solve, to use learning strategies, and to apply information and experiences to real-life situations.

She's cheating. She's looking at the pictures.

A teacher who was visiting our program to learn how to teach children to read, was observing a reading session. Four picture cards, with the name of the object in each picture written underneath them, had been placed on the table, in front of Kim, the five-year-old student. I would show Kim a flash card with one of the words on it, and she would read the word and match the flash card with the word under the picture. If Kim was uncertain of a word, she would look down at the words under the pictures, find the word, look at the picture, and tell me what the word was. The teacher, standing behind me, stepped forward, unable to tolerate such stupidity and leniency on the part of the teacher, and whispered in my ear quite emphatically, "She's cheating! She's finding the word on the cards and looking at the pictures!"

I was teaching, *not* testing. Kim was a model student. She was effectively using the strategy that was provided for her to help her learn to read the words. She was in the process of *learning* to read words, not taking a test. I was demonstrating a teaching strategy, not how to give a test.

(Thank goodness, that teacher came for some training! I'm not sure that it helped her, but I know it helped me. It helped me to pinpoint one of the major problems teachers have. Many have difficulty discriminating testing from teaching.)

Remember that learning to read is a gradual process. The learner does not have to learn everything at once. Take your time and go at his pace. Be sure that he masters one set of words before new words are introduced. Introduce letters, letter sounds, and new concepts gradually. Give the learner time and keep reading a positive, successful experience. We like to do what we do well. Be sure that he is doing well, each step of the way, and give him an opportunity to enjoy his success.

Individualize for Your Child

This program is about individualizing for the individual learner. This means that we are going to let *the child* determine what words will be taught (words that are meaningful and useful for the individual); the rate at which words will be taught; when new concepts will be introduced; when to try a different approach; when and if he will move to another reading program; whether learning phonics is feasible for him; and how long the reading sessions will be. In time, we want the learner to set his own reading goals. If you are individualizing for your child's success, and he is not succeeding, something is wrong.

Plan for the Stages of Learning

The stages of learning, on which the sample lessons provided in this book are based, are: acquisition, practice to fluency, transfer, and generalization. These stages often overlap, but to give you a clearer understanding of the purpose of the steps and activities presented in the reading program, they are each described separately.

Acquisition is the first stage. During this stage, the child does not know the information or have the skill. In the case of reading, the child does not know the words, letters, or letter sounds—it is *new* to him. During this stage we are going to tell him what the word is, show him how to match it, and prompt him on selecting and naming it. We are going to do all we can to help him *acquire* the word (or letter, or letter sound) and to understand its meaning.

The second stage is **practice to fluency.** The child has been introduced to the word; he has matched it, selected it, and named it, but he needs *practice* to become *fluent*. During this stage he will play matching, selecting, and naming games, using the picture and flash cards, and can move on to bingo, lotto, and other games for more practice. This stage overlaps with the next stage, transfer.

During this third stage, **transfer,** the child *transfers* his ability to read the word to different presentations of the word (stimuli). For example, if he has been reading handwritten words on flash cards, then he will need to transfer his skill of reading these same words in different type fonts and font sizes, as used in games and books. This stage can overlap with the practice to fluency stage, and is the start of the generalization stage.

In the last stage, **generalization,** the student learns to use his reading ability in all situations; wherever and whenever he has the opportunity and need to read and use his skill. He can read the words in books; in sentences, notes, directions, recipes, letters; on labels, shopping lists, name tags, signs, greeting cards, maps, and place cards—and he knows what the words mean and is able to use his reading whenever he has a need or desire to do so.

Daddy! Daddy!

Back when the prisoners of war were coming home from Vietnam, there was a cover on *Time* magazine, showing a family with a big sign that said, "Welcome Home Daddy!" This magazine was in a rack in the supermarket, next to the check-out counter. B.J., four years old, was sitting in the shopping cart as her mother wheeled it up to the counter. She saw the magazine and recognized "Daddy" immediately, and pointed and shouted, "Daddy! Daddy!" She had generalized. She recognized and read the word in a different place, written a different way, and presented in a different manner. (She also impressed the check-out clerk.)

We are going to make *butter?*

In the kindergarten class, I would sometimes write messages for the children on the chalkboard. One day I wrote, "Today we will make butter." We were in a unit on farm animals and learning about cows, and an activity planned for the day was "making butter" by passing around a container of cream and letting the children shake it until it became butter. For our snack we would spread the butter on bread. This was a new activity for this class. When Kari entered the classroom, she looked at the chalkboard, studied it, and asked in disbelief, "*We* are going to make *butter?*"

Kari was able to use her reading to understand and react to a novel message that she had never seen before. Reading was, indeed, a meaningful, useful skill that was well generalized. (See figure 5.1.)

In writing the objectives for the lessons in this book, I have not written objectives for the transfer stage, because this stage is embedded in the practice to proficiency and generalization stage. However, if your child has difficulty transferring his ability to read words when they are printed differently, add a step. Develop activities and games in which he can practice matching the word (on the flash card that he can read) with the same word written in different fonts. You may also develop

Figure 5.1. Kindergarten children reading a message on the board. Note that the alphabet is low, at the children's level.

some sorting games, where your child sorts the same word written in different fonts. For example, if your child can read *Sally, Mommy,* and *Daddy* on flash cards, but does not recognize them when written in any other way, make several flash cards of each name, each in a different font style and/or size. Your child finds all the cards that say *Sally,* then all the cards that say *Mommy,* and then all the cards that say *Daddy*.

Chapter 6

PREPARING YOUR CHILD TO BECOME A READER

Parents often ask what they can do to prepare their child, who has Down syndrome, to become a reader. Generally, the key is the same as for any child: Provide a nurturing family that facilitates learning in an enriching environment. Children with Down syndrome respond to good parenting, as do typical children. They learn their limits, that they have choices within these limits, and that different choices have different consequences, natural and logical. These consequences are consistently carried out by their caregivers, so they learn the impact of their behavior on their environment.

In addition, early intervention programs, preschools, and kindergarten programs help parents in meeting their child's special needs. Many parents are choosing inclusive preschools over special education preschools. This choice is generally becoming the preferred choice, and, in time, special education preschools may not be options. However, the most important consideration when choosing a preschool and kindergarten is the quality of the program: The program must be effective in meeting the child's objectives. She needs to belong where she is and *grow* where she belongs.

How Can I Prepare My Child for Reading?

If you are a parent, and you are reading this book, chances are very good that you have done a good job of preparing your child to read. You read for information and pleasure, and you value reading. You are providing a model for your child. Reading is an essential part of your life, and your child observes this. She notices that you often choose to read, and that it is a pleasurable and useful activity for you. In addition, you most likely have provided your child with appropriate books to look at and talk about since she was able to sit and point. You routinely read these books to her. You take her to the library with you, and allow her to choose books to check out. You have taught her that reading is a pleasurable, positive experience, and a desirable skill to have. She knows how to handle and respect books. They are a source of pleasure to her.

If you provided your child with books and read to her, you probably also sang to her, taught her songs, provided her with tapes of her favorite songs, and gave her opportunities to listen to words that rhyme. In addition, you provided her with appropriate toys and materials, engaged her in play with these materials, and allowed her to explore and learn about her world. If your child is four years or older, and does not have severe disabilities, she most likely has the attending, interaction, and discrimination skills necessary to start this reading program.

If you are concerned that perhaps your child does not have these skills and you want to know the types of toys and material that will help prepare her for reading, here are some suggestions, in addition to reading books to her.

Provide your child with games and toys that develop skills in discrimination, problem solving, communication, and imagination. Allow your child to choose the toys she wants to play with, letting her take the lead. Interact with her, taking turns, first imitating what she does with the toys on your turn. When the interaction is going well, on your turn, take it further, teaching her the next step, showing her a new strategy, and modeling the next level of communication or speech production. Provide her with ample opportunity to take a turn on her own and praise her for her efforts. (See Chapter 2 for more information on turn taking.) Make your interactions with her positive, and your time with her enjoyable for both of you. If either of you is not having fun, chances are very good that little learning is taking place, and a power struggle is in progress.

Some basic suggestions of toys and materials to have available for your child are listed below. (If I go too thoroughly into preschool curriculum and materials, I'll never get to reading, and that is why you are reading this book! If you need more help in this area, consult a preschool curriculum.)

(1) Shape boxes and balls, that require the child to find the correct openings for each object that goes in the box or ball, are excellent for young children. The child learns to attend to the object and task, find the hole with the matching shape, and turn the object the right way, in order for it to fit. She learns to discriminate shapes, to problem solve, and about the nature of objects. In addition, she experiences the satis-

faction of completing a task, learning that activities have a beginning, a middle, and an end. (Form boards teach the same skills.) Learning to open these balls and boxes is also a learning experience.

(2) Puzzles develop discrimination and problem-solving skills, much the same way as form boards. Start with simple, single-piece puzzles, and move on to the interlocking type. Generally, children enjoy puzzles. If this is the case with your child, reward her interest and provide her with many interesting puzzles.

(3) A large writing surface, such as a good quality chalkboard with lots of colored chalk available, is essential. (Research on early readers—typical readers—showed that every preschool reader had a large writing surface in their home, and had access to it.) Also, provide your child with various other drawing and writing materials, such as felt pens (great because they do so much with so little effort), crayons, and easy-to-use primary pencils. Have an unlimited supply of inexpensive paper (newsprint and used computer paper, or any paper you can let her recycle).

(4) Blocks, animals, cars, trucks, and "little people" that can be used together in construction and pretend play (building zoos and farms for animals and garages and roads for the cars and trucks).

(5) Dolls, stuffed animals, little tables and chairs, tea sets, and housekeeping equipment, lend themselves for practicing interaction, for pretending, and for learning the use of objects and family relationships and roles.

(6) Ordinary things around the house such as pots and pans; old clothes, shoes, hats, scarves, gloves for dress-up; boxes, all sizes (a big box that can be used for a house is nice); and, of course, a sandbox.

(7) *Sesame Street:* Children who watch, attend to, and enjoy *Sesame Street* generally have a head start. They often learn the alphabet and letter sounds and are very interested in learning to read. (If your child is not interested in *Sesame Street,* it most likely means that it is not meaningful to her, or that it moves too fast for her to comprehend. Turn it on anyway, in case something catches her interest, but don't try to force her to watch it. You'll have a power struggle on your hands.)

(8) Provide your child with experiences in the community to help her learn about her environment and how the community works. Foreshadow, let her know what to expect, and what she can do on the outing. Give her a goal, a reason for going to these places, so they will be meaningful to her. For example, she could put a picture she drew in an envelope addressed to Grandma and carry it on the way to the mailbox or post office and drop it in the slot, and on the way, you can discuss

what she is mailing and to whom she is sending it. Give her some dirty clothing to take to the cleaners, show her the spots, and talk about what the cleaners is going to do about it. If she can, ask her to show the spot to the person at the cleaners. Let her decide on something that she can buy at the supermarket. Give her the label from the can or package it comes in, or draw a simple picture of it. Let her carry this market order (her goal for going to the store) and show her how to find it. Let her help plan outings, such as going to feed the ducks—she can put stale bread in a bag to carry; going to the park—she can put a snack in a bag or help make sandwiches for a picnic, or choose a ball or other toy to take.

(If an outing has little meaning to your child, or she has no goal for the outing, such as on long shopping trips, when you will be trying on clothing and looking for items of no interest to her, it is better not to take her. The experience is most apt to teach her to misbehave by trying to escape the situation that is unpleasant to her.)

(9) Picture cards (often called pre-primary cards) and lotto picture games are excellent for developing matching, selecting, and naming skills used in the reading program described in this book. They are good for building vocabulary as well. The picture cards are generally about the size of playing cards and have pictures of simple, familiar objects on them (doll, ball, bus, car, bird, dog, etc.). These are generally found in variety stores and book stores in the section where children's books are sold. Buy two sets, so you can play matching and selecting games.

Lotto games consist of a larger card with six or eight pictures and smaller matching picture cards. There are games with pictures of simple, familiar objects and games that feature objects in different categories, such as all farm animals, zoo animals, flowers, fruits, vegetables, etc. In addition, there are lotto games that feature math concepts, perception, and symbols.

How Do I Know If My Child Is Ready to Learn to Read?

The same procedures used to teach children to discriminate and name the picture symbols on picture cards or lotto cards are used to teach sight words. When preschool children are able to match and select lotto cards that require fine discrimination skills, they are generally able to begin sight reading. If a child is not able to match and select lotto pictures, chances are, she is not able to match and read words, and will not be successful. (If she can do it, but refuses, that's another story.)

In the program developed at the University of Washington (described here), children were taught to match, select, and name lotto cards. When they were able to match lotto that required fine discrimination, they were moved into this beginning reading program. For children who had not been in the program and did not have this experience, matching lotto that required fine discrimination was used to test the child's readiness for reading. However, I have found that sometimes children are not interested in matching lotto—they are tired of it, it is meaningless to them, or they are older and think that matching lotto is something that preschoolers do (not age appropriate for them). These same children will often show interest in words and pictures of their families.

I think that it is generally best to test for "readiness" by presenting the first step in the reading program, matching words to words under photos. (See Chapter 8 for a full description of this step.) If your child can match words and responds to the tasks, she should have the discrimination skills to start this reading program. If she can't match words, perhaps she would profit from learning to match lotto or symbols (line drawings) for objects, but do not try to continue with the reading. If she is not responding with awareness of or interest in the tasks, reading will not be meaningful to her. Most likely, she does not yet have the behavioral or cognitive skills necessary to succeed in the program. Wait a couple months and try again.

Subjects who were taught reading readiness were best in reading readiness; subjects who were taught reading were best in reading.

During a presentation to a class, Dr. James Moss reported on a research project. There were two groups of special education subjects. One group was mainstreamed into the first grade. The other group was assigned to a special education class. The group in the first grade was taught reading with their peers; the group in the special education class was taught reading readiness skills. At the end of the school year, both groups were tested. The group that was taught reading was better at reading; the group that was taught reading readiness skills was better at reading readiness tasks.

Children generally learn what they are taught. It is important that we teach them skills that are meaningful and useful to them.

Chapter 7

ABOUT THIS READING PROGRAM

Characteristics of this Reading Program

Perhaps the most distinctive components of the reading program described in this book are: it breaks reading down into simple steps that provide tasks and activities that allow the child to practice at his success level before moving to the next step; it is functional—activities are planned so that the child can immediately use the words; it utilizes a number of methods and techniques that can be applied to meet individual needs and learning styles; and it is systematic. More specifically:

(1) It is carefully programmed for the success of the learner: The child first matches the word (simplest response, matching word to word); second, selects the word (selects the word on verbal cue); and third, says the word (says the word verbally, or signs it). Words are added gradually. After the learner masters the words introduced, then new words are added. The alphabet and letter sounds are taught after the learner has experienced success reading sight words. Care is taken that the child is successful at each step, before moving to the next.

(2) It is an adaptation of the language experience approach, individualized for each learner, and is functional: The words and sentences that the individual learns to read are within his experience and are meaningful to and useful for him. The child has opportunities to use these words throughout the day. The child's interest and progress determine the words taught and the rate of adding new words and new concepts.

(3) It builds success and confidence: Meaningful sight words are taught first, and alphabet and letter sounds are introduced after the child is reading some sight words. After letters have been introduced, sight-words and phonics are taught concurrently. In addition, the use of mnemonics and other learning aids are encouraged to meet individual needs of the learner.

(4) It provides meaningful practice: Games, books, and activities are used to provide practice in reading words, learning letters and letter sounds, generalizing reading skills, and comprehending the meaning of the written word.

(5) It is versatile: It can be a functional, language experience program within itself, and may be the only program used for some children. It can be a "beginner" program used to enhance language and to build confidence for later success in a basal reader. And the programming and teaching techniques can be adapted to supplement other reading programs.

(6) The materials are simple, inexpensive, and individualized for each learner: Flash cards, games, charts, and books have to be custom made in order to provide individualized, personalized, instruction. This does require more work on the part of the instructor. However, the materials are simple and inexpensive to make.

(7) It is fun for the learner and the instructor: If it is not fun for both of you, you are not following the program. You should discontinue the program if your child does not find the activities fun and meaningful. Likewise, if you, the instructor, do not find it an effective program and don't receive satisfaction and pleasure from teaching your child, you should discontinue the program. If you find it drudgery, you will be ineffective in implementing the program. This will result in your child being "mistaught" and is sure to lead to failure.

(8) It is systematic: Goals and objectives are stated; there are procedures to follow; records of the words learned are kept in a systematic manner (alphabetized word bank and alphabet book-dictionaries); data on the child's progress are kept; new words and letters are introduced based on data; and activities are described for each stage of learning—acquisition, practice to fluency, transfer, and generalization.

How This Program Can Be Used

The procedures and guidelines described in this book are not intended to fit every child to a T, and the instructor is not expected to always follow each step as described. In fact, it is my goal to give enough information for you to tailor it to your child and his needs. Take into consideration the skills and experiences your child has and determine how the methods and techniques can be used to his best advantage. Following are some possible uses of the program described in this book:

(1) As a success-oriented beginning reading program: For some children, the program is used as a starter program, an introduction to reading. This program introduces reading in a fun, non-threatening way and builds confidence in the child. (If this is not the case, the instructor is not following the program and the program should be changed or discontinued).

While in this program, some children will demonstrate an aptitude for reading, learning words readily and rapidly, making it difficult for the instructor to make materials fast enough to keep up with them. These children can generally move into a basal reader successfully, and eliminate a lot of work on the instructor's part.

Basal readers are generally well programmed, teaching all the intricacies of reading. A few children will be able to keep up with their peers in inclusive classrooms, and others will continue in the basal program but will be reading at a lower grade level than most of their peers. They can continue in the basal reader as long as the material is interesting and meaningful to them, and their success continues. It is important that the child continues to make good progress and enjoys reading.

(2) To help supplement a basal reading program: The techniques and methods described here can be adapted to teach the student words and concepts he is having difficulty with in a basal program. Also, some of the games and activities can be used to teach him the functional use and practical application of reading, and will give him opportunities to demonstrate comprehension in practical situations.

(3) As a language experience, functional reading program: Some children may not be successful in basal readers that have stories about Peter and Jane going to the pet store, and they may have difficulty answering comprehension questions as to how Jane felt when the puppy licked her nose. And, they may simply not be interested in the stories. For these children, this will be the only reading program used. They will be dependent on the reading skills they learn in this program to obtain information, to enhance their memory, to read directions and labels, to communicate with others, and for reading pleasure. Using this approach and programming books for recreational reading should not put the child at a disadvantage over children who are in basal readers, as long as he continues to grow in reading skills. The child should continue in the program in which he is most successful and is most meaningful to him.

(4) To "program" recreational reading material: Children with Down syndrome can be taught to read books, magazines, newspapers, and other materials they are interested in reading. The choice of reading material depends on the child. The techniques and methods presented in this book can be adapted to any reading material that is within the child's understanding and experience. In some cases, it opens the doors to recreational reading, and makes it possible for the child to entertain others with reading as well.

Are you my mother?

Rudy was nine years old, and his class was having a Mother's Day Program. When his teacher asked him what he would like to do, he said that he wanted to read *Are You My Mother?* (by P. D. Eastman, Beginning Books, Random House, Inc.), a story about a newly hatched bird who fell out of his nest, never having seen his mother. The baby bird went out looking for her, asking a kitten, chicken, dog, cow, and even a car, airplane, boat, and crane, "Are you my mother?" Rudy's teacher taught him to read the words in the book that he did not already know. He learned to read it very well. His performance was impressive. His mother, and all who attended, were touched. (Chapter 16 describes how to program books.)

(5) As a visual language to enhance communication: As mentioned earlier, the program described in this book was first used to help a non-verbal child to communicate. Most people with Down syndrome have speech and language problems that make it difficult for them to communicate verbally. For some children, the focus of this program will therefore be on using reading as a means to improve speech and language. Some of the ways reading can be used to enhance communication include:

(a) *It can help with articulation:* When a child learns the sounds of letters and can *see* the word, he can *see* the letters and syllables and determine how the word should sound. Often, the individual does not hear all the sounds in a word. He does not hear the beginning, middle, or end. The spoken word lasts a second or less. The written word is there for as long as it is needed. It is there for the child to study and think about.

But nana *doesn't start with a b.*

When my own son was a preschooler, we were in the supermarket together. He looked at the big sign above the bananas and said, "But *nana* doesn't start with a b." I told him he was right, but the word was not *nana,* but *banana,* as I showed him the *ba* and the *nana.* He was amazed. On the way home, he repeated several times, as if he had made a great discovery, "It's ba nana!" He had never heard the *ba,* but when he saw it, he could see that it was there. He remembered and practiced it.

Generally, children with Down syndrome articulate better when they are reading. It is a good exercise in helping them to practice good articulation. I cannot promise that reading is going to improve articulation, only that it can be used as a tool to help. Some individuals with Down syndrome will always have difficulty with articulation and most people will have difficulty understanding them.

(b) *It can help in learning sentence structure.* When children learn to read simple sentences, they are learning to put words together, and practicing speaking in sentences. And just as they do not hear all the sounds in a word, they frequently do not hear all the words in a sentence. When they see the word there on paper, they become aware that it is there.

Read am *Mom, read* am.

Scott, five years old, had a long ferry ride to the University program, so he came to school only once or twice a week, and his mother tutored him in between. He was learning to read a made-for-Scott book called *All about Me.* One sentence in it was, "I am a boy." He would read, "I a boy." But he skipped *am.* I had him match, select, and name *am* (usually did the trick), but still, when he read the sentence, he skipped *am.* I told his mother that I thought the word had no meaning for him. He did not hear it when others spoke, as we seldom say "am," we usually say "I'm." *Am* is a strange word, as we can use it only with *I.* I suggested to his mother that she use the word *am* a lot, emphasizing it in her speech. She could say, "I *am* your mother. I *am* driving the car. I *am* eating dinner," etc.

When his mother picked him up after school the next time he attended, she said, "Scott, what did you do in school today?" He answered, "Read *am,* Mom, read *am.*" He let her know that he had received the message.

I want apple juice, please.

Jason was six years old and reading sentences, but he did not usually communicate using sentences. His mother used sentence strips to encourage him to speak in sentences. I was visiting in their home and had the opportunity to observe her method in practice at breakfast time. He sat at the table, and she placed a sentence strip on the table in front of him that said, "I want apple juice, please." He read it enthusiastically, and his mother, just as enthusiastically, responded with, "Apple juice is coming right up." After the apple juice was served, she presented him with another sentence strip that said, "Apple juice is delicious." He read it as he enjoyed his juice, and there was little doubt that he did, indeed, think apple juice was delicious, and he expressed it well as he read the sentence. His mother presented him with yet another sentence strip that said, "I want oatmeal, please." And, again, she responded and brought him the oatmeal and another sentence strip that said, "Oatmeal is delicious." Both mother and son enjoyed this game. He had a script, and was learning to ask for and comment on things in sentences, using written cues, rather than the usual verbal cues that we are constantly giving our children, continually pointing out their inadequacies, correcting them by saying, "Remember to say the whole thing." Or "Say, 'I want apple juice please.'"

Jason's mother felt confident that he would soon learn this breakfast dialog and would no longer need the sentence scripts. She told me that this approach had been successful in teaching him to ask for his car toy properly. Previously, he would get in the car and yell for it. Before he started yelling, she presented him with the sentence strip, "I want my toy, please." As soon as he read it, she rewarded him with the toy—and a nice smile and kind words. After reading the sentence strip just two times, he asked for the toy properly, and even said "please," without the help of the sentence strip.

> (c) *It builds vocabulary, provides information, and facilitates learning concepts:* When a child does not know or understand the meaning of a spoken word, we may not be aware of it. The child is unlikely to call our attention to it by saying, "What was that word? What does it mean?" When teaching the child to read, it becomes very apparent what he does and does not understand. This helps us to identify some specific needs of the child. A good example of simple vocabulary building was mentioned above—Scott learned the word *am*. And he learned how to use it.

Simpsons! Simpsons!

I was teaching Travis, who was six years old, to read. His mother told me that *The Simpsons* was one of his favorite television shows. I thought that he would enjoy reading about how he liked watching the Simpsons. In addition, he would have the pleasure of reading "The Simpsons," when it appeared on the screen (functional use of his reading). I presented a picture of the cartoon character Bart Simpson. His response was, "Simpsons!" My reaction was, "He's *Bart*. His name is *Bart. Bart* Simpson." Travis ignored my insistence that the character's name was Bart. He was excited with having Bart there, but would respond to the photo with only, "Simpsons! Simpsons!"

His mother said that she did not think that he had the concept that Simpson is the family name, and that each character has a different first name, or that families, in general, have family names. I put Bart aside, and made a family lotto game featuring Travis's own family, to teach him the concept of family names. This is valuable, functional, general information. After he learns about his own family, then he can apply the concept to other families. And, I hope, have a better understanding of the Simpsons. The program should then have more meaning to him.

(d) *It gives the reader the option of using notes to make speeches and relate experiences:* I have heard and seen several persons with Down syndrome make speeches at conferences, workshops, and school assemblies. All of them read their speeches. Reading enables them to make public speeches. It gives them the security to stand before several hundred (in some cases thousands) of people and share information, ideas, and feelings. They do not have to worry that they might forget what they are going to say, or how they are going to say it. They have the advantage of having the same prop the rest of us have.

When students with Down syndrome go to middle school and high school, they are often included in speech and drama classes. Reading is very helpful. They can organize their thoughts, write their speech (perhaps with help), read it, and participate fully. Also, in drama they can practice their lines by reading, or use cue cards. I am sure that actor Chris Burke finds reading very helpful to him in his profession.

It was a very impressive Bar Mitzvah.

Reading English can help when making speeches or saying prayers in a foreign language (or even learning a foreign language). When Eliot was preparing for his Bar Mitzvah, he was having difficulty memorizing the Hebrew prayer using the audio tape of the prayer his parents had prepared for him. The Hebrew words were sounds that did not make sense to him, and he had no way of connecting them to any experiences or information he had. The solution to this problem was a transliteration of the prayer into English. He read his speech, using his knowledge of phonics to say the Hebrew words. It was a very impressive Bar Mitzvah. (See figure 7.1.)

Figure 7.1. Eliot and his very proud mother at his Bar Mitzvah.

What did you do in school today?

In addition to making formal speeches, the child can use notes, written reports, or journals to relay his school experiences to his parents, and to relay home experiences to the teacher and classmates. Parents often complain that when they ask their child, "What did you do in school today?" the child responds, "Nothing." Perhaps the child does not remember, or thinks that nothing worth talking about happened. Completing "reports" that can be used as a guide for discussion about what happened is a functional use of reading and is explained in detail in Chapter 18.

Where the Program Has Been Used

The Program for Children with Down Syndrome and Other Developmental Delays was funded for outreach from 1972 through 1987. During those years, Dr. Valentine Dmitriev and I provided training to early intervention programs, public and private schools, and parent groups, throughout the United States and in several foreign countries. (I have provided training on every continent, except for Antarctica). The reading program described in this book was presented during most of these training sessions. In addition, we have presented the program at many state and national conferences. We do not know to what extent these techniques are being used today. Two programs, one in Australia (Down Syndrome Program at Macquarie University, North Ryde, New South Wales), and one in the United Kingdom (Portsmouth Down Syndrome Project), used this basic method and published reading data. Susan Buckley, from the United Kingdom project, published a manual, *Reading & Language Development in Children with Down's Syndrome,* and a videotape that describes the program as she used it.

Currently, I am providing on-going consultation services to a program for children with Down syndrome in Saudi Arabia. I have taught the teachers how to teach reading using this program, and have developed a curriculum for them. The children are making impressive progress, reading in Arabic.

PART 2

Getting Started

This section focuses on the "how to" in getting started when teaching sight words, the alphabet, writing, spelling, and beginning phonics. Each of these areas are presented in different chapters for organizational purposes, but are generally taught concurrently. For example, Chapter 8 describes how to teach sight words; Chapter 9 describes how to teach the names and the sounds of the letters in the initial position of the sight words taught. Usually, after a child has a strong sight vocabulary and has been introduced to most of the letters, he can learn to use letter sounds (phonics) to read "word families." A child can start spelling when he knows the names of the letters (Chapter 10), and writing when he is able to recognize letters by name and copy letters using pencil and paper or keyboard (chapter 11). Your child's success in each of these areas (sight words, the alphabet, phonics, writing, or spelling) will be your guide in determining the rate at which you will move through these areas and into new areas. It is important for your child's success—and yours—to follow the program, one step at a time, so that neither of you are overwhelmed. You do not need to teach everything at once, and your child does not have to learn everything at once.

This is a language experience approach to teaching reading. Once you have familiarized yourself with the methods and techniques described in this section (Part 2), you should be able to use them to teach any words that are within your child's experiences, interests, and needs. To give you a clearer understanding of how to develop

teaching units based on your child's experience, interests, and needs, and to apply the methods and techniques described here, sample lessons are provided in Part 3. For most children, it will be appropriate to first teach the sight words in Chapter 8; then introduce the beginning letters of these words as described in Chapter 9; and then move on to a unit in Part 3 (or develop a unit yourself). Most children will need to experience considerable success in reading sight words before moving on to writing, spelling, and phonics (Chapters 10, 11, and 12).

This book describes methods and techniques designed to get your child off to a successful start. When his success is established, he may be able to move into a basal reader or into another reading program that provides methods and materials for teaching higher-level reading skills. However, some children will make better progress by continuing in a language experience program. It is not within the scope of this book to provide detailed instruction on teaching these higher-level concepts—compound words, word endings, digraphs, consonant blends, vowel combinations, prefixes, syllables, etc. If you wish to move forward and teach your child these higher-level concepts within the language experience approach, and he is able to learn and apply these higher-level concepts, you can adapt the techniques described in this book to teach these concepts as well.

To assist those of you who wish to continue with the language experience approach in teaching higher-level concepts, some guidelines are provided in Appendix A-2. These guidelines suggest a

sequence for teaching reading, and outline some
rules to help in teaching hard and soft sounds of
"c" and "g" and syllabication.

Chapter 8

TEACHING SIGHT WORDS

Introduction

This is an individualized, language-experience, functional reading program, adapted for children with Down syndrome. It is impossible to describe exactly how, what, and when to teach each child; therefore, I am providing sample lesson plans, organized by units. The instructor will need to make decisions about which units will be most appropriate for their student and adapt these lesson plans and units to fit her. In some cases, there may not be a unit that is appropriate for your child, or you and your child may decide on a theme or subject that is not presented in a unit, or your child may finish all the units provided and you will need more. In these cases, you will need to develop your own units by using these sample lesson plans as models. These sample lessons are arranged in units that represent typical themes and subjects that are functional for most children. They are intended to provide you with techniques, strategies, procedures, and material that can be applied and adapted to teach your child to read about any subject that is meaningful to her. The words taught and the reading activities will vary with the individual, and will be determined by each child's interests, experiences, age, existing skills, environment, and her responses to the activities.

In the true language experience approach, the teacher provides the students with experiences, such as field trips (visits to zoos, museums, parks, historical monuments, stores, airports, universities, factories, buildings, and all that the community has to offer that would be of interest or value to the students), art projects, science experiments, cooking projects, films, books, stories, games, role playing, etc. These experiences are usually centered around specific subjects or themes (units), and the students each write (or dictate to the teacher or another student) about these experiences using their own words. In the process, they learn to read, spell, write, and speak about their experiences. (When we speak or write, it is important to have experiences, information, and vocabulary—we must have something to write about and the tools to write; when we read, we need experiences, information, and vocabulary before the reading material is meaningful and useful to us.) It is my goal to give you, the reader, the tools to use this approach, using these adaptations for children with Down syndrome. Strategies and ideas will be provided for various age groups, environments, and skill levels. These are basic guidelines to follow. Individualize, use your own creativity, and use options that appeal to your child.

These procedures are generally directed to parents of elementary-age children to use at home. Suggested adaptations for the classroom and for older learners will be provided for units in which adaptations may be needed.

I read a recipe, then I put in what I had on hand.

When I returned from a trip, my husband served me some spaghetti with a delicious sauce. I asked him if he followed a recipe or just made it up. He said, "I read a recipe, then put in what I had on hand." This is what I want you to do. Read the instructions, learn the sequence and strategies, and adapt them to your situation to meet the needs of your child. It's the product—the happy and inspired reader, in this case—that's important.

FAMILY NAMES: READING SIGHT WORDS USING MATCH, SELECT, AND NAME SEQUENCE

"Sight words" are the words that a reader recognizes instantly, with fluency and proficiency. Any word, if read enough times, becomes a sight word. Most of the words we read, we read by sight—that is, we recognize them instantly—we do not stop and "sound them out." Each person's sight vocabulary will vary with his or her reading interests and occupation. "Basic sight words" are words that are used frequently in most reading material. There are many lists of basic sight words. These lists are usually graded, starting with a basic sight vocabulary for each grade level. Appendix B contains a list of 200 basic sight words that make up 50 to 75 percent of the words in material used by elementary school students. Words such as *I, the, and, is, a,* and *to* are words of highest utility. If a reader has 200 of these high-utility words in her sight vocabulary, she very likely has mastered over half of the words she is apt to encounter in her reading. However, these words, in isolation, have little meaning and the reader has little use for them. They are best taught in context when the child can use them in reading sentences and phrases. The first sight words taught should be words that are meaningful to the child, and words for which she has an immediate use.

This chapter describes in detail the materials and procedures for teaching sight words. Refer to this chapter whenever you need more information about materials and procedures for teaching sight words. These procedures will be used and referred to in Part 3.

Goal: *Your child will build her sight reading vocabulary to include the names of family members and additional words used in a simple book; she will practice reading, comprehending, and generalizing these words by using them in games and home activities, and by reading an individualized book.*

Lesson Plans for Teaching Sight Words

Figure 8.1

Introducing Family Names: Acquisition

Objective 1: *Your child will match, select, and name (verbally or by sign) the names of family members using picture cards and flash cards.*

In the following sample lesson the words *Sally* (the child), *Mommy, Daddy,* and *Will* (Sally's brother) are used.

Materials:

Flash cards and picture cards (figure 8.1).

Supplies for making:

(1) Cards, approximately 5 by 8 inches (standard 5 x 8, index cards or other cards approximately that size, large enough for mounting a photo and having about a 2–inch space at the bottom to write the name on).

(2) Photos, approximately 5 x 3½ inches, of the child and each family member (one person on each photo, not group photos—if there are more than 4 children in the family, you may choose to use photos of the siblings closest to the child).

(3) Tape (Scotch Magic™ works well, and when used on the back of the photo, does not damage the photo).

(4) Black felt pen, either wide (such as Mr. Sketch™, or fine point (such as Vis-a-Vis™ markers).

(5) Scissors.

(6) Paper clips, rubber bands, or other device for holding cards together.

(7) Shoe box or large envelope (to keep it all in).

How to make:

(1) Mount the photos on the 8 x 5 cards: Use the tape and make a "doughnut" with the sticky side out, place a "doughnut" on the back of each photo and stick each photo to a 8 x 5 card, leaving about 2 inches at the bottom of the card. (Use tape, rather than glue, so the photo can be taken off the card later).

(2) Print the name the child calls the person in the photo in the space at the bottom of the card, using the felt pen. For example, if she calls her father Pop, print *Pop;* Daddy, print *Daddy;* Dad, print *Dad.* The same is true of her mother and other family members. If the child does not yet call a person by name, print the name that you use when referring to that person to the child. For example, if you call Stephanie, Step, print *Step* (good to use simple, easy-to-say names when possible); if you call William, Will, print *Will.*

Print well, making letters approximately ¾ to 1 inch high using upper and lower case letters appropriately. If you need them, draw lines to print between, to help keep the letters in their proper position, above and below lines as they should be. Leave ample space between words so that it is clear where one word ends and another begins when writing sentences and phrases. Refer to the standard for printing letters in Appendix B-2, if you need to refresh your memory.

Using a computer program that prints large fonts is an option, if it is available to you and you find it efficient. If a computer is used for flash cards and picture cards, cut the words out and glue them on the cards, or copy them on card stock; if your printer is designed to print on card stock, print directly on the card stock. Paper of standard weight is a bit too flimsy. Cards printed on card stock will need to be cut out.

If you are concerned about your printing and don't have a computer, use a stencil. It is important that the words are written properly. Your child is learning to read, and it is necessary for the printing to be of a high standard, so she can recognize the word, properly printed, anywhere. If she sees "MoMmY" one place and "Mommy" in another, she may not recognize them as the same word. We want her to be able to read standard text.

(3) Make matching flash cards for each picture card (figure 8.1). Using the scissors, cut 8 x 5 inch cards into four 2 x 5 inch cards. To begin,

you will need as many as the number of family members you have. Print the word on the card, just as you did for the picture card. (If your child drools or has a tendency to put her fingers in her mouth, laminate both the picture card and the flash card (or use clear Contact™ paper; otherwise, the ink will smear and you will have to start over again).

Procedures:

Conduct the reading sessions anywhere that is comfortable for you and your child, at a table or on the floor. It is generally easier to keep track of the materials and to keep a child engaged at a table, but if the structure of sitting at the table is threatening to her, or she finds it aversive, use the floor.

This is the acquisition stage; your child is just "acquiring" these words in her sight reading vocabulary. Words she did not previously read are being "introduced" to her. The procedures for this stage, described here, provide errorless practice at three levels of difficulty.

Level 1: Matching. Matching is the simplest response. The child matches a word to a matching word.

Level 2: Selecting. Selecting is more difficult. The learner has to be able to select the correct word on verbal or verbal and signed cue.

Level 3: Naming. Naming (saying or signing the word), in response to the written word, is the most complex response.

If your child does not speak, or if her speech is not intelligible or very limited, teach her manual signs for the words you teach her to read. Model the manual sign by signing the word each time you say it. (This method of communication is known as "Total Communication.") If signing is used with her at school, consult with the teacher or the speech clinician and use the signs they use. If signs are not being used at school, and you want to use signs, purchase a book on sign language. If sign language is used, and if your child will be expected to use sign language to communicate her needs, it is important that those with whom she interacts can read her signs. Being able to sign the word gives the learner a means of "naming" or "reading" words at this highest level. For more information on using signs with children with Down syndrome, consult *Communication Skills in Children with Down Syndrome,* by Libby Kumin (Woodbine House, Bethesda, MD).

If Your Child Makes Mistakes

If your child takes the blank distractor card, rather than the Sally card, she may: (1) not have any idea what you are talking about (no concept that those symbols on the card are symbols for her name); (2) not be attending and/or is uninterested; (3) be teasing you (deliberately making the wrong response); (4) have "learned helplessness" and be trying to avoid the possibility of failure (if she does not cooperate, she won't have to do it anymore); or (5) be non-compliant in general, and unwilling to cooperate. Try to avoid mistakes; remember, you want to make it an almost errorless process. Your child is learning and you want her to practice the correct response. It is rare that a child would make a mistake at this point, but I am giving you correction procedures, just in case, and you can refer to them when you need them.

Correction Procedures:

(1) Remove the choice (distractor). Hold up the Sally card and say, "This card says *Sally*; take *Sally*. Good! Now put Sally on Sally."

(2) Put the two flash cards in front of your child again, and, pointing to the Sally card say, "This says *Sally*. Take the card that says *Sally*." Place the Sally card closer to her, so it is easier to reach than the distractor card. If she reaches for the distractor card again, hold on to it and say, "No, this one says *Sally*." Point to the Sally card.

(3) Hold up the two cards, holding the distractor card away from your child in one hand, and the Sally card close to her in the other hand, making it very obvious what the correct choice is, and again, say, "Take the card that says *Sally*." Or "Take *Sally*." If your child goes for the blank card, hold on to it and say, "No, this one says *Sally*. Take it."

(4) If your child is still insisting on taking the blank card, perhaps she is in a power struggle with you and is not willing to cooperate at this time and is making a statement about her lack of interest in reading. If this is the case, put the materials away, and say, "You can tell me when you are ready to read and look at the words and pictures."

(5) If you think your child is teasing you, make it into a game. Bring in two small jars (empty spice or baby food jars). Put a jar by her and one by you. Tell her that when she gets it right, she scores, she gets a marble in her jar. If she gets it wrong, you have "tricked" her, so you score. (See "Setting the Stage for Success" in Chapter 5.) (She can count the marbles and plot the scores on a chart later, if she likes—math and fine motor bonus.)

(6) If the above strategy does not work, and you think that your child has the ability to learn to read but lacks motivation and/or has "learned helplessness," you may try to use a desired food as a reinforcer. (See Chapter 5.)

(7) If the above strategies do not work, and your child does not cooperate, put it away and try again in a few months. Your child is not ready, or not interested in learning to read, or it is meaningless to her. Do not continue with this method if your child is not cooperative. Nothing will be achieved but a power struggle.

DURING ALL PROCEDURES GIVE YOUR CHILD FEEDBACK AND PRAISE FOR CORRECT RESPONSES; FOLLOW CORRECTION PROCEDURES FOR INCORRECT RESPONSES.

Introducing the First Word
LEVEL 1:
MATCH 1:1 (NO CHOICE)

Show your child the picture card with her picture on it. Let her look at it and talk about it, and if she does not say who it is, tell her, "It's *you*, Sally" (be natural). Then show her, pointing to her name under the photo (chances are, she can already read it, which is good, because it is good to start with something the child already knows). Say, "*Sally*. It says *Sally*." Then show her the flash card with Sally printed on it, and say, "This says Sally. Put Sally on Sally." If she does not understand what she is to do, model, putting Sally on Sally, then give her the card so she can do it herself. You may need to gently guide her hand to put Sally on Sally, if she does not understand the task. When she matches the flash card with the matching word on the picture card, praise her, be excited, say, "You did it! You found *Sally!*" Or, "You put *Sally* on *Sally!* Good for *you!* You were *looking!*" (Praise/feedback/reinforcement.)

LEVEL 2:
SELECTING 1:2 (BLANK CARD DISTRACTOR)

Next, take the Sally flash card, and hold it and a blank card at your child's eye level (or place these cards on the table by her) and say, "Take the card that says *Sally*." Or, simply, "Take *Sally*." When your child takes Sally, say, "Good! Now, put *Sally* on *Sally*."

When she matches it, say, "Great! You found Sally!"

LEVEL 3:
NAMING (VERBAL OR
SIGNED RESPONSE)

Hold up the Sally card and say, "This card says _____." Allow your child to supply the word. If she does, say, "*You* are right; it says *Sally!* You read it!" Accept any approximation to Sally. If your child cannot say Sally, teach her to sign it by signing (modeling) every time you say "Sally," and supply the word for her.

The entire match, select, and name procedures for one word, described above, should take only 30 to 45 seconds, unless there is a lot of discussion or corrections. Of course, each time you go through the procedure, it will take an additional 30 to 45 seconds.

Introducing the Second Word

Your child has read one word (matched it, selected it, and responded by orally reading or manual signing); now she is ready for another, *Mommy.* Follow the same procedures in levels 1, 2, and 3, using the Mommy picture card and flash card.

Now that your child has been introduced to two words individually, provide practice that will require her to discriminate these two words.

LEVEL 1:
DISCRIMINATING WORDS, MATCH 1:2 (MATCH ONE WORD, TWO CHOICES-ONE DISTRACTOR)

(In Select 1:2, there was a distractor, the blank card, so the child could make a mistake; however, this distractor made it very easy to make the correct choice. In this exercise, we are using the words that have been introduced to the child as distractors.)

Place the two picture cards (Sally and Mommy) in front of your child. Hold up the Sally flash card, present it to her, and say, "It says Sally. Put Sally on Sally." (If your child spontaneously reads Sally, say, "Yes, it says Sally, put Sally on Sally." This is a matching task, don't ask her to read the word, but if she does, GREAT! These are procedures to provide errorless practice, but if she gives a more advanced response, reinforce her. Perhaps she can start skipping some of these steps.) Hold up the Mommy card and say, "It says Mommy. Put Mommy on Mommy."

LEVEL 2:
DISCRIMINATING WORDS, SELECT 1:2 (SELECT ONE WORD, TWO CHOICES)

Leave the two picture cards in front of your child. Place the Mommy and Sally flash cards on the table, beside the picture cards. Calling attention to the cards say, "Point to (or show me) Mommy; point to Sally." This accomplished, rearrange them as you would dominos in a domino game. (Children generally enjoy this little routine, as it gives it a game-like quality. Soon your child will want to do the mixing; let her.) Say to her, "I'm mixing them up."

Then say, "Now where is Sally? Where is Mommy?" Respond, "You are right, I can't fool (or trick) *you!*" (Of course, saying this is optional. Use your own judgment. It generally increases the child's interest in the task, makes it a game, and challenges her to try hard to avoid being "tricked" or "fooled.")

Next say, "Put Sally on Sally." Then, "Put Mommy on Mommy." (She selects the correct flash card and matches it with the name on the picture card; more errorless practice.)

LEVEL 3:
DISCRIMINATING WORDS, NAMING 2 CARDS

Leave the picture cards in front of your child. Hold up the Sally flash card and say, "This card says_____?" Then hold up the Mommy flash card and say, "This says_____?" As your child responds, give her the card and let her match again (more practice). If she doesn't respond correctly, point to the picture cards and show her the name, so she can learn to use the picture cards as a strategy to figure out what the flash cards say.

Introduce Additional Words

When your child can successfully match, select, and name the first two words introduced, then introduce new words, one at a time, using the match, select, and name method described above. As new words are introduced, increase choices by adding distractors of words introduced. For example, when Daddy is introduced, your child will match and select 1:3 (choices, Mommy, Daddy, Sally). When brother Will is introduced, match and select 1:4 (choices Mommy, Daddy, Will, and Sally). At this stage, for these practice sessions, keep the choices at four. For example, when the family pet, Sam, is introduced, the instructor can drop a previously introduced word to keep the choices for practice during this acquisition stage at 1:4.

Use Mnemonics When Needed

Figure 8.2

Mnemonics, the use of memory aids that employ vivid imagery, can be used to help your child remember words and letters. For example, if your child has trouble with remembering "see," draw eyes (for seeing) in the top part of the e's; the same can be done for the word "look," the o's can be made into eyes for looking.

Sometimes simple color coding of a letter can be helpful. For example, Dennis confused *Dennis* and *Daddy* because they both started with D. The *y* in *Daddy* was colored red and Dennis was told that it was like Daddy's tie. He needed to look for the *y* like Daddy's tie; if he found the tie, the word was Daddy, rather than Dennis, who did not wear ties (figure 8.2).

(More information on using mnemonics is in Chapter 11.)

Evaluate: Do a Probe

Now is your chance to *test*. At the end of each session, put the picture cards away. Present the flash cards of the words that have been introduced to your child, one at a time, and ask her to read them. Cue her any way that is natural for you, such as, "What word is this?" or "This says _____." (Showing the card may be the only cue your child will need.) If your child misses a word, simply supply the word for her. Nonverbal children can respond with sign language or gestures (for example, when the *Sally* flash card is shown to Sally she may point to herself, gesturing rather than using a manual sign).

As your child responds to the words, put the flash cards in two categories, one for words read correctly, one for the ones she missed. (An open file folder with a "+" on one side and a "-" on the other works well for this sort.) After the session, use the two piles of cards to record the data on a chart, placing a "+" by the words that were in the correct category and a "-" by the words in the "-" category (see sample data). This simple sorting after each response allows you to take accurate data, and it does not interrupt the flow of reading, as recording after each response does. This method is also easy for peer tutors to use, and, in time, your child herself can record her own data.

Keep adding words (and letters) to the probe, as they are introduced, until ten words (and/or letters) have been introduced. Then, keep the number of words in the probe at ten, dropping words mastered from the probe, and adding new words as they are introduced. The criteria for mastery (proficiency) here is defined as four correct responses to a word out of five trials of reading the flash card during the probe (80 percent). Until this criteria for mastery is met, continue to provide practice at the acquisition stage, matching, selecting, and naming using the picture cards and flash cards. When criteria for mastery are met, it is not generally necessary for your child to continue the match, select, and name practice, unless your child "misses" the word often when playing games and reading in books.

Length of Time for Reading Sessions

The amount of time for each structured reading session will depend on your child and her interest in the activities, her attention span, age, rate of learning, and in the number of different activities you plan for each session. Generally, for a beginner, I plan about 5 minutes per session for the acquisition stage activities. As new words are introduced (more words to practice) and new activities (alphabet book, Bingo games, lotto games) are introduced, the time is increased to about 20 to 30 minutes per session, depending on your time and your child's interest in the tasks. The games can be played at other, nonstructured times during the day, and can last as long as those playing are enjoying them. Just be sure that your child is not getting burnt out and the activities remain fun and motivating. Again, this is an individualized program, and you will need to determine what is appropriate for your child.

Example of Time Line and Probe

First Session (9/6/94): *Sally* and *Mommy* were introduced, so there were two words in the probe. At the end of the session, the instructor put the picture cards in the box, and Sally was asked to read "Sally" and "Mommy" from the flash cards, without picture cues visible. As Sally read the cards, the instructor placed them on an open folder that had a "+" on one side (for correct responses) and a "-" on the other (for incorrect responses). Sally read both cards correctly; the instructor put them on the "+" side, then recorded the results: 9/6/94 Sally +; Mommy +. (If your child does not respond correctly to both words, provide match, select, and name practice during subsequent sessions until she is correctly reading both words during the probe, before introducing new words. Your child is not ready to learn new words.)

Second Session (9/7/94): The instructor started Sally with some match, select, and name practice with *Sally* and *Mommy* as a "warm up," and then introduced *Daddy*. Sally practiced matching, selecting, and naming, using *Mommy* and *Sally* as distractors (1:3, three choices). Sally responded well, so the instructor introduced *Will*, and provided some practice using *Mommy, Sally,* and *Daddy* as distractors (1:4, four choices). At the end of the second session, there were four words in the probe (Sally, Mommy, Daddy, and Will). The instructor recorded her responses: Sally +; Mommy +; Daddy +; and Will +).

Third Session (9/8/94): The instructor reviewed Sally with some matching, selecting, and naming practice, and then introduced two new words, *I* and *see* (see next objective). Now there were six words in the probe, and probe data were as follows: Sally +; Mommy +; Daddy +; Will +; I +; see -.

Fourth Session (9/9/94): Sally moved into the practice to fluency, transfer, and generalization stage. She played Word to Picture Lotto and read her *I See Book* (these are described later in the chapter). At the end of the session, her data showed that she made correct responses to all six words in the probe.

Fifth Session (9/12/94): The instructor introduced the word *Book*. In this case, the *I See Book,* and a flash card were used to introduce the word. Sally matched the *Book* flash card to the word *Book* on the cover of the *I See Book*. She also practiced matching, selecting, and naming *I* and *See*. She then read the book, played lotto, and learned to put place cards around the table. Her probe had 7 words; she needed to be prompted with *Book* and *Will*.

Sixth Session (9/13/94): The instructor started the session with matching, selecting, and naming practice with *Will* and *Book*. Sally played lotto, read her book, and learned to use labels with family names on them. Sally read all words correctly on the probe.

Seventh Session (9/14/94): The instructor introduced the *S M D W B Book* and the letters *S* and *M* (see Introducing the Alphabet, Chapter 9). Sally went on an "S hunt" and played Alphabet Bingo using the "S" and "M" columns. She read her *I See Book*, and used the labels and place cards. The instructor added the letters *Ss* and *Mm* to the probe (9 words and letters in the probe). Sally read all words correctly, but had to be prompted on *S* and *M*.

Eight Session (9/15/94): Sally enjoyed reading her book, playing lotto and bingo, and using the fam-

Session	1	2	3	4	5	6	7	8	9	10
Date	9/6	9/7	9/8	9/9	9/12	9/13	9/14	9/15	9/16	9/19
Sally	+	+	+	+	+	+	+	+	drop	
Mommy	+	+	+	+	+	+	+	+	drop	
Daddy		+	+	+	+	+	+	+	+	+
Will		+	+	+	-	+	+	+	+	+
I			+	+	+	+	+	+	+	+
see			-	+	+	+	+	+	+	+
Book					-	+	+	+	+	+
Ss							-	+	+	+
Mm							-	+	+	+
Dd								-	+	+
Ww									-	+
Bb									-	+

DATA CHART

ily names. She went on an "M hunt" and reviewed the "S hunt" (walked through the house, finding the S's and saying, "S for sink; s for stove; s for skirt.") The instructor introduced *D*. Now the probe had ten words and letters. Sally read all words and letters correctly, except *D*.

Ninth Session (9/16/94): Sally continued to read her book, played games (lotto, bingo, alphabet basketball), and used labels and place cards. She went on a "D hunt" and reviewed the M and S hunt words. The instructor introduced *W* and *B*. *Sally* and *Mommy* were dropped from the probe to keep the number of words and letters at 10. Sally had exceeded criteria for mastery of these words. Probe: Sally needed to be prompted on *W* and *B*.

Tenth Session (9/19/94): Sally continued with her practice, playing games and reading her books (*I See Book* and *S M D W B Book*). She was correct on all letters and words in the probe.

When the next new word was introduced, *Daddy* was dropped. Actually, at this point, criteria for dropping (4 correct responses out of 5) had been met for all words, but in order to keep the number of words and letters in the probe at 10, only *Daddy* was dropped from the probe. Criteria for dropping had not been met for any of the letters, except *I*. It is wise to go slowly and provide lots of fun practice, so it can all "soak in."

Start a Word Bank

The word bank consists of flash cards of words that your child can read. When your child reaches mastery for a word, add it to her word bank. At this stage, the word bank can be kept in an envelope. As the alphabet is introduced, instructions will be given for alphabetizing and organizing words. The word bank is a storage of words for future use. The probe is a means of taking data to determine your child's proficiency in reading the words and letters she has been introduced to and to determine when your child is ready for new words to be introduced.

Match, Select, and Name Using Two Sets of Flash Cards

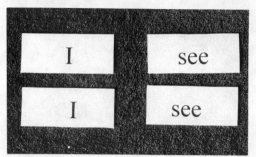

Figure 8.3

Objective 2: *Your child will match, select, and name words using two sets of flash cards.*

Materials:

Two flash cards for each word taught—in this case two flash cards each for *I* and *see* (figure 8.3).

Procedures:

After your child has learned the family names, teach her to read words that can be put with the family names to make simple sentences. For example, *I* and *see* are simple words that children may use in a sentence. These words, as well as other pronouns and verbs, plus articles, conjunctions, adjectives, adverbs, and prepositions are difficult to illustrate. At this point, now that your child can read a few words, it is not usually necessary to have illustrations for these words, because they will be put in the context of a sentence for meaning. If, however, an illustration is necessary for the reader's understanding, a drawing of the sign language sign for these words can be used on the picture cards.

To introduce words that are not illustrated, use the same method described above, except, instead of matching the flash card to the picture card, your child matches flash card to flash card.

Example: To teach *I* and *see*: You will need two flash cards for each word. Show your child the two cards. Pointing to the cards say, "This says *I,* and this says *see*." Then present the matching flash cards, one at a time, saying, "This says *I,* put *I* on *I*; this says *see,* put *see* on *see*." After she has matched the words, continue with the selecting and naming activities as described for using picture cards and flash cards.

After she can read these cards, make sentences for her to read using the flash cards. For example, "I see Daddy. See Mommy. Mommy see Sally." (Don't worry about the grammar just yet.)

Adaptations for Older Learners

For most older learners, picture cards are not necessary for teaching most words. Use the method described above, "Match, Select, and Name - Using Two Sets of Flash Cards." As stated above, words taught will depend on the interest of your child, her environment, and her needs—the words that would be meaningful and useful for her to learn. Talk with your child and discover what she wants to learn to read about. Use these words to grab her interest and keep it. In most cases, your child's name is taught first. Most often, she can already read it;

however, it is good to start with a word she knows, as success is assured, and she can learn the match, select, and name procedure using a word she knows.

Adaptation Examples:

Example 1: Brett, 16 years old, wanted to write a letter to his special kind of hero, Chris Burke, and tell him that he liked his show. He learned to read: *Dear, Chris, Burke, I, like, your, TV, show, Love,* and *Brett.* By the end of his first session, he could read these words on flash cards, arrange them in order, read his message and copy it to send to Chris. Before, his mother wrote letters for him to copy, but he could not read them.

If Brett maintains his interest in Chris Burke, words for expanding the letter could be taught. For example, he could tell Chris about himself: "I am 16 years old. I live in Kent, Washington. I have a twin brother. His name is John. We go to Kent High School." He may also ask for something from Chris: "Please send me a picture of you and Andrea. How much does it cost? Do you have a fan club?" Interest maintained, he could learn to read his own address and Chris Burke's and copy the addresses on the envelope in the correct places. In addition, map activities could be planned so he could look up Kent and Los Angeles on the map and expand his knowledge of geography. He could arrange these words and write to others as well: "Dear Grandma. I like Chris Burke on TV. I sent Chris a letter. Chris Burke lives in Los Angeles. Los Angeles is on the west coast, like Seattle. I love you, Brett."

If your older child has trouble copying words, if he has access to a computer or typewriter, teach him to write using the keyboard.

Example 2: Gloria, 18 years old, had a boy friend, James. The first words she learned to read were: *Gloria, James, are, friends, and, TV, like,* and *popcorn.* She learned to read sentences: "Gloria and James are friends. Gloria and James like TV and popcorn." In time, she can read and write about the places they go and other things they do together. Example: "On Tuesday James and I go bowling. On Friday James and I watch a movie on TV." She can write these events on the calendar on the correct days. And, she can place words in order, copy them, and send or give James written invitations, such as, "Come to my house on Friday, 7:00 p.m. We will have pizza and watch a movie. You bring the video." In addition to using reading and writing as a means of communicating, she is learning to use calendar and time concepts and to plan ahead.

Example 3: Neal, 26 years old, wanted to be able to read the menu at his favorite fast food restaurant, Wendy's. During his first session he learned to read: *Wendy's, cheeseburger, fries,* and *Sprite.*

After he successfully read these words, Neal told me that he really missed his mother, who had died recently. The next words that he learned were: *I, miss, my, mother,* and *love.* He learned these words and could arrange them in order to say, "I miss my mother. I love Mother." He could copy well, and could now read and write this message. In this case, he used his reading and writing to express his feelings, and hopefully, to help deal with his grief.

As Neal was leaving this first reading session, his eyes filled with tears, and he said, "This is the happiest day of my life." He had told me that he had gone to school for 20 years and had never been taught to read, and he wanted to learn—that's why he came to the workshop. His dream had come true. He could read some words that were meaningful and useful to him.

Example 4: Raymond, who was 42 years old, lived in a group home. When he was asked what his goals were for the upcoming year, he said that he wanted to learn to read. We started with his name, first and last (he recognized these words), the names of his closest friends in the group home, and the name of the group home. He learned to read "Raymond, James, Val, and Donald are friends" and "Evergreen Home friends are Raymond, Val, James, and Donald."

When asked what he liked to watch on TV, he said, "King Kong." He learned to read "I like King Kong" and "Evergreen Home friends watch King Kong on TV."

Games and Activities: Practice to Fluency, Comprehension, Transfer, and Generalization

Figure 8.4

Objective 3: Your child will practice and use her reading skills by using place cards and labels with family names.

Place Cards (figure 8.4)

Materials:

Place cards, one for each family member. You can be creative and make fancy ones, or you can simply take the 8 x 5 inch cards, cut them into two 4 x 5 inch cards, fold each of these in the middle so they will stand (like a tent), and print the names on both sides. Your child (and everyone at the table) can look across the table and read the cards.

Procedures:

Your child places the cards on the table where each person sits. She may: (1) place the cards before the family sits down (this requires more abstract thinking, as she will need to remember where everyone sits, if each family member habitually sits in the same place); (2) be given the power to decide where each person is to sit, if the members of your family are willing to cooperate and sit where she places their cards; or (3) wait for family members to sit, and then place each card where each person is seated. Be relaxed and do what works best, and you can do it differently from time to time. The idea is to provide meaningful practice using the words. (If your child learns to read a pet's name, she can also place a place card by the pet's dish.)

Bedroom Labels

Materials:

Flash cards with family names and tape.

Procedures:

Place names on the bedroom doors, at your child's eye level. As she walks by, she can read the name or names of the people who sleep in each room.

I had to take the names off the door.

One mother reported that each time her son walked by the bedroom doors, he not only wanted to read the words, but he insisted on tracing the letters in each name with his finger. This presented a problem when the school bus was waiting. His mother took the names off the doors. It is important to recognize when reading activities interfere with other important matters. As always, use your common sense to determine which activities you choose to use. This child did not need extra practice. He was very motivated and fascinated with letters and reading.

Self-Sticking Labels

Materials:

File folder labels, or other pull-off, self-sticking labels, or blank stickers with the names of family members printed on them; envelopes, names of family members printed on each.

Procedures:

Figure 8.5

Place each strip of labels (all labels on the strip will have the same name on them) in a separate envelope; write the person's name on the outside of the envelope. Teach your child to read "to" and "from." Whenever she creates a product, such as drawings and paintings, print "to" and "from" on the paper. Your child: (1) decides to whom she wants to give the product; (2) finds the correct label (Mommy, Dad, Teacher, Grandma); (3) places it by the "to"; (4) finds her own name and places it by "from." Your child then delivers the product to the correct person, or, perhaps, helps mail it to Grandma.

This can be done with products going to and coming from school. This provides a functional use for reading; your child is actually using the written words to communicate. Pulling the labels off and sticking them in the right place also provides practice with fine motor skills. Of course, when your child is able to write, she does not need the labels.

It was my best Christmas present ever.

Sean's mother wrote me: Two months had passed since I heard your presentation about reading in Denver. We'd been working on name matching. Sean had also been practicing writing many of the letters of the alphabet that he recognized, especially those in his and our names. We were wrapping Christmas presents. Sean was watching me write names on the tags. I picked up one and said, "This one's for Dad." "Dad," he said excitedly, "D-A-D, I know Dad. D-A-D." He grabbed the pen from my hand and wrote his first word independently, "dad." That was the best Christmas present ever.

Adaptations for the Classroom

Place cards and labels can be used in the classroom: (1) If children eat in the classroom, at a table other than their desk, place cards can be used. Each child can put her own place card on the table, or students can take turns putting on the place cards. (2) Names can be on place mats, and place mats can be used as placards. (3) Place cards can be used when small groups sit at a table for a project. (4) Students can wear name tags. (5) Lockers, hooks, or cubbies and desks should be labeled with names.

Your child can store envelopes with labels in his desk or cubby. When he produces a product, he can select the appropriate labels for "To" and "From" and place them on the product.

Lotto Games

A lotto game set consists of a lotto card with four to eight words or pictures, and individual cards or disks with matching words, pictures, or symbols. For our purposes, the match can be: (1) word-to-word; (2) picture-to-word; (3) word-to-picture; (4) symbol-to-word; or (5) word-to-symbol. Interesting, colorful materials help to maintain your child's interest and give the reading practice a game-like quality.

In addition to providing practice in reading and comprehension, lotto games can help your child build social skills (learn to play games, take turns, follow rules). Another important skill that she can learn from lotto games is to put words, objects, and people in categories (organization skills). Therefore, it is important to give each lotto set a title. In the case of the family words, the game may be called, "Family," "My Family," "Family Lotto," or "James Family" (if you want to introduce the family name, and your last name is James). The important thing is that the title is at your child's level of understanding. She can learn to read the words *family* and *James* and learn the concept of family (a category), and that family members share the same last name, if this is the case. If not, in time the exceptions can be taught and for now you can stay with "Family" game.

Objective 4: *Your child will practice reading, comprehending, and generalizing words by playing word lotto games.*

How to Make Lotto Games

Figure 8.6

Word-to-Word Lotto

OPTION 1:
ONE-COLUMN LOTTO (Beginner's Lotto Game)

Supplies:

Index Cards, 8 x 5 inches; felt-type pen; ruler; scissors; lamination; large paper clips, envelope, or files with sides stapled or taped together to keep each set together.

Making Lotto Game Cards:

To make lotto game cards with four words, draw lines, 2 inches apart, on the 8 x 5 card, making spaces 2 x 5 inches. Print in the family names (or other words) in these spaces. Laminate. (One-column, first lotto games do not need the title; wait until your child graduates to two columns.)

Making Matching Flash Cards:

Use the flash cards you already have as matching cards, or make a duplicate lotto card (as above) and cut on the lines to make more flash cards. Laminate before cutting.

OPTION 2:
TWO-COLUMN LOTTO

Supplies:

Standard size 8½ x 11 inch tag-board or card stock, available in most copy centers and stationery shops; felt pen; ruler; scissors; lamination; large paper clip, envelope, or file folders with sides stapled or taped together to keep each set together.

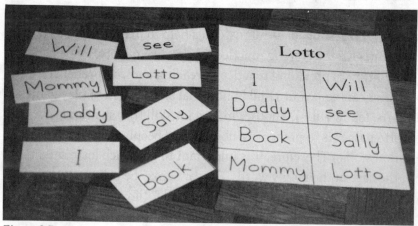

Figure 8.7

Using different colors is optional. The color makes the game more attractive and the color serves as "coding" in keeping the lotto sets (card and matching flash cards or disks) together, later on, when your child has more than one game. For example, the family lotto game may be pink; the food word lotto may be green. When putting the games away, it's easy to match the lotto card with the flash cards. Color can be used to teach children to use color coding.

However, if more than one game card is to be used for games (later on, when she is playing with others) the game cards and the flash cards should all be of the same color so your child will be required to use her reading and ability to put words in categories to determine to which game card the word drawn belongs, rather than using color coding. This will be explained in "How to Play," below.

Making Lotto Game Cards:

Lotto Game Cards are found in Appendix D-1, D-2, and D-3. The simplest way to make a game card is to copy the desired form onto 8½ x 11 card stock. (It's a good idea to make several copies while you are at the copy machine—you'll need them.) If you want to do it the hard way, or don't have access to a copy machine, simply copy the forms by hand, or design your own to individualize for your child. (You may have nine family members and you may need to use an open file folder in order to accommodate all family members.) Print the title of the game in the space at the top. You can title it "Lotto," if all the words are not in the same category, or "Family Lotto," "James Family," "Name Lotto," or any title appropriate. As you make more lotto games, the title will become more important, because the title should identify the category of the words on the card and help your child learn categories.

Print the words on the card in the spaces marked off. Laminate.

Making Matching Flash Cards:

Make another lotto card identical to the one above. Laminate. Cut out the words, making individual matching cards, of all words, including the words in the title. (If you are using stick-on lamination, it is safe to laminate and then cut. However, if you use a laminating machine, you may need to cut the cards out first, then laminate. Sometimes the lamination comes off if there is no seal around the edges. Also, lamination is not usually necessary if the children using the cards do not drool or put their hands and fingers in their mouth.

OPTION 3:
WORD-TO-WORD LOTTO WITH DISKS

Supplies:

Standard 8½ x 11 inch card stock; lids from frozen concentrate juice cans; glue stick; scissors; felt pen; ruler; lamination; large envelope or file folders with sides stapled or taped together to store each set.

Figure 8.8

Making Lotto Game Cards:

You may choose to turn the lotto game card either horizontally or vertically. If you have a long title, such as "Kiladopheram Family," horizontal works better. Print the title of the game at the top. In the space under the title, make circles (one for each word to be used in the game), by tracing around a juice can lid, or by copying Appendix D-2 or D-3, if the number of spaces is right for you. Print the words in the circles. Laminate.

Making Lotto Disks:

On a matching piece of cardboard, make circles, like the ones on the card, except make these a little smaller, so the circle will fit inside the rim of the lid (trace around a lid, cut out the circle, trim to fit inside the rim, then use this circle as a model for the other circles, rather than the too-big lid). Print matching words in these circles. Laminate. Cut out the circles and glue to the lid, inside the rim (the side that has printing on it—to cover the printing or logo, if there is any).

Picture-to-Word Lotto with Disks

Supplies:

Standard 8½ x 11 inch card stock; lids from the frozen concentrate juice cans; glue stick; scissors; felt pen; ruler; and photos or symbols (for non-name words). If you are using photos, you will need to cut the photos to fit on the disks. If you do not want to cut photos, or to pay to have extras printed, photocopy the photos (you can get several on a page). If you photocopy photos, make a few extra; they will come in handy for books and other activities.

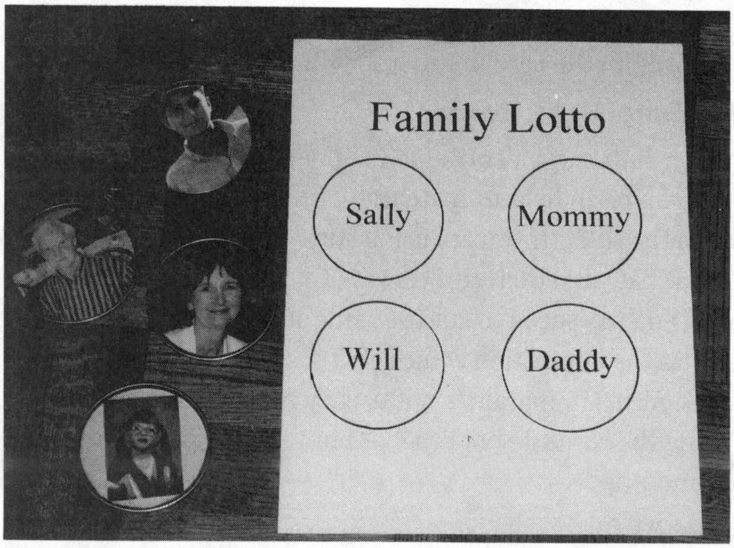

Figure 8.9

Making the Lotto Game Card:

Copy Appendix D-2 or D-3, or design your own to individualize for your family. Print the title of the game at the top of the card. In the space under the title, make circles (one for each word to be used in the game), by tracing around a juice can lid. Print the words in the circles on the card. Laminate the lotto card. (If you made a disk word-to-word lotto using the same names, you may use the same lotto card for this one; only the disks will change. If your child has mastered the word-to-word disk lotto, recycle the lids by gluing the photos over the words.)

Making Lotto Picture Disks:

On a matching piece of card stock, make circles, like the ones on the card, except make these a little smaller, so the circle will fit inside the lid (trace around a lid, cut out the circle, trim to fit inside the lid, then use this circle as a model for the other circles, rather than the too-big lid). Cut the photos, or the photocopy of the photos (symbols/line drawings will be used in most other lotto games), to fit inside the circles, so the colored paper forms borders around the photos. Laminate. Cut out the circles and glue on the inside of the rim of the lid.

Word-to-Picture Lotto with Disks

Supplies:

Same as Picture-to-Word Lotto.

Making the Game Cards:

Copy Appendix D-2 or D-3, or create one on your own. Write the title, such as "James Family," at the top of the card. Tape or glue the photos in the circles on the card. (These can be the same photos from the picture cards, or photocopy photos. For lotto games in other chapters, symbols/line drawings will usually be used instead of photos). If you have more than four people in your family, or need more room, extend the card by taping two cards together (you can make it so it folds, like a book), or get a bigger piece of tag board or use a file folder. (This game, and all lotto games described that use disks, can be made without using disks. Simply tape or glue the photo or symbol/line drawing on the game card, creating rectangles or squares rather than circles. Use flash cards for matching. The disks simply provide more of a game-like quality and generally make it more appealing to the child.)

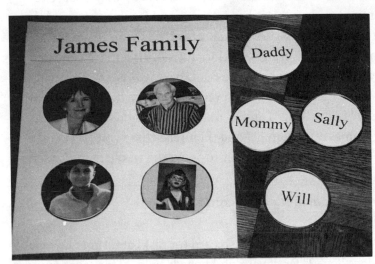

Figure 8.10

Making Word Disks:

Make disks as described in Word-to-Word Lotto, above, or, if you make them for Word-to-Word, use the same disks for this game.

How to Play Lotto

Procedures:

Lotto games can be played any way that is fun and natural for you and your child, so long as both of you are having fun and she is getting practice reading, matching, and comprehending. Following are steps in how to teach her to play lotto, if she does not already know how to play, or if you need some guidelines.

Step 1: *Present the lotto card.*

Show her the lotto card, placing it in front of her. Tell her, "This is a game, the James Family game—a game about our family, the James family," pointing to the words in the title, reading them to her, or with her. Point to the family names, on the card, reading them to her, with her, or let her read them. Or, in the case of the word-to-picture lotto, name the people in the photos.

If your child does not read "James" and "Family," you may want her to learn to read these words at this point; or, you may choose to play the game a few days to get her interest, and teach her to read these words later, if her data (the probe) indicates that she needs more practice with the words she's learning before introducing more words. Whenever you decide to teach her to read these words, use the match, select, and name method described previously. Have her match flash cards that say "James" and "Family" to these words on the lotto card, then select "James and "Family," and then read these words. You can also have her put the words together to "read the whole name," such as "Doug James."

Step 2: *Present matching flash cards or disks, one at a time.*

Word-to-Word: Present one flash card (or disk) at a time, saying, "What does it say?" Or, if your child needs help, "This says *Mommy*. Put *Mommy* on *Mommy*." If she does not respond correctly, show her how to match it with the word on the card.

Picture-to-Word: Present one disk at a time, saying, "Who is this?" Give it to her and show her how to match it up with the word on the lotto card.

Word-to-Picture: Present one flash card at a time, allowing her to read them, or read them for her, and show her how to match the flash card with the correct picture.

When the card is full, say "Lotto! You did it! You got them all right!" (Or anything else that feels natural to you and is reinforcing to your child, emphasizing her accomplishment and the joy of finishing the game.)

Step 3: *Present all cards or disks at one time.*

Place the flash cards (or disks) on the table, word side down. For fun, move them around, mixing them up like you would dominoes, saying, "We need to mix them up." (This gives it a game-like quality and usually helps to maintain the interest of the child.) Show her how to "draw," or take one at a time, and match it with a card.

Variations:

(1) If you are using flash cards, teach your child to "shuffle" them and "draw" one a time.

(2) Put the cards or disks in a bag or box, and allow her to "draw" from the bag or box.

(3) Let your child choose how she wants to do it. Children often have their own ideas, and this gives them some control and ownership of the game. They can be creative, and we want to encourage this.

No! I want to hold them.

One child took all the disks and held them to his body. When I asked him to put them on the table, so we could play, he said, "No! I want to hold them." I told him that he could hold them, if he wanted to. He then took one disk at a time and matched them with the words perfectly, obviously enjoying the game and demonstrating his comprehension. The point of playing lotto is to provide fun practice in reading words, and, in the case of the word-to-picture and picture-to-word, practice comprehension. We do not want to turn it into a power struggle of our will against the child's. Respect her ideas. When she feels that her ideas are respected, she will respect yours. You are actually modeling how to respect another person's ideas and to compromise. The child did what I wanted him to (match the disks to words), and I allowed him to do what he wanted to do (hold the disks). Actually, I was pleased that he liked them so much.

Step 4: *Teach her to play lotto by herself.*

She should be able to get a set out, turn the cards or disks over, mix them up, and take one at a time and match them up. In time, she can learn to do this with more than one card. It's self-entertainment like playing solitaire or working a puzzle. Something she can do and *use* her reading.

Step 5: *Teach her to play lotto with others.*

With one lotto card:

"Play" the game with your child, taking turns with her, "drawing" a card or disk on your turn. You may choose to let her show you where the card goes, so she will be getting more practice. You may say, "I have Daddy. Where should I put it?"

With more than one lotto card:

In time, your child should have several lotto game sets, each with words in the same category, such as "Family Lotto," "Action Word

Lotto," "Food Lotto," "Schedule Lotto," etc. When she has as many as two lotto cards, she can play lotto with another person, and each person will have their own lotto card. You can make up your own rules, based on your child's understanding and social maturity. Remember that social skills are embedded in this reading game. This is a way of teaching her how to play board games, take turns, and follow rules. Different rules are needed for the games played with lotto game sets that are the same color and games that are played with lotto game sets that are different colors. Below are some guidelines to help you play the games.

Same Color Lotto Sets:

Each person playing will have a lotto card (start with two players and more players can be added after your child has learned the game well). Mix individual cards that match the lotto cards being used in the game together, as you would a deck of playing cards, with the word side face down. Teach your child to do this; it is a fun part of the game, and good fine motor practice. She may not be ready to actually "shuffle," but you can show her other ways to mix them up, such as putting them on the table and pushing them around and then stacking them, or leave them face-down, mixed up on the table. (This can be one of the choices the player has, "Do you want them stacked, or spread out?")

Each person playing has a lotto card and takes turns drawing a card from the stack. When a card is drawn, the person who draws it determines if it is in the right category for her card. If it is, she matches it up. The player may say, "It says *Daddy*. It's a family word. I have the family card, so I get to play it." If the player draws a card that she cannot play on her card, she has to relinquish her card to the person who has the card on which it can be played. The player may say, "It says *jump*. That's an action word. Who has the action card?" If the player has to relinquish the card to someone else, she gets another draw, and continues to draw until she draws a card she can play. The person who fills up her card first, is "out" first. The rest of the players continue until their cards are filled.

It is important that the game remains fun for your child and that she wants to play it. I would rather emphasize cooperation (giving the card to the person who can use it, and trying again) to competition (if you cannot play your card, you have to put the card back in the pile, losing a turn, and making the "winner" the person who fills up her card first). With the "cooperative" game, everyone "wins" when a card is filled. Some finish earlier, and it's okay. It's a cooperative game, and we all helped. Older children may find it more interesting if the game is made more competitive, but, for the most part, I think that everyone generally has more fun, if there are not winners and losers. We would not want a child to not want to play because she was afraid of losing.

Lotto with Disks:

Because the disks look the same when turned face-down, games with disks can be played the same as same-color games (the player does not see the color until they have drawn the disk). Instead of using cards, you will be using disks, "shuffling" them as one shuffles dominoes.

Different-Color Lotto Game Sets:

Option 1: Teach your child to use color coding. Mix up all the cards in several lotto sets and place them face up on the table. Each person needs to select a card that is the same color as her game card, when she draws. When the correct color is selected, the card can be played. This gives your child an opportunity to practice color skills and adds another component to the game.

Option 2: Use the "blind" draw. Place the cards in a bag (cloth bag with a drawstring works well) or a box (with a hole big enough for players' hands to go in). This blind draw prevents the person from selecting only cards that match her card. When a player draws a card from the bag or box, she determines who can play the card by looking at the color. If it matches her game card, she plays it; if it does not match her card, she gives it to the person who can play it. As the game is played, you may emphasize the categories: "It's green, a family word."

Adaptations for the Classroom

All or any of these games can be played at school, either alone, or in groups. The games can be an option at the game or reading center. Make games using functional words taught at school. Examples:

(1) Classmates Lotto: Word-to-word or picture-to-word (can use photocopied photos). If children typically work in set groups, lotto games can be titled Group 1, Group 2, Group 3, etc. and students can play multiple-card games.

(2) School Lotto: Played with school words, such as school, name of school, teacher's name, lunch, recess, bus, teacher, principal, friends.

(3) Schedule Lotto: Word-to-word, or symbol-to-word lotto with schedule words, such as group time, reading, centers, recess, PE, library, etc. Symbols for these can be used, rather than photos.

Note to teachers: Team with an art teacher or a teacher of fourth-, fifth-, or sixth-grade students. His/her students can make materials (books and games) and play the games and read the books with the students as projects. It will be a learning experience for each group, and you don't have to do all the work.

First Book: Reading for Pleasure

Figure 8.11

Objective 5: *Your child will practice reading sentences in a personalized book (figure 8.11).*

Now that your child has learned to read the names of those nearest and dearest to her, make her a book that she can read. Individualize, by making a book that is appropriate and functional for her age and interest and uses her reading vocabulary. Use your own imagination and material available, if you wish. Following are suggestions and guidelines.

Supplies for making book:

Standard size (8½ x 11 inch) tag-board weight colored paper (card stock), construction paper, or other material appropriate for the cover; standard unlined white paper, heavier weight preferable, so words do not show through on the back side; stapler, rings, or binder holder to hold the book together; black felt pen for printing; tape, made into "doughnuts"; photos from picture cards; and colored felt pens for decorating and illustrating.

How to make a book:

For the first book, take the photos off the picture cards (or use other photos). On each page, turned horizontally (to give more space for sentences across the bottom), tape a photo near the center of the page, using the doughnuts so the tape does not show. Make a frame around each photo, by drawing designs around them, using the felt pens. (Some parents enjoy drawing fancy frames using the computer. This is nice, if you have the equipment and the time for this desk-top publishing, but it is not necessary for producing books that children enjoy. Frames make the page more interesting and attractive.)

Now that there is a photo of a family member on each page, write a simple sentence that the child can read under each picture, making the letters near the same size as those on the flash cards, and leaving ample space between words. (Draw some light lines as guides to print on, if you have trouble printing straight across the page. Some talented parents who have computers enjoy writing the sentences with larger fonts on their computer. If you don't have a computer, and feel insecure about your printing, use a stencil.) It is important that the printing is very readable and clear and that the words do not run together.

After the pages are completed, put them together in the order that you want, then put the front and back cover on, and staple it all together. Print the title on the front cover.

Some parents have used photo albums for books, placing sentence strips under the photos and covering it all with the plastic cover. This makes a sturdy book.

Content of the first book:

The first book is usually very simple. Often the child has a limited reading vocabulary, and a limited speaking vocabulary as well. It is important that your child will be able to read the book with ease and feel successful. A simple book is the *I See Book:* on each page, print at the bottom of the page, under the photo, "I see (person's name)." Example:

"I see Sally."

"I see Mommy."

"I see Daddy."

"I see Will."

The book will have as many pages as there are people or pets in the family whose names the child has learned.

This first book is usually titled, *I See Book,* or *(Child's Name) Book,* such as *Sally's Book*. (Examples of other books are given following these procedures.)

Procedures:

Show the book to your child, allowing her to look at it and talk about the pictures. Then point to the words and ask her to read them to you, or you may want to read the book to her before you ask her to read it to you. As she reads the book to you, give her as much help as needed, pointing to the words and giving her cues or supplying the word as needed. (She should know these words quite well as she should have had the match, select, and naming practice.) Teach her the word *Book* by giving her the word *Book* to match with the word on the cover of the book. Practice can be provided selecting and naming *book* using the other words as distractors.

Evaluation:

Make a note of words your child needed help with while reading the book. Provide extra matching, selecting, and naming practice with these words.

Other Examples of "First Books"

I LOVE MOMMY.

Troy, who was six years old, had learned the family names during the first week of February. Rather than learning "I see," he learned to read *I*, *and*, and *love*. (A heart was used as a symbol of love on the picture card. *I* and *and* were taught without picture cards.) Being able to read the word *love* was especially functional for the time of the year. He was able to read "I love Mommy" and "I love Daddy" on the valentines he made for them at school.

His first book was titled *Troy's Book*, and there was a big heart drawn around the title. (If you want to go all out on this theme, you could make the whole book in the shape of a heart.)

The pages, with the photos framed in hearts, were:

"I love Mommy." (Mom's photo)

"I love Daddy." (Dad's photo)

"I love Annie." (Annie's photo)

"Daddy, Mommy, and Annie love Troy." (Troy's photo)

I LIKE TO EAT AT GRANDMA'S HOUSE.

Nathan, who was also six years old, had learned family names and a number of unrelated words. He had been reading these words on flash cards and in unrelated phrases, such as "Nathan eat" and "big dog." His vocabulary, both in reading and speaking, was beyond the "I see" stage. We incorporated many of the words he could read in this book, and the words that he did not know, he learned quickly. (He was "ripe and ready.")

The content of *Nathan's Book*:

"My name is Nathan. I am a boy." (Nathan's photo)

"I am six years old." (drawing of a cake with 6 candles, 6 balloons with "Happy Birthday" written on them, or a birthday photo could be used).

"This is Daddy." (Dad's photo)

"This is Mommy." (Mom's photo)

"My brothers are Tom and Brian." (photos of Tom and Brian)

"My sister is Alisa." (photo of Alisa)

"This is my dog Butch. Butch is a big dog." (photo of Butch)

"I like to eat at Grandma's house." (photo eating at Grandma's)

(Nathan's favorite treat was eating at Grandma's, and he could read about it.)

His mother said that she was going to put this book on rings, so she could add pages to it.

Adaptations for the Classroom

If you do not have pictures available and are unable to get them, teach the words with two sets of flash cards, using match, name, and select. This can be done in large and small groups and with peer tutors.

For the classroom, start with the child's name and, as always, with words that are meaningful to and useful for the child. For the younger child, his name, and Mommy and Daddy, or the name that he calls his caregivers, are generally appropriate. After these words are learned, and the child is using them, the names of other class members and other words that can be used throughout the day can be introduced. Examples: the name of the school, teacher, and calendar and schedule words. (See Part 3 of this book.)

Children who are speaking using three or more words together can learn to read a book about themselves and their school. Books can be made by copying photos of the school, the student, and the other students in the class (group or individual), and symbols (line drawings) for activities can be added. The teacher can make the pages, including the sentences, and use them with other students as well.

Sample pages:

"My name is Peter Forest." (his photo)

"I go to Emerson School." (photo of school)

"My teacher is Ms. Johnson." (photo of teacher)

"I am in the first grade." (photo of door to classroom, or a line drawing of the door with the number and teacher's name on it)

"Friends in my class." (group photo, or single photos with each child's name printed under their photo)

"Tuesday and Thursday we go to the library." (photo of library, or class in library, or line drawing of books to represent library)

"We play at recess." (photo of children on the playground, or line drawings of playground equipment)

"My schedule." (class schedule printed on the page)

"My bus is number 32." (photo of bus with number, or line drawing of bus with "32" on it)

Keep it at the student's level of understanding and add pages as he learns to read the words. This book becomes the student's textbook that helps him to learn about his school and his school day.

If your child is speaking (or signing) using only one or two words per utterance, an adaptation of the above book can be made. A child at this stage may need picture cards for learning some of these words. Use the photos or line drawings on picture cards before putting them in the books. The pages may be simply:

"Peter Forest" (Peter's photo)

"My school" or "Emerson School" (school photo)

"My teacher" or "Ms. Johnson" (teacher's photo)

"My friends" (photo of class)

"Recess" (photo of children at recess, or line drawing of playground equipment)

"Lunch" (photo of children eating lunch, or line drawing representing lunch)

"My choices" (photos or line drawings of choices in learning centers)

"My bus" (photo of his bus, or line drawing with the number in clear view)

Why bother!

In the 1970s, I was taking a graduate course in reading from a professor who was nationally known as a reading expert. As a class project, I wrote up this program and presented it to the class, with the help of video tapes of my students reading. My professor's comment at the end of the presentation was, "Why bother."

I was crushed. He viewed what I considered my single greatest professional achievement to date as a bother. His comment indicated to me that he thought that if one had to go through all those steps to teach children with Down syndrome to read, they were not worth the effort and/or they would not be able to use their reading skills. He was a bachelor and had no children of his own, and I do not know how much experience he had with children in general, but if he had any experience at all, he would have known that all children are a bother. They all require and deserve a great deal of our time and energy. And, in my case, I was a teacher, paid for my bother, and I wanted the time students spent in the classroom to be productive and to make a difference in their lives. It was a wonderful opportunity and challenge to me. And it was exciting to see them learn, and to be a part of their education—and their lives. If I—and the other staff members—had viewed the planning, making materials, breaking tasks down into small steps, data taking, and the time we spent with the children as bother, we would not have taught them anything. Almost everything we taught them had to be broken down into steps and carefully programmed—so that the child could experience success. We used the same effective techniques to teach reading. We did not expect our students to learn by osmosis from just being in a classroom where we were not bothered. Our pupils deserved all the time, energy, talent, education, and training that each of us brought to the classroom.

We have the power, right here, within our own grasp.

After one of my very early presentations on teaching reading to children with Down syndrome (before the above classroom presentation), Dr. Alice Hayden, the project director of the program, summed up the presentation with this comment: "We often look to the medical profession for the answers—for the magic pill—to help these children, but we have the power, right here, within our own grasp."

This power that is within your grasp is the follow-through. Reading this book will not teach your child to read unless you, or someone else follows through and implements the program. Reading a cookbook does not put gourmet meals on the table; watching an exercise video does not build physical fitness. It's the follow-through that makes things happen. It is within your grasp to teach your child to read (provided that your child is able and ready). It's up to you to grasp the power—or see to it that someone else does. And this follow-through should not be a painful, but rather a joyful, satisfying experience. The "no pain, no gain" rule does not apply here. If there is pain, there is very likely to be little gain.

A Word of Encouragement

The teaching techniques and procedures described in this chapter may seem a little overwhelming as you read it, but remember:

(1) **You are a learner too; you are learning new teaching techniques and procedures.** I have attempted to give detailed, step-by-step instructions to assure your success—to give you enough information to implement the program. The instructions may look tedious and rigid as you read them, but remember that you do not teach everything at once, and you do not have to understand and remember it all at once. Learn and follow the instructions, one step at a time. As you learn the procedures and get a feel as to how your child responds and learns, you can use your own judgment and adapt the procedures and use the activities that your child enjoys most. As your child learns to read, the chances are very good that you will be able to skip some of the steps.

(2) **You do not have to play all the games and do all the activities that are described here.** Several options are described so you can select those that appeal to your child and fit your schedule, living environment, and lifestyle.

(3) **You do not have to make all the materials before you start.** Take it one step at a time and prepare just what you need for the time being. To begin, all you need are the picture cards and the flash cards. As your child learns these words, you can decide what materials to make next. Preparing materials becomes an on-going process, as you learn to individualize for your child and make materials she enjoys. For example, you may make the place cards one week, a lotto game the next week, a book the next week, an alphabet book the next week, and an alphabet bingo game the next. This project can be a family project. Include extended family members as well as immediate family members (and in some cases your child can help as well). Supportive friends may also want to help. Share the work and the joy with others. You do not have to do everything yourself. (I like to make materials when a favorite TV show is on—mix my pleasures and make the most of my time.)

(4) **You do not have to follow a specific time line or schedule.** However, making reading a part of your daily routine provides structure and consistency that assures that the program is implemented. I rec-

ommend a scheduled time for the acquisition stage and the more structured activities, such as the probe (about 10 to 20 minutes 3 to 5 times a week—plan with your child and put it on the calendar for her to see and anticipate). The other games and activities can be available at any time that is convenient for your child and for you or other family members and friends available to play with her.

(5) **You do not have to do it alone.** In addition to involving other family members and friends, share what you are doing with your child's teacher and speech clinician and ask them what they are willing to do to help. Ask that reading objectives—that are consistent with where your child is in this program—be added to her IEP. (Or if the teacher is using another program, find out what she is teaching and adapt this program to supplement her program, or if your child is doing well, you may not need to use this program). If the materials are made, incorporating activities and games into the classroom can often be done with little additional work on the teacher's part. She can have the materials available at learning centers, arrange for peers to play the games with your child, or arrange for older tutors from other classrooms to play reading games with her (and they can make materials too). Let others participate in and share ownership in the project. Share the joy.

Chapter 9

INTRODUCING THE ALPHABET

Knowledge of the alphabet—the names of letters, letter sounds, and the sequence of the alphabet—gives any child valuable tools that will help her learn to read new words, to spell, to write, and to organize and find information. Knowing the letter sounds will help her to learn to read new words and to remember words she already knows. Knowing the names of the letters will give her the vocabulary to communicate using letters, as in spelling and writing. Knowing the sequence of the alphabet, in addition to the names of the letters, will enable her to organize words and information using the alphabet, and will enable her to have access to information that is alphabetized, such as dictionaries, phone books, computer files, and encyclopedias.

Before introducing the alphabet, I recommend teaching sight words, as described in the previous chapter. This will give your child instant success with reading and capture her interest. When your child has experienced success with a few words, reading them on flash cards, in books, and in playing games, and understands the value of reading, it is usually a good time to start teaching the alphabet.

When the alphabet is taught first, out of the context of the written word, some children with Down syndrome do not understand that learning these symbols and sounds will help them learn to read. They most likely do not even understand the concept of reading. Letters are just strange symbols that don't make sense to them. Therefore, they are not motivated to learn letters and sounds, often express little or no interest in the alphabet, and make little or no progress toward learning it.

Some children will already know the alphabet, or some of it. That's great. No harm done. She has a head start, and this is an indication that she may have a natural potential for learning to read, or that she has had a good reading environment at home. Of course, she may also have been taught the alphabet at school. This section will be useful for these children as well as those who do not yet know the alphabet. They will learn functional uses of letters.

This chapter describes procedures, in the format of lesson plans, to systematically teach the alphabet, starting with the first letters of the words your child can already read by sight. Using these letters will give more meaning to the letters and the sounds they make. If you have done the activities in Chapter 8, your child is already familiar with how the letters look and may be using them to discriminate the words she can read. In addition, if she has been verbally reading the words, she has been practicing the sounds of these letters; if she has been using sign language when reading the words, she most likely has been using these letters (signed) when signing some of the words she reads. In either case, she has heard the words and the sounds of these letters many times.

Lupita took those letters and threw them across the room.

The first child we taught to read was Dennis, who was basically nonverbal. Inspired by his success, a graduate student working in the program decided to teach Lupita, who was 3 years, 10 months old, to read. She reasoned that Lupita had language, and she would be able to learn to read starting with phonics— letter sounds. I thought that it was worth a try. After all, we just might make a great discovery. The student took Lupita to a small lab room and started teaching her the letter sounds. Lupita showed little interest in these symbols and the sounds her instructor put with them. In a few days, the student reported to me that Lupita had taken the letters and had thrown them across the room, and that she wanted nothing to do with them. She did not even want to go to the lab room with the student. The activities in there were meaningless to her. Given her aversion to the room, we decided to label objects in the classroom and have her match, select, and name using matching flash cards. Lupita matched, selected, and named these words readily, and in two weeks had mastered 17 sight words.

Her mother had been busy with her business, and had been unable to observe Lupita at school during this time. Lupita's teenaged sister picked her up from school one day. I told her to tell her mother that Lupita could read the words on the labels in the classroom. The next day, her mother appeared at school, with tears streaming from her eyes. My first thought was that something terrible had happened, but that was not the case. Her sister had told her mother the words Lupita could read. Her mother wrote them on paper, and Lupita, without hesitation, read them flawlessly to her. Her mother was crying with joy. She said, "When Lupita was born, they told me that she would be but a vegetable, but she has learned to read at an earlier age than any of my other children."

Lupita was, and still is, a talented reader, but the letter sounds, taught in isolation, had no meaning to her. Sight words, however, were meaningful and she learned them readily.

One of the reasons some children never learn to read is because some instructors think that it is necessary for a child to master the alphabet and/or letter sounds before they can be taught words. Years can go by waiting for some students with Down syndrome to reach this criteria, which many may never reach, because the alphabet, in isolation, has little meaning. Even if the student learns the letter sounds in isolation, she may be unable to transfer and use these sounds to read words. Some students are unable to grasp how letters (the visual symbols of sounds), put together, form words.

Mmmm aa er ya

Mary, who was seven years old, had been in a reading program that taught letter sounds first. She had been drilled on these sounds and could identify letters by sound, but she could not read a word, not even her name. When asked to read a word, she would sound out each letter, but could not blend them to make a word. When asked to read the word, "Mary," she responded, "mm aa er ya." I would say, "*Mary,* it says *Mary;* say *Mary.*" She would repeat the word, saying, "Mary," but again, when presented with the printed word (without modeling) and asked to read it, she sounded out each letter. Mary did not understand the relationship of these symbols, their sounds, and words. She was "stimulus bound," responding to the visual stimulus (each letter) as they had been drilled into her memory. She had learned letter sounds, but she did not know how to use them to read.

For some children, the concept of letter sounds, and how they work to form words, is too difficult. They learn best by sight, and all words they learn will need to be taught to them using the sight word method in Chapter 8. These children will, very likely, not develop as great a vocabulary and will learn to read only words that are the most functional to them. Even though most words eventually become sight words, words are learned and remembered much easier when your child has more tools —the ability to apply letter sounds, phonic rules, and rules of syllabication to reading words that are not already in their sight vocabulary. These learners will be able to continue to increase their reading vocabulary independently, by "sounding out" words, whereas learners who are not able to use these concepts are dependent on others to teach them new words, limiting the number and variety of words they will learn.

Sample Lesson Plans for Teaching the Alphabet

Goal: Your child will match, select and name the upper and lower cases of letters in the initial position of words that she can read; will identify words and objects that start with the letters sounds; and will categorize words by initial letter sound.

Alphabet books

Rather than starting with ABC, start with the first letter of your child's name, and then the first letter of each family member's name. These learned, keep adding the beginning letters of other words he reads. The reader's first alphabet book will have only a few pages, as letters will be introduced a few at a time, just as words are. In the case of Sally, her first alphabet book is the *S M D W Book* (for Sally, Mommy, Daddy, and Will); the next one may be *B I J R Book*. These books become a dictionary of the words in the child's reading vocabulary. In time, the books can be taken apart, and the pages can be re-arranged in alphabetical order.

Objective 1: Your child will match, select, and name upper and lower case letters, S, M, D, and W, using the alphabet book and alphabet flash cards.

Materials:

Book-cover paper; paper for pages; felt pen; stapler; index cards; paper clips.

How to Make Alphabet Books *(figure 9.1):*

Each page will have the upper and lower case of the featured letter at the top, with matching alphabet flash cards clipped to the page. Words in the child's reading vocabulary that begin with the featured letter will be listed on this page.

At the top of the page, print the featured letter, upper and lower case, the same size as the letters of the words on the page. To make them clearly upper and lower case, draw guidelines and print within these guidelines, so your child can see clearly how the letters fit on the lines. Using an index card, make matching alphabet flash cards, one for the upper case letter, one for the lower. Clip these matching flash cards to the top of the page. (These will be used for matching—to the letters at the top of the page, and to those in the words on the page.)

Below the featured letter, print the words in your child's reading vocabulary that begin with this letter. For example, in Sally's case, at

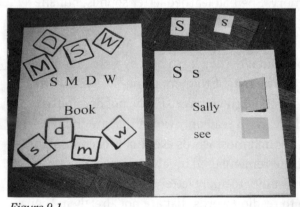

Figure 9.1

the top of the page are the upper and lower case S (Ss). Under that is printed "Sally," and "see" (the two words she knows that start with S).

Alphabet books can be made on the computer as well. Save the pages in your computer, add new words as they are learned, and print out a new page when words are added. Some children will be able to maintain their own dictionary using the computer. Encourage this independence.

When the pages are made, staple the cover on. On the cover write the title of the book, such as the *S M D W Book.*

For some children, a book with no pictures will have little or no appeal. You may choose to put pictures or symbols/line drawings with flaps on them by the words, as shown in figure 9.1. To do so, by each word, place a small photo or drawing to represent the word (remember that you can photocopy photos and cut them up—in this case, you may want to use just the face). Over the photo or drawing, tape a paper flap, with the tape on the left side, so the flap will open as a book, or at the top, as a tablet. Make a little handle with tape so that the flap will be easier to open (and your child can practice that pincer grasp as she opens it). The reader reads the word without the picture cue, then she opens the flap for self-correction. This adds novelty and fun to the book.

How to Use the Alphabet Book:

Teaching Upper and Lower Case Letters:

Teach the upper and lower case letters together, so that your child will learn that letters come in pairs, big and little, and she will not be confused when the upper and lower case of the same letter looks different (as Aa; Bb; Dd; Ee; Ff; Gg; Hh; Ii; Ll; Mm; Nn; Qq; Rr).

As you talk about the big and little letters, try using a deep voice for the big letters, and a high voice for the little letters. Most children really enjoy this. It adds novelty and interest to the task, and gives them an auditory stimulus support that will help them to discriminate between the big and little letters. Emphasize the sound of the letter, and repeat the sound whenever it seems natural to do so. (For the older learner, the terms "upper and lower case" will be more appropriate, and it might be patronizing to use the changes in your voice. Keep in mind that you will need to adapt these tasks so that they will be age-appropriate for your child.)

When introducing the book, read the title to your child, if your child does not know the letters. If she does, let her read them.

As you open the book to each page, first discuss it with her. Point to the letter and then the word, saying, "This is *D* for Daddy." (Start with the child's name first; Daddy is used in the example because it has both upper & lower case D.) Then present the flash card with the upper case D, and say, "This is a *big D* for Daddy." Give the card to her, and say, as you point to the first letter in Daddy, "Put the big *D* on the big *D* for Daddy." She matches it. Then give her the lower case d, pointing to the little d's in Daddy and say, "This is the little *d*. Daddy has two little *d's*. Put the little *d* on a little *d* in Daddy." Point to these letters in the word again, pointing to the d's and emphasizing the d sound as you do (Dad-dee).

Next, have her match the letters to the letters at the top of the page. As you give her the letters, one at a time, point to these letters saying, "Put the big *D* on the big *D*; put the little *d* on the little *d*."

Matching completed, selecting is next. Place the two letters on the table. Say, "Show me (or point to) the big *D*; the little *d*." Now she is ready to name: Hold up the big D and then the little d saying, "This is a *big* _____; this is a *little* _____." Allow your child to fill in the name of the letter. If she is unable to say the letter, teach her the sign, and accept a signed response.

(When a letter has been systematically introduced, point it out to your child when it appears in any word that your child is reading, or learning to read. Emphasize the sound of the letter and where it appears in the word.)

Teaching Vowels:

When you introduce a vowel, tell your child that it is tricky, it does not always "say its own name." When it does "say its own name" your child can reward it by "patting it on the head" by drawing a mark across the top of it. For example, if Sally has a brother named Alan, and she learns *A* for *Alan,* you can tell her that the *A* is not saying its own name, most of the time it just says *A* (the short sound). When she comes to a word that has the long *A* sound in the initial position, such as *ape,* (or, if her brother's name is Adrian) tell her that the *A* said its own name, so she gets to "pat it on the head" by drawing a long line on it, rewarding it for saying its own name. When she goes "Alphabet Hunting" (see end of chapter), and is hunting for *A's,* when she places the Post-it ™ on the object, she gets to decide if the A on the Post-it gets a pat on the head.

After she has learned a vowel, she can look for it in words that she knows or that she is learning, and if it is saying its own name she can "pat it on the head" on the flash card, or in the book, or wherever she wants. For example, after the letters *E, A,* and *O* have been introduced, and she has learned, or is learning words such as *see, make,* and *boat,* ask your child to listen carefully and tell you if a vowel is saying its own name (say the word, emphasizing the long vowel sound), then let her reward it. (Of course, this is just a little game that makes it more interesting, and will, perhaps, motivate her to be on the lookout for those vowels that will help her to sound out words.)

Add Letters to the Word Probe

Systematically teach the letters as you teach words, one at a time, and add them to the probe. After D is introduced, add it to the probe, and when probe data show that another letter (or word) can be introduced, then start systematically teaching the next letter. (Chapter 8 explains in detail how to conduct a probe.) Be careful not to overwhelm your child with too many letters at once, and try not to work on the matching and selecting tasks too long. She may lose interest. If she does, put it aside. She can learn letters other ways—by playing games.)

Alphabetize Word Bank

As letters are taught, start using the letters to put the words in the word bank in alphabetical order. This may be done in a number of ways: (See Chapter 11 for uses of the word bank.)

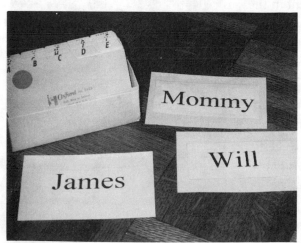

Figure 9.2

Option 1: Index Card File (figure 9.2): Use a simple card file (3 x 5 index cards, recipe type). Remove all the letter dividers from the file box. As letters are systematically taught, place the letters in the file box and show your child how to place the words that start with that letter behind the letter. The word-bank words are printed on 3 x 5 index cards.

Option 2: Rolodex Guide (figure 9.3) (Set No. AG35J has 3 x 5 cards): This file can be used the same as the Index Card File. The advantage is that the cards are easier to flip through when looking for specific words.

Option 3: Envelopes in a Box (figure 9.4): Print the letters on envelopes; place the words in the appropriate envelopes. Keep the envelopes in alphabetical order in a box.

Option 4: Use Rubber Bands (figure 9.5): Keep all the words that start with the same letter together with a rubber band around them. The "letter" card is the first card in the group. Store in a box in alphabetical order.

Option 5: Use Pinch-Spring-Type Clothespins (figure 9.6): Print the letters on the clothespins. Clip the appropriate words together with the clothespins. Store in a box in alphabetical order with the clothespins sticking

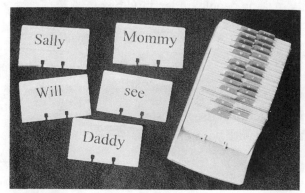

Figure 9.3

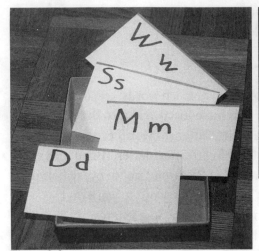

Figure 9.4

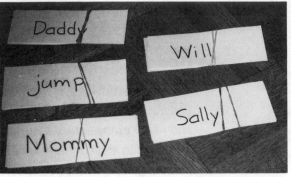

Figure 9.5

up so the letters show. (This is fun and using the clothespins builds strength in your child's hand.)

Option 6: Use cups with letters printed on them (figure 9.7): Find a shallow box to keep them in.

Option 7: Use a large key ring or bracelet that opens (figure 9.8) Figure 9.8 demonstrates organization by category. Although it is not apparent in the black and white photo, each category of words is in a different color. The categories are foods, feelings, activities (book and tape deck), and people. This can be used as a spelling reference or as a

Figure 9.6

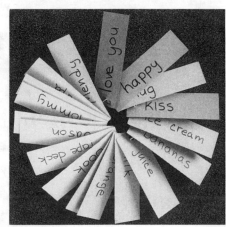

Figure 9.8

Figure 9.7

communication board (the user points to the word if she has difficulty making people understand her.)

Alphabet games

To provide fun practice, functional use, transfer, and generalization, make games and play them with your child.

Bingo Games

For our purposes, bingo games differ from lotto games in that the columns on the bingo card will have a heading, as a standard bingo card does, where the columns are labeled B I N G O.

Objective 2: Your child will practice saying letter sounds, naming upper and lower case letters, and categorizing by letters by playing Alphabet Bingo.

Upper and Lower Case Bingo *(figure 9.9)*

Materials:

Standard size 8 ½ x 11 inch tag-board weight colored paper or card stock; black felt pen; ruler; scissors; lamination; large paper clips; large envelope or large file folder with sides stapled or taped together for storage of each set; and, if you choose to use disks, frozen juice can lids. Color coding, making each set a different color, is recommended. Use the form in Appendix D-4 for two column bingo.

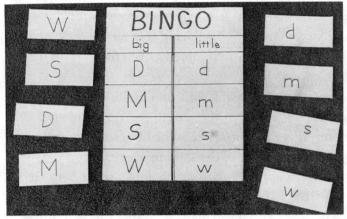

Figure 9.9

How to Make Bingo Game Cards:

(If lids are used, follow the directions for Making Lotto Games with Disks, Chapter 8, except draw a line down the middle of the page to form two columns and label the columns "big" and "little.") Copy the form provided in Appendix D-4. Because these bingo game cards and flash card sets will become a part of a complete bingo game, make each set with the same measurements. Make two copies on card stock and use one for the game card, and one for the matching cards or lids.

Above the left column, in the first space, print "big"; above the right column, print "little" (or upper case, and lower case, if more appropriate). In the spaces under "big," print the upper case letters that you are working on; under "little," the lower case. (If your child has not learned to read *big* and *little,* and you do not want to teach them just yet, symbols, such as a big ball and a little ball may be used beside the words.) Sally's first bingo card would have *S M D W* in the left column; *s m d w* in the right, with upper and lower case letters on the same line, divided by a vertical column line. Print these letters within guidelines drawn on the card. Laminate.

Making Matching Letter Flash Cards or Disks: Make a second bingo card, identical to the first (or copy it on the tag board-weight same-color paper), and cut it up to make matching flash cards or disks to be glued inside the rim of the juice can lids. If the reader needs practice reading *bingo, big,* and *little,* these cards will be used as well.

How to Play Upper and Lower Case Bingo:

Present the game the same as for lotto, pointing out that big letters are under the word "big," and little letters are under the word "little." Mix up the cards or disks, turned face down. The players take turns drawing cards (or the child takes all the turns, whatever works best). As a card is drawn, if the player does not spontaneously say the letter (give her a chance), cue her ("What is it?"). If she does not answer, or if you know that she does not know the letter yet, say, "It's a *D*, a *big D* for Daddy. Look for it on the *big* side." As you say this, point to the big side. If your child said or signed the letter spontaneously, but did not indicate that it was big, you may ask, "Is it a big *D* or a little *d?*" If she just takes the letter and matches it right up, say, "You found it on the *big* side. It's a *big D.*"

If you are taking turns, and playing with your child, on your turn, you can model how to play the game, if you need to. You could say, "It's an *M* for Mommy! It's a *little m.* Here is the little side, and here is the little *m.*" As you say this, point to the appropriate spaces on the bingo card. If your child does not need this modeling, ask for her help on your turn. Say, "What did I get?" as you show your child what you drew, and "Is it big or little?" Then you may ask, "What side is it on?"

When the card is filled up, say, "BINGO!"

Word-to-Word Bingo (*figure 9.10*)

Figure 9.10

Materials:

Same as for Upper and Lower Case Bingo.

How to Make:

Make the same as Upper and Lower Case Bingo, except, instead of *big* and *little,* print the featured letters, upper and lower case, at the top of each column. In the spaces below, print the words the child can read that start with the letter at the top of the column. (Start with only proper nouns, and the word *I* with upper case). For example, Sally would have a bingo card that has *Ss* at the top of one column, and *Mm* at the top of the other. Under *Ss*, *Sally*, *see,* and *stop* would be printed (provided Sally has been introduced to *see* and *stop,* as well as *Sally*). Under *Mm*, *Mommy* is printed. The other spaces on the card are left blank, until your child has been introduced to more words that start with that letter. As new words that start with these letters are introduced, add them to the card, and make matching flash cards.

If the same color is used for all the Word-to-Word Bingo sets, the players will not have color as a cue to determine which flash card goes with which bingo card. This will be more challenging for the players when they are playing with more than one card at a time, or with other players. (As with lotto, color coding is optional. See "How to Play Lotto": "Same-Color Lotto Game Sets," and "Different Color Lotto Game Sets" in Chapter 8.)

How to Play Word-to-Word Bingo:

Introduce the game card, pointing out that the letter is at the top, and the words starting with the letter are under it: "Here's *S* for *Sally, see,* and *stop.* Here's *M* for *Mommy.*" Place the matching flash cards on the table and mix them up. As your child draws the cards, she reads the words, determines what letter it starts with, looks under that letter, finds the words, and matches it up. Provide assistance when needed. If your child matches the word without attending to the letters at the top of the column, you may comment, "That right, it's under *s: see* is an *s* word!" When more words are added, your child will learn the value in using the column title cues.

When the card is filled, say, "BINGO!"

Word-to-Letter Bingo (*figure 9.11*)

Figure 9.11

Materials:

Same as other bingo games, except use the form in Appendix D-5.

How to Make:

Print the letters in the spaces at the top of the column as shown in figure 9.11. Make flash cards (of words your child can read that start with the letters at the top), that fit into the spaces.

How to Play Word-to-Letter Bingo:

Follow the same procedures as Word-to-Word Bingo, except show your child how the words go in the column under the letter each word starts with.

Word/Symbol-to-Letter Bingo with Disks (*figure 9.12*)

Materials:

Same as Picture-to-Word Lotto with Disks (Chapter 8), except use the form in Appendix D-6.

Figure 9.12

Figure 9.13

The same disks made for the lotto game can be used with the bingo game, as some of the same words will be used. For this game, you can combine disks with pictures or symbols and disks with words. The disk the player draws may have a picture, or it may have a word on it.

How to Play Word/Symbol-to-Letter Bingo:

Play the same as Word-to-Letter Bingo, except, instead of the child drawing a card, she will draw a disk. She looks at the photo, symbol, or word that is on the disk she draws; says the word; determines what letter it starts with; looks under that letter; and places it in the correct column.

Object Bingo *(figure 9.13)*

Materials:

Use the same game card as Word-to-Letter Bingo. Instead of flash cards, use small items and toys that start with the letters to be practiced; storage container (bag, box, can with plastic lid, or plastic container such as the cottage cheese type—clear ones that you can see through are best) to keep the objects in.

Objects and toys: Collect some items whose names start with the letters to be practiced and which are small enough to fit in the empty spaces on the bingo card. Examples: For the spaces in the *Ss* column, a small spoon, a doll-house stove, a star, sand (in a small bottle with a lid on it), sugar cubes (in a small jar with lid); salt (in a small salt shaker), small scissors, and soap (little hotel bar all wrapped up works well, or just a piece of soap); for the *Mm* column, matches (use an empty match book to represent them, for safety), money (coins in a little jar or plastic bag—or any small see-through container), little toy monkey and mouse, and moon (make a little crescent moon, or any type that the child will recognize as a moon), man (doll-house man doll), and milk (cut the logo off a milk carton to represent milk); for the *Dd* column, little toy animals that start with *d,* such as dog, duck, dinosaur, and dime; and for the *Ww* column, a toy watch, toy wolf, whistle, wood (a little chunk of firewood or a popsicle stick), and woman (doll-house woman doll).

This same game can be played using picture cards, or you could put pictures and drawings in the lids and use them. Real objects add novelty, interest, and variety. In addition, it helps with generalization. We want your child to start hearing the sounds in the words she uses and the names of things in her environment. Remember, too, this is a language/speech lesson as well.

How to Play:

Show your child the card. Tell her that she needs to find things that start with these letters, pointing to the letters at the top of the card. You may model by showing her how it works, by picking up an object and saying, "This is a *dog*. *Dog* starts with a *D* like *Daddy*. Put it under the *D*." Or, you can ask her what the object is, and help her to decide by emphasizing the sound of the initial letter. Give her as much help as she needs while she is learning the game. In this case, she does not have the written word to help her, and it may be harder for her.

To play the game, the players select an object (objects are either displayed on the table, or they may be taken out of a bag, box, or can as a "blind" draw). As a player takes an object, she names it, then decides what letter it starts with, then places it in a space in the column under the correct letter. When all spaces are filled in, "BINGO!"

Active Games

Children generally enjoy moving around. Games can be made and played that allow more activity on the part of the players, and your child can practice motor and math skills as well. Demonstrate all games to your child. You may choose to play with your child, have other players, or have your child play alone.

Scoring: It is generally more fun and reinforcing for the child when score is kept. There are a number of ways you can do this. Following are some options that can be adapted for other games as well.

Option 1: Tape the letters used in the game on little jars (such as baby food jars or spice jars) or cups, as shown in figure 9.7. Use one letter per jar or cup (you will need as many jars as letters in the game). When the player names something that starts with the letter she hits, she gets to drop a marble or coin in the jar that has that letter on it. After the game, she counts to see how many words she said for each letter. She could even put her score on a graph (figure 9.14, left score sheet). In doing so, she would be using her math, reading, and fine motor skills. In addition, she could learn how to interpret graphs by talking about her scores, using numbers and the words *more* and *less*.

Option 2: Print the letters used in the game on index cards, one letter per card (figure 9.15). Place the cards on a table or other flat

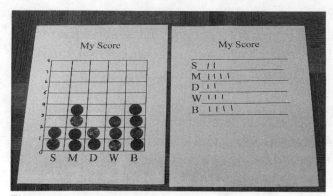

Figure 9.14

Figure 9.15

surface. When the player says a word, place a block (the toy kind kids use for stacking) on the index card with the corresponding letter (or have the child do it). As other words are said, add blocks, stacking them up. This makes a three-dimensional graph for her to talk about and interpret, or to transfer to paper.

Option 3: Keep a simple tally (figure 9.14, score sheet on the right). Write the letters on a paper and put a mark by the letter each time your child says a word that starts with that letter. Make it big, so she can look over at the score.

Beanbag and Ball Alphabet Games

There are a number of games you can play using beanbags. Make and play the games that are most appealing to your child, and for which you have materials.

Objective 3: Your child will practice naming letters and recalling words with initial letter sounds by playing beanbag and ball alphabet games.

Alphabet Beanbag Toss

Materials:

Floor alphabet board: Standard 8 ½ x 11 tag board-weight color paper (or poster paper, butcher paper, or newsprint); wide felt markers; beanbags.

How to Make:

If the 8½ x 11 paper is used, write a large letter on each one (letters that the child knows or is working on; for Sally's first floor beanbag game, S, M, D, and W). You may choose to place both the upper and lower case, or you could put upper case on one set, and lower case on another. If a large piece of paper, such as poster paper, butcher paper, or newspaper is used, make large letter boards by dividing the paper into four equal parts (easy to fold the paper and draw on the fold lines), and put a letter in each section. As more letters are introduced, make more cards or letter boards.

How to Play:

Place the letter cards (or the paper with letters in sections) on the floor. Players take turn throwing the beanbags at the letters. When the beanbag lands on a letter, the player says the letter and a word that starts with that letter. It can be a word she can read, or any other word that starts with that letter. (Or she may simply say the letter or the letter sound; adapt the game to meet your child's current objectives). As new letters are introduced, add them to the game. The number of letters displayed at one time can increase as she learns more letters. If you are playing with her, on your turn, you can think of new words, modeling for her.

Alphabet Basketball (figure 9.16)

Figure 9.16

Materials:

Letter "baskets" and ball. Containers for the "baskets," such as gallon-size plastic milk cartons or plastic bleach bottles, large coffee cans, mop buckets, or shoe boxes; index cards, 5 x 8, or other paper to print the letters on; wide felt markers; tape; beanbags or balls safe for the setting (soft sponge balls or tennis balls can be used).

How to Make:

If you are using plastic milk cartons or bleach bottles, cut the top off with a knife or scissors, so the opening will be the largest possible. Print the letters (upper and lower case) your child is learning on index cards, making them big enough so that she can see them from a distance. Tape these letters on the containers, one letter per container. Use up to four containers. You can change the letters on them, as additional letters are learned, or have letters on all sides, and turn the containers so that the letters you want your child to see are visible to her.

How to Play:

The player "shoots" the beanbag or ball into a container. She names the letter on the container she got the ball in and says a word that starts with the letter. (Or she could just say the letter, or the letter sound, whatever she needs practice on). Or, she draws an object or a flash card out of a box. She is to aim for the letter that the object or word on the flash card starts with. Example: she reaches in a bag and brings out a toy dog; she tosses for the *D*. If she gets it in the *D* container, she scores.

Alphabet Bowling *(figure 9.17)*

Figure 9.17

Figure 9.18

Materials:

Bowling pins: Large plastic pop or water bottles; sand or water; funnel; tennis ball; index cards; wide felt markers; tape.

How to Make:

Let your child help you by putting some water or sand in the bottles, using a funnel, and screwing on the lids. This will give the bottles some weight. Print the letters or words to be used on the index cards, large enough for your child to see from a distance. Tape index cards on the bottles.

How to Play:

Same as for alphabet basketball, except this time the player knocks the bottles over and then proceeds to say the letter and a word that starts with it. (See figure 19.18.)

Alphabet Relay *(figure 9.19)*

Objective 4: *Your child will practice recalling letters and letter sounds by selecting words or objectives that start with specific letters while playing alphabet relay.*

Materials:

Index cards, 5 x 8 inches; wide felt markers; objects; pictures; two stations, and space to run between stations (perhaps in the back yard).

How to Make:

Write the words or letters to be used on the index cards. Have two "stations": Station A, where your child starts with the "assignment"; Station B, where your child runs to find the letter, word, objects, or pictures.

Figure 9.19

How to Play:

The player starts at Station A with an "assignment" card, runs to Station B, picks up a designated letter, word, or object, and returns to Station A. Examples:

Option 1: Word/Letter Relay: The player draws a word, such as *Mommy,* at Station A; takes the word and runs to Station B and exchanges it for the *M* (printed on an index card); runs back to Station A with the *M;* and then draws another card and goes for another letter. (Can be reversed, as can all examples; she draws a letter and runs for the word.)

Option 2: Letter/Object (or Letter/Picture): The player draws a letter at Station A, such as a *D,* and runs with it to Station B; exchanges the *D* for an object or picture that starts with *D,* such as a stuffed dog; runs back to station A with the object; and draws another letter and repeats the run.

Option 3: Upper/Lower Case: The player draws an upper case letter at Station A; runs to Station B; selects the lower case letter; runs back to Station A with it; draws another letter and runs to Station B for the lower case letter, etc.

Figure 9.20. Gini plays reading relay.

When all of the items used have traded places, the game is over, but could be played in reverse. (See figure 9.20.)

Alphabet Hunting

Objective 5: *Your child will practice reading letters, saying and recalling letter sounds, and identifying objects that start with specific letters.*

Materials:

Post-it™ notes; wide felt marker; safety pins; small jar; marbles.

How to Play:

Go on a hunting trip around the house with your child to find things that start with a specific letter. Example: If your child's name is Sally, and she is learning that *S* is for *Sally,* take her around the house on an *S*-word hunt. When you find something that starts with an *S,* print an *Ss* (you can put both the upper and lower case on it, if you like) on a Post-it note ™ and let her stick it to the object, or pin it on, if necessary. You may model to show her the concept, but let her take the lead as much as possible, so she can think about words and sounds. You could ask her what *Sally* starts with, and when it is established that *Sally* does start with an *S,* pin the Post-it with an *S* printed on it to her clothes. Then go from room to room looking for other things that start with *S,* such as the stove, sink, soap, sheet, shirts, skirt, shoes, etc. Ask her to find *S* words, or, if she is having trouble, ask her, always emphasizing the sound of the first letter, "Does *bed* start with an *S? Socks? Scarf?*" (She may need to look in drawers, closets, and cupboards—after, all, it is a hunt. This activity should increase vocabulary and help articulation as well, as she becomes more aware of the sounds in words.)

After the labeling session is over, go around the house with her with a small jar that has an *S* taped on it. Every time she finds an *S,* she drops a marble in the jar. Then she can count the marbles and determine how many *S* words she found.

Give her a few days to wander around the house and repeat these *S* words and practice the *S* sound. As other letters are introduced, repeat the activity. In Sally's case, the next letter would be *M,* then *D,* and then *W.* And, of course, as she learns new letters, repeat the activity using these letters as well.

These labels can be left there until they fall, if they do not interfere with your decor. If you take them down or they fall, and your child misses them, needs more practice, or wants them back up, go hunting again. If she knows all four letters, she can go around telling you what letter she needs to put on things: *"Wall,* need a *W* here; *mirror,* need *M* here."

Option 1: After a few letters are up, let her go around and collect them, then show her how to sort them, putting the *S'*s in one pile, *M'*s in another, etc. She can count to determine how many there are of each letter, and fill in a simple graph showing how many words she has found that start with each letter (figure 9.14). This incorporates math, fine motor, and cognitive skills. She can come to some conclusions, such as, "We found more *S* words than *W* words."

Option 2: The letters can be taken down each day, and your child can go on the hunt all over again the next day. The same Post-its can be used each day. If your child has some letters left over, she knows that she needs to keep on hunting. This is a good memory exercise, as well as a letter-sound activity.

Option 3: Your child can also "go hunting" for letters in words. Words and/or sentences that your child can read are written on a page. Your child draws a letter that she has learned or is learning; then she hunts for that letter in the words (not just in the initial position), and circles or marks the letters in some way. You place a penny or token on each letter marked that is correct. Your child counts the tokens/pennies to get her score.

Evaluation: Measure letter recognition mastery by probe as described in Chapter 8; letter sound comprehension and association by accuracy when playing games.

Teaching the Sequence of the Alphabet

The best way I know to teach the sequence of the alphabet is to teach your child the "ABC Song" (to the tune of "Twinkle, Twinkle Little Star."). You can start singing it to your child even before she knows the alphabet, just to familiarize her with it. When she has learned a few letters, you can start pointing to the letters as you sing the song, emphasizing the letters that your child has learned or is learning by holding the note on these letters. For Sally you may sing, A B C *Deeeeee* E F G; H I J K L *Mmmmmm* N O P; Q R *Sssssss* T U V; w *(double u)* X Y and Z. Strips of the alphabet in sequential order (you can make them or buy them in school supple stores) should be attached to the top of your child's desk for easy reference for the sequential order, as well as for a reference for how to write the letters. When your child is introduced to a letter, circle it, or highlight it with a felt tip highlight pen.

In addition to having the alphabet across the top of your child's desk, the alphabet can be displayed, in order, any place that you choose—across the wall of the family room, bathroom mirror, her bedroom wall, on the ceiling above her bed, etc.

Magnet letters can be used as well; your child, using a model, can place these letters in order. When she recognizes the letters, she can place them in order using the "Alphabet Song." Also, you can "feature" the letters that she is learning on the refrigerator, and she can find these letters in the sequence.

In my kindergarten class, the alphabet (typical large classroom type) was placed on the wall, low, at my pupils' eye level. When we sang the "Alphabet Song," I pointed to each letter with a pointer as it was sung. In time, my pupils took turns using the pointer and pointing to the letters. It is important to sing the song slowly, keeping pace with the child's pointing.

M is for Martha

In addition to singing the song, I showed the group, one at a time, letters (on flash cards) that were in the initial position in each pupil's name, asked them to identify it, determine whose name started with that letter, and then let them match it to the matching letter in the alphabet, displayed on the wall at their level. One pupil, Martha, was from a Spanish speaking family, and her use of English was more delayed than most of the children's. The first day I played this game with the class, when I held up an *M* and asked, "What's this?" Martha responded, *"M, Martha! Martha!"* and rushed forward to take her turn matching her M with the M in the alphabet. It was a real thrill to observe that it was a meaningful game for Martha and that she was using

Figure 9.21. Patrick and Kari have graduated to a primary dictionary.

her reading to help her learn English. She was in the spirit of the game, and soon learned the letter for all the children's names.

(When I had two pupils whose names started with the same letter, I would have two flash cards with that letter on them, so I could give each child a card to match.)

Chapter 10

BEGINNING PHONICS: WORD FAMILIES

Introduction

Phonetics is the branch of linguistics that deals with the study of the sounds of speech represented by written symbols. It includes the production, combination, and description of sounds. *Phonics* is the term for the use of phonetics in teaching reading—the use of letters (the written symbols) and the sounds they represent in isolation and in combination to form words. When we "sound out" or "decode" words using our knowledge of letter sounds, letter combinations, and "rules" of long and short vowels and hard and soft *C* and *G,* and the rules of syllabication, we are using phonics.

Learning to use phonics to decode words is a long, on-going process, and concepts can become very complex for some children with Down syndrome. As mentioned earlier, for many of these children, learning phonics is more difficult than learning sight words. When learning words purely by sight, each word is practiced enough times for the learner to immediately recognize the specific combination of symbols as a word, without the clues of letter sounds. The learner does not have to know the names of the letters or their sounds. The use of phonics involves learning letter and letter combination sounds and the rules concerning the use of them, then transferring this knowledge to decode words. It involves problem-solving skills in determining which rules apply to what situation. In addition to having difficulty using these concepts, many children with Down syndrome have hearing impairments that make it difficult for them to discriminate sounds (Chapter 4). Also, low tone in their speech production muscles and other problems, such as tongue thrusts, can make it difficult for them to reproduce certain sounds in isolation and in words.

As difficult as phonics can be for children with Down syndrome to master, even the most basic knowledge of phonics —letter sounds— can be a very valuable tool in helping children with Down syndrome learn to read, look up words, and alphabetize. Therefore, they should be given the opportunity to learn the concepts they are capable of learning, one step at a time. This chapter provides fun and simple techniques for introducing the use of the most basic phonics—consonant sounds—using "word families."

The first step in learning phonics is learning to recognize and sound out letters in the initial position of a word. The alphabet book and alphabet games described in this chapter are designed to provide practice in this skill. Once a letter and its "sound" has been introduced to your child, it should be used to help him read words that contain this letter—to help in "sounding out" the word. Sight words and phonics should be taught concurrently—your child should be able to use all the information he has, as he is learning it. He learns that *D* is for *Daddy,* and when *dog* is introduced, he learns that it starts with the same letter and the same sound as *Daddy.*

This chapter describes techniques for teaching the use of consonant sounds using "word families." For those of you who wish to continue with this reading program, it should serve as a model for teaching more advanced phonic concepts. (See "Typical Sequence for Teaching Reading" in Appendix A-2.) It is not within the scope of this book to go beyond this "how to" model, repeating these steps for digraphs, consonant blends, diphthongs, prefixes, endings, etc. After teaching these "word families" using the techniques presented here, however, you should be able to transfer and apply these techniques to the more advanced phonic concepts. You will have learned what works for and appeals to your child, and what concepts will be most useful for him to learn. You have enough experience to make the necessary adaptations and materials. Just as Chapter 8 gives the general methods for teaching sight words, and the instructor is expected to transfer and adapt the techniques described there to teach any sight word, this chapter gives the basic techniques for teaching phonics—broken down into simple steps designed for pupil success.

I started her with the word families in May, and when she entered first grade in September, she was the best reader in the class.

One mother told me that after she attended a workshop in May (in which I presented the techniques described in this chapter), she was inspired to start teaching her daughter, Tina, to read. She started with the "at" family, using the techniques described here, and Tina took to it "like a duck to water." When Tina started school in September, she had a head start. She started the school year as the best reader in her inclusive class, and was successful in the regular reading program. Her mother added that first graders tended to judge each other on their reading ability, and that her daughter ranked very high.

Some children with Down syndrome have a special talent for reading, as Tina has. This talent needs to be tapped and developed. These children typically do well in the regular basal readers and develop skills using more advanced phonics with their classmates. Others find reading more challenging; regular basal reading programs are not meaningful to them, and they are unable to comprehend the concepts taught and the content of the stories. These children are more apt to become successful readers by continuing in a functional language experience reading program, learning useful words primarily by sight. They should, of course, be encouraged to use their knowledge of letters and letter sounds, and the techniques presented in this chapter to "decode" words, and other phonetic concepts should be taught as the need arises.

Your child's success and interest in reading is most important. If too much emphasis is placed on sounding out words, this frequently "turns off" and frustrates the reader. Having to stop and sound out a word often interferes with the flow and can become so distracting that the child loses the meaning of the text, and, in turn, ceases to find reading a meaningful and pleasurable activity. In most cases, when a child is reading and comes to a word that he does not recognize, I think that it is best to supply the word for him, so he can continue reading with minimal interruptions and little attention given to words missed. Practice on words missed can be provided later, and "word attack skills" can be demonstrated in a less threatening, programmed-for-success, way.

When to Introduce Word Families

My general recommendation is to introduce the word families after the learner has 50 to 100 words in his sight vocabulary and recognizes most letters. However, this is no hard rule, as each child is unique, and some children (such as Tina) have been successful starting with the word families rather than with sight words. If you teach the word families before sight words, or before your child has 50 to 100 words in his sight vocabulary, and he is successful, that is wonderful. No harm done—he now has more tools for learning to read. It is your child's success that is important. If he succeeds, then it was right for him; your decision was right. If, however, your child is not successful, teach each word as a sight word.

Word Families

If you implemented the procedures described in Chapters 8 and 9, your child has been learning letters and letter sounds. He has been playing Alphabet Bingo, Alphabet Hunting, Relay Alphabet, Alphabet Bowling, and Alphabet Basketball, and has been using letters as cues and clues when reading. Now he is ready to learn how letters go together to make words, or rather, how to "break the code."

It's magic! It's just magic!

Several years ago, a teacher of an "outreach class" told me this story. At the end of the school day, Jason, a student who did not have Down syndrome, came to her classroom to wait for his bus at the end of each school day. The teacher, concerned that the "trainable" class in which he had been placed offered no opportunities for learning to read, decided to use this waiting time to teach him this skill. She started him with this beginning phonics program. When she showed him how he could change a word by changing the first letter, he was amazed and became very excited and exclaimed, "It's magic! It's just magic!"

The activities described here should be fun and exciting for readers, as they discover the magic as Jason did. We all like to use our skills, and these activities and games give the child opportunities to have fun while practicing and using his phonetic skills.

Teaching Word Families

The short vowel-consonant families for which instructional materials are provided are: *at, an, ug,* and *en*. Materials for making books are provided for the *at* and *an* families; poems to inspire you to make your own books for other families are also provided.

To illustrate procedures, the "at family" will be used in this chapter. The same procedures can be followed with all short vowel-consonant families for which materials are provided here (and can be used to teach other concepts such as blends, prefixes, and suffixes).

As always, not every child will need every step or will need to play all the games. Use these steps as guides and adapt them to your child's interest and level of understanding.

STEP 1: TEACHING "WORD FAMILIES"

Materials:

Two flash cards that say *at*.

Procedures:

Teach the word *at* as a sight word, using the two *at* flash cards, and no picture cards, and the match, select, name method explained in Chapter 8. (The meaning of the word *at,* as it is used here is not important. The meaning should be taught in context, when it appears in a phrase or sentence. Other "word families," such as *en, an, ug, oy,* and *ig* are not words, but simply short vowel-consonant combinations. It is just coincidental that the vowel-consonant combination *at* also happens to be a word.)

STEP 2: INTRODUCING THE "FAMILY" WORDS

Materials:

Picture cards (Appendix C-3) and flash cards for *cat, bat, sat, rat, Pat, Nat, vat, mat,* and *hat* (Appendix C-2). (Picture cards are used to be sure your child knows the meaning of these words, but are not necessary for most children. Sometimes they may be necessary to get your child's attention, or he may feel more comfortable starting with a familiar procedure.)

Procedures:

Introduce these words as you would sight words, two or three at a time (examples used in these procedures use *cat, mat,* and *bat* as the first "at words" introduced), using the match, select, and name method. As you do so, tell your child that these are all "at words" that belong in the "at family." Point out that they all have *at* in them, but each word starts with a different letter. You may say, "This says *cat,* can you find the *at* in *cat?*" Or, "It says *cat.* See, the *at* is right here." You can also give your child the *at* to match with the *at* in *cat.*

Then say, "Cat starts with a *c,* show me the *c* in cat." Repeat the hard *c* sound (*k*), and encourage your child to say it, but if he does not, just keep going. Some of these sounds are difficult to say in isolation, and I think that it is better to keep it fun and not try to "require" your child to say it. If he is able to, most likely he will spontaneously imitate you. If your child responds, accept any approximation. Do not put him on the spot by insisting that he replicate the sound. That takes the fun out of it, and he is going to get lots of practice using it in words, the natural way.

STEP 3: MAKING WORDS BY CHANGING THE INITIAL CONSONANT

Materials:

The *at* card and the initial consonants, *c, b, m, r, h, s, v, P,* and *N* (figure 10.1). (Appendix C-1)

Figure 10.1

Procedures:

(1) Demonstrate how adding different initial consonants to *at* makes different words: Place the *at* card on a surface to your child's right. To the left put the *c, b,* and *m* cards (or the letter cards for the initial consonants of any of the words that you have introduced). Then say, as you move the *c* to the *at,* "Watch me, I'm going to make a new word." When the word is together, ask, "What word did I make?" If your child does not respond, say, "I made *cat.*" Repeat, demonstrating again how adding the letter *c* to *at* made a new word. Repeat the procedure with *b* and *m.*

(2) Your child makes his own words: Say to him, "You make a word." If necessary, assist your child in moving a letter to the *at.* Then say, "What word did you make?" If he does not respond, say, "You made *bat.* You put the *b* (and say the sound) with *at* and made *bat!*"

(3) Your child makes specific words: Place the letters to the left, and the *at* to the right. Then say, "Listen carefully, and make the word I say. Make *bat.*" Give assistance as needed. Repeat, using each letter that is displayed.

(4) Your child makes words using letter sounds: Letters placed to the right, *at* to the left, say, "Take the letter that says *mmm* (making the *m* sound) and put it with *at.*" Task completed, ask, "What word did you make?" (Anytime he does not respond, model the answer for him.) Repeat with other letters displayed.

(5) Your child makes words using the name of the letter: Letters to the right, *at* to the left, say, "Take the *c* (saying the name of the letter), and put it with *at.*" Then ask, "What word did you make?"

When these first three words and initial consonant sounds are mastered (your child can successfully perform the above tasks), teach the other words and letters, one at a time, until your child can read and "make" all words in the family. (This usually goes fast.)

As new words and letters are introduced, the initial consonants are added "to the left" to increase the choices. For example, after all words in the *at* family have been introduced, all the initial consonants in the family, *c, b, f, r, m, s, h, v, P* and *N* will be placed to your child's left and he can make any word in the *at* family.

STEP 4: PLAY WORD FAMILY GAMES

Slide-Through Games (initial consonant slides)

Materials:

Slide-Through Games, made by using the materials provided in Appendix D-7 and D-8. Make slide-through games, so that the initial consonant matches up with the family word and makes a word (figure 10.2).

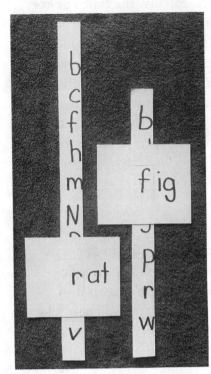

Figure 10.2

Procedures:

Show your child how he can move the strip with the letters up and down, forming words. As each word is made, your child reads the word.

Self-Correcting Wheel Game

Materials:

Self-Correcting Wheel Game, made by copying materials provided in Appendix D-9 to D-12 on card stock. Cut out the pieces and cut on the dotted lines to form a window over the letters and a flap over the drawings. Attach in the middle with a paper fastener (the little round-headed metal device with two flat prongs that you may remember from elementary school art class). (See figure 10.3.)

Procedures:

Show your child how to turn the wheel so the letter meets the family word and makes a word. Your child reads the word, then opens the "window" to self-correct, as a line drawing of the object will appear.

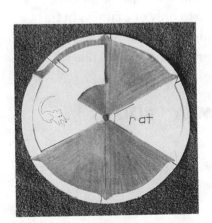

Figure 10.3

Lotto Games

Materials:

Picture-to-word lotto games, made using forms provided in Appendix D-2 and D-3 and symbols/line drawings provided for picture cards in Appendix C-4. You will need to reduce the flash card pictures on the copy machine for this one. Copy on card stock.

Procedures:

Give your child opportunities to play single card lotto as each family is introduced. As each "new" family is introduced, multiple card lotto can be played. For example: One person has the *at* family card with the *at* words on it; the other person has the *ug* family card with the *ug* words on it. Players take turns drawing the cards or disks that have the line drawings for the words on them. When each player draws a card, he says what it is and determines who can play the card. For example, if a player drew a card with a drawing of a bug on it, he might say, "*Bug,* it belongs in the *ug* family. You get it. You have the *ug* family." The player gets to draw, until he draws a card he can play on his card. (Or, of course, you can make up your own rules. Most children give the card to the other person more cheerfully if they do not have to sacrifice a turn. A different "rule" could be that the player would have to put the card back on the "deck," if he could not play it, rather than helping someone else fill up their card.)

Bingo Games

Materials:

Bingo game card and matching flash cards. Make Bingo games using materials provided in Appendix D-4, D-5, and D-6. This time, instead of putting initial letters at the top of the column, put word families. (Copy the forms and card stock; remember, you will need a lot of these.)

Procedures:

Give your child opportunities to play Bingo, after the families on the cards have been introduced. As your child draws a card, he determines which family it belongs in, finds the family name at the top, and looks under the family name for the word. This bingo game can be played when your child has been introduced to only one family. In this case, he will use only the words in the family he is learning and will use only one column. As additional "families" are learned, your child will use these columns.

STEP 5: READING "WORD FAMILY" BOOKS

Materials:

Word family books made by copying pages provided in Appendix E-1 (*at* family) and E-2 (*an* family).

Procedures:

After your child has learned to read the words in a word family, teach him to read the books that use these words in stories. For words (other than the family words) that your child does not know, teach these words as sight words. Or, you may choose to start by reading the book to your child and allowing your child to supply some of the words, as you point to them. Example: "Pat the fat cat sat on the _____." Or, let your child supply the family words, and you supply the other words. Example: as you and your child read "Pat the fat cat sat on the mat," point to each word as your child reads. If he does not know *the* and *on,* supply these words for him. It is important that your child enjoys the book and has an opportunity to use these words in the context of a story that he understands.

Published books can also be used, such as *The Cat in the Hat* by Dr. Seuss.

Poems for making other "family word" books are provided in E-3 for inspiration in making other books using your own creativity. Picture cards to help your child learn the words used in these poems are in Appendix C-5, C-6, and C-7. You can individualize these poems to your child, his experiences, and his interests.

STEP 6: MAKING WORDS BY CHANGING THE FAMILY WORD

Because your child has been focusing on the initial consonant, when other word families are introduced, he may not attend to the new family word and substitute a family word that was taught previously. For example, if the *at* family was taught first, and the *an* family taught next, your child may confuse *man* with *mat, can* with *cat, fan* with *fat.* Therefore, activities that teach your child to attend to the whole word are important. When as many as two families have been introduced, play the word-making games by changing the family word, rather than the initial consonant.

Materials:

Family word cards and an initial consonant card. The same materials are used as in figure 10.1, except this time you will have one initial consonant and more than one word family. Examples: Small flash card with *b* on it; cards with family words *at, ug,* and *ig.* You may print the materials yourself, as in figure 10.1, or you may choose to make an extra copy of the materials in Appendix C-1 on card stock and cut them out to form letter and family word cards.

Procedures:

Place the initial consonant card on a surface to your child's left, and the family word cards to your child's right. Your child selects the correct family word to make specific words. Example: if your child has been introduced to the families *at, ug,* and *ig,* place these cards to the right, and a *b* card to the left. Ask your child to "Take the *at* (the *ug,* the *ig*), put it with the *b*." Then ask, "What word did you make?" Or, say, "Make a word— put any family with the *b*." Then ask your child, "What word did you make?"

Slide-Through Games (family word slides)

Use materials in Appendix D-9 to make slide-through games (copy on card stock and cut them out) in which the family word slides through and the initial consonant remains the same. Play as described above for slide-through games in which the initial consonant slides.

Where to Go from Here

More Word Families

It is not usually necessary to teach *all* the vowel-consonant combinations, especially by going through all the steps above. The above activities are used to teach your child the *concept* of how phonics work to form words. You should not have to go through all the steps to teach each "family," but you may want to do the "word making" routine (Step 3) with other word families, and make bingo, lotto, and slide-through games and books as you choose, depending on the amount of practice your child needs.

To determine what word families to teach next, choose "families" that contain words that your child will have the most use for, or choose a family from which he already knows a word. For example:

(1) If your child reads the word *dog,* or has an interest in dogs and you want to add stories about dogs, teach the *og* family (*dog, fog, hog, jog, log,* and *tog. These words could be used in a story— about a dog that goes for a jog and finds a hog in the fog, jumps over a log, and goes home and puts on a tog).

(2) If your child is reading the *All about Me Book* (Chapter 14), and reads, "I am a boy," then the *oy* family can be taught—*boy, coy, joy, soy, toy, Roy.* (A poem that combines the *oy* and *ay* families is provided in Appendix E-3.) You could also choose to build on the *am* (I *am* a boy. I *am* 5 years old.) Teach the *am* family—*ham, jam, Sam,* and *yam*—get him ready for *Green Eggs and Ham* by Dr. Seuss—or you can read it to him and let him supply the words he knows.

(3) Or, in the same book, if he is reading "My foot is this big," teach the *ig* family—*big, dig, fig, jig, pig, rig, wig,* and *zig.* A poem using these words is provided in Appendix E-3.

(4) If he is reading *hug* in the action word unit (Chapter 12), you may want to teach the *ug* family—*bug, hug, mug, rug, tug, lug, pug.* A poem using these words is in Appendix E-3.

(5) If your child is playing treasure hunt and using a map (Chapter 13)—or is learning to read a map of his home, school, or commu-

nity, teach him other *ap* words—*cap, map, gap, nap, rap, lap, sap, zap*—he and you can write a *rap* using *ap* words.

(6) Other word families are: **ag**—*bag, gag, hag, lag, nag, rag, sag, tag, wag;* **od**—*cod, nod, pod, sod;* *ot*—*cot, dot, got, hot, jot, lot, not, pot;* **ob**—*Bob, cob, hob, job, mob, rob, sob;* **op**—*cop, hop, mop, pop, top;* **it**—*bit, fit, hit, kit, lit, pit, sit, wit;* **in**—*bin, fin, gin, kin, pin, sin, tin, win;* **im**—*dim, him, Kim, rim, Tim;* **id**—*bid, did, lid, mid, rid, Sid;* **un**—*bun, dun, fun, gun, Hun, nun, pun, run, sun;* **ut**—*cut, gut, hut, nut, put, rut;* **um**—*bum, gum, hum, mum, rum, sum;* **ed**—*bed, fed, Jed, led, Ned, red, wed;* **et**—*bet, get, jet, let, met, net, pet, set, vet, wet, yet.*

These word families can be used for "sounding out" practice; your child does not have to know the meaning of all these words. When one of these words is introduced, you may choose to point out the family word, and do some practice with him. Also, when he is learning to spell one word in a word family, show him how he can spell several words, using the family word and changing the first letter.

Digraphs and Consonant Blends with Word Families

In English, single letters are used to represent certain sounds, and letter combinations are used to represent certain other sounds. Letter combinations that appear in the initial position of words are digraphs (*ch, sh, th, wh*) and consonant blends (*bl, cr, fr, pl, sc, sl, sp, st, thr, br, dr, gl, pr, scr, sm, spr, str, tr, cl, fl, gr, qu, sk, sn, squ, sw, tw*). (Letter combinations also appear *within* words, but for now we are working on the initial position. Vowel combinations and diphthongs usually appear in the middle of words and sometimes at the end.) The methods described in Chapter 9 and this chapter can be adapted to teach these initial letter combinations. For example, when the digraph *ch* is introduced, a "ch" page could be added to the alphabet book; your child could go on a *ch* hunt, putting *ch* on objects that start with *ch* (chair, chain, chicken, check, china); and in the word bank, the *ch* words (as well as the *cr* and *cl* words), can be clipped together and placed in a sub-file under *c*.

Some digraphs and consonant blends that belong to word families are: **ag**—*shag, slag, stag, brag, drag, flag, snag, swag;* **an**—*clan, plan, bran, swan, scan, span, than;* **at**—*flat, slat, brat, drat, swat, scat, spat, that;* **am**—*clam, slam, cram, gram, pram, tram, swam, scam, sham;* **ap**—*clap, flap, slap, crap, trap, wrap, swap, snap, chap;* **od**—*clod, plod, prod, trod;* **op**—*stop, chop, shop;* **og**— *clog, flog, slog, frog, smog;* **ot**— *blot, clot, plot, slot, trot, spot, shot;* **ob**—*blob, slob, snob;* **it**—*flit, slit, grit, writ, spit, split;* **in**—*grin, twin, skin, spin, chin, shin, thin;* **im**—

slim, brim, grim, prim, trim, swim, skim, whim; **id**—*slid, grid, skid;* **un**—*spun, stun, shun;* **ug**—*slug, drug, grub, snug, chug, thug;* **ut**—*smut, shut, strut, glut;* **um**—*plum, slum, drum;* **en**—*Glen, then, when;* **ed**—*bled, fled, sled, bred, Fred, sped, shed.*

Remember that you can make games that require your child to join different word families to these consonant blends and digraphs, changing the last two letters rather than the first two. For example, to *fl* your child can join *ag, ap, og,* and *ed;* to *br, ag, an, im, ig, and ed.*

Three-Letter Word Families

You may also identify some common "three-letter word families" and make some games that allow your child to change the first letter, blend, or digraph to change a word (as described in this chapter). Examples: **ame**—*came, dame, fame, game, lame, tame, name, same, flame, blame, frame, shame;* **ain**—*gain, pain, rain, plain, slain, drain, train, stain, grain, Spain, stain, chain;* **ock**—*sock, dock, rock, hock, jock, lock, mock, block, clock, flock, crock, smock, stock, shock;* **ook**—*book, cook, look, hook, rook, nook, took, brook, crook, shook;* **amp**—*camp, damp, lamp, ramp, vamp, clamp, cramp, gramp, tramp, champ;* **are**—*care, bare, dare, fare, mare, rare, tare, blare, flare, scare, stare, share;* **oat**—*goat, coat, boat, moat, bloat, float;* **ing**—*ding, ping, ring, sing, wing, zing, cling, fling, sling, bring, swing, sting, thing.*

As stated earlier, select word families—and teach words—that appear in the literature that your child has an opportunity to read and can understand. ("Program" a book for him, or make one using the words and concepts—or provide this practice to supplement another reading program that has reading books that use the words and concepts.) He must have a use for the words and concepts presented and opportunities to practice them in order for the words and concepts to be of value to him.

Green Eggs and Ham, Hop on Pop, The Cat in the Hat (all by Dr. Seuss) are fun and easy to understand, and provide practice using word families. Use the techniques described above to first introduce your child to the word families that are "featured" in the book you choose.

Summary

This chapter has discussed some techniques for teaching phonics to children with Down syndrome. Phonics concepts have been broken down into small steps and interesting activities have been described to increase the probability of your child's success. If your child is making mistakes—less than 80 percent correct responses—chances are, your child is not getting the concept, you are going too fast, or he is getting tired of the activities. If you and your child are not having fun with these phonics games, but enjoy the sight reading games more, I recommend that you continue with the sight words and just point out letter sounds. It is most important that your child enjoys his reading activities and feels successful. Teach him to read using the methods that work best for him.

Chapter 11

WRITING AND SPELLING

Introduction

As with spoken language, there are two components to written language: *receptive,* what we understand when we hear or read words; and *expressive,* what we can say by speaking or writing. Reading is a means of *receptive* communication using written symbols. When the reader comprehends and understands the written language, he is a *receiver* of information and ideas expressed by others in writing. Writing is a means of *expressive* communication using written symbols. The writer uses written symbols to *express* or send information and ideas to other readers. We hear and understand the spoken language before we are able to speak; we read and understand written language before we are able to communicate by writing.

Writing involves arranging specific symbols (letters) of the language so these symbols communicate information, ideas, or feelings to readers. We can write by using handwriting or keyboards (typewriters, computers, and other electronic means). This chapter is primarily about handwriting and spelling; the use of keyboards will be referred to as an alternative means of writing.

Handwriting involves the ability to create specific symbols, in the correct order, to form words on a writing surface. Creating the symbols (letters) on a writing surface by hand is the "writing" part, and selecting the correct symbols and putting them in the correct order to make the desired word is the "spelling" part. It is possible for individuals to copy words and express themselves in their own handwriting, and lack the ability to spell the words. Conversely, it is possible for individuals to spell words orally or by using letter tiles or a keyboard, and lack the ability to write them by hand. If your child has more difficulty in one area than the other, adaptations, or alternatives, that allow your child to move forward by expressing himself in writing should be provided. A lack of skills in one area (writing or spelling) does not have to interfere with progress in learning how to express oneself by using written symbols.

WRITING

Writing and Down Syndrome

Figure 11.1

Generally, children with Down syndrome have difficulty learning to write. Perhaps the primary cause for this is decreased muscle tone and lack of strength in the hands and fingers. One study found that motor scores in children with Down syndrome between the ages of 12 and 36 months were lower than mental scores by as much as 10 months (LaVeck and LaVeck, 1977). This difference may be even greater as they grow older; in addition, poor motor skills may influence mental scores, because so many cognitive test items require motor ability in order for the child to demonstrate that he has the concepts or the ability to problem solve. On top of motor problems, some children with Down syndrome may have difficulty with visual perception; motor memory, planning, and control; spatial relationships; and eye-hand coordination.

And, of course, vision problems can be a very important factor.

As stated earlier, it is very important to have vision problems properly diagnosed and corrected. Of the samples of writing given in this chapter, two are from writers—Patrick and Glenn—classified as legally blind (20/200 vision or less in the better eye, even after the best possible correction with glasses or contact lenses). Both of these young men, however, are able to read, write, commute to work by bus, and hold responsible jobs in the community. Patrick works at Microsoft as a media assistant and Glenn is a merchandiser in a drug store. Aggressive treatment and glasses from early-on enabled these young men to use the vision they have, and they have certainly made good use of it. (Figure 11.1 is a photo of Glenn at five years of age, drawing a face on the chalk board. Around this time it became apparent that he had trouble seeing; he had to tilt his head in order to see.)

Just as with any other skill, children with Down syndrome vary in their ability to write. Some children are able to learn handwriting and spelling along with their same-age peers in inclusive classrooms with little special help. For others, progress is very slow, but, eventually, they learn to write. Some children may not learn handwriting, but learn to use a keyboard. And for some children, neither writing by hand nor using the keyboard is an effective means of communication.

For most children with Down syndrome, writing is a difficult task. However, with perseverance and encouragement, most can learn to write, and by adulthood, some can learn to write very well. Those who have the opportunity to learn the keyboard, like the rest of us, usually prefer this method of writing.

I could not believe it; it was as if he learned to write overnight.

Danny had the same special education teacher for several years, both in elementary and middle school. His teacher told me that she had struggled with him during those years, determined that he would learn to write, but he made little progress. Writing was very difficult for him. Then, as if a miracle had taken place, when he was 12 years old, he started writing very well, forming his letters perfectly and making them uniform in size. She said it was as if it had happened overnight.

As I reflected on this story and remembered Danny as the student who received the "best reader" award when he "graduated" from kindergarten, I wondered why it had taken him so long to learn to write, and why there had been such a dramatic change so suddenly. The possibilities I thought of were: (1) Developmentally, in his fine-motor, eye-hand coordination skills, perhaps he was functioning at about half his age, putting his fine motor development age at about six years developmentally, the age when most children learn to write. Perhaps his neurological development had just reached the stage when it was possible, and something "just clicked" when it was. (2) Perhaps the writing program the teacher was using was not programmed carefully enough for him. It could have been that the teacher expected him to make letters before he became proficient at making lines and strokes, and she was not giving him the "writing language" and prompts he needed to understand and remember how to form the letters; but, somehow, suddenly, it all "came together" for him.

He copied all the signs in the cafeteria and gave them to me.

When Danny was 16 years old, he and some other former students had lunch with me in a cafeteria. He was shy, and did not talk much, but when he finished his lunch, he took a notebook and a pencil from his book bag, and copied all the signs in the cafeteria. As he was leaving, he tore out the page and gave it to me. It was a gift, and although the material on it was not original, it communicated to me what I think he wanted to communicate: "See how well I can write. I want to share it with you." He did, indeed, write very well, and it was, indeed, a wonderful gift. I'm sorry that I lost it and cannot share it with you now. However, Dan (he now uses a more "grown up" version of his name) recently wrote me a note and sent his prom picture. I am sharing them

Figure 11.2

Dear Pat Olewein,
I hope you come your places
visit sometime 1 days! come down
to evey thuns How are your doing
wood you come down my Brithday
parry October 30, 1994 (10/30/72)
my Mom make you A help you
finD my House Baing your frinads
So I miss you Pat Olewein
I like you Bast friend, Dan Mitchell
P.S. Senior Prom is fun
Graduation is great
Nathan Hale High School is
Good

Figure 11.3

with you, with his permission (figures 11.2 and 11.3). Also see the box on page 149.)

Some children with Down syndrome become very capable writers and write letters, stories, poems, assignments, and speeches. Reed (age 9) wrote a speech to read at his church (figure 11.4). (Reed says that he *use* to have Down syndrome, when he was little; now that he is in inclusive education, he insists that he no longer has Down syndrome. Figure 11.5 is a photo of Reed and the pet he said he needed in his speech.) Patrick, who was 24 at the time, wrote a note to me when he sent an article about himself that appeared in *The Advocate,* the paper published by Bellevue Community College, where he was a student (figure 11.6). Lupita, a young adult, typed a speech to read at a meeting with state legislators (figure 11.7). Becca Winegar, who, at age 15, enjoys sitting at the computer three hours at a time, transcribing scripts from audio tapes, and copying text from the encyclopedia (on subjects of current interest), also writes creative essays (figure 11.8). Glenn, a young adult, stopped by my office to see me, but I was not there, so he left a note (figure 11.9). (I am always *very* touched when former students write to me.)

Dan, Patrick, and Glenn wrote in cursive, as do many people with Down syndrome. However, some people with Down syndrome experience considerable difficulty in making the transition from printing to cursive. In these cases, it may be best not to burden these individuals with the agony of continuing to work on *perfecting* cursive, unless it is something *the learner* really wants to learn and is very motivated to do. Printing is functional and meets the needs of most people with Down syndrome; legible printing is certainly preferable over illegible cursive. Usually, however, I do think that it is worthwhile to teach them to write their name in cursive so they will have a signature, even if it is not all that legible—it does not have to be. They can sign their checks, and sign their name when they vote. Most of the time when a signature is used, the person's name also appears in print, or they are asked to print their name by their signature. Of course, it is okay to sign your name by printing, but this may be embarrassing to some people with Down syndrome. Give them the opportunity to learn to write their name in cursive.

I recommend teaching cursive writing to learners with Down syndrome in order to help them learn to *read* cursive. While learning to

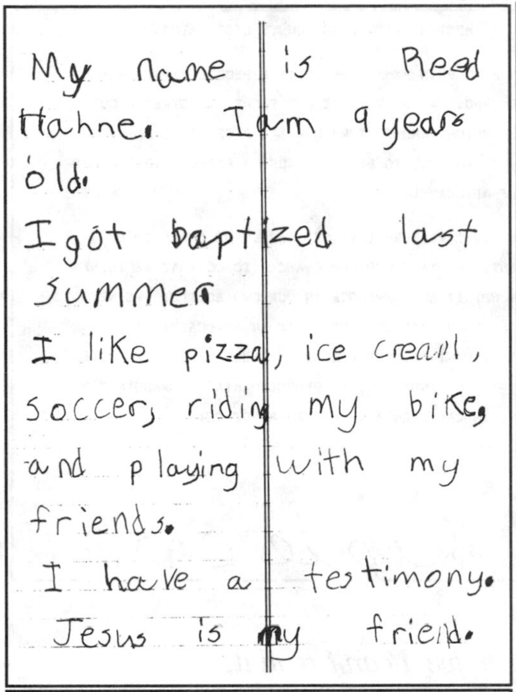

My name is Real Hahne. I am 9 year old.
I got baptized last summer
I like pizza, ice cream, soccer, riding my bike, and playing with my friends.
I have a testimony.
Jesus is my friend.

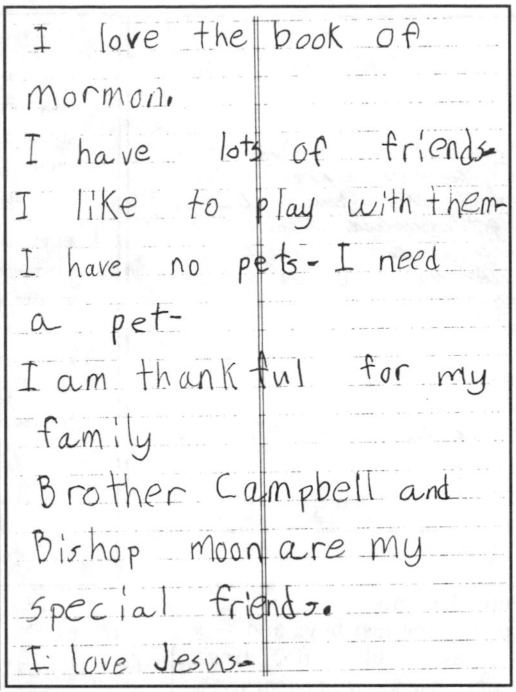

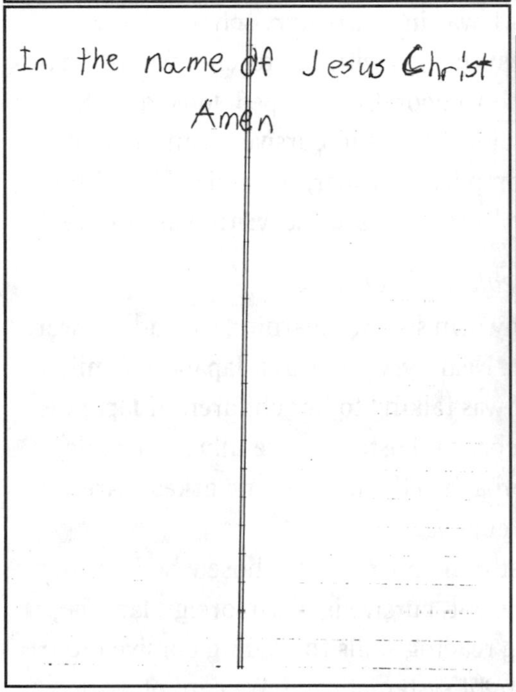

In the name of Jesus Christ Amen

I love the book of Mormon.
I have lots of friends.
I like to play with them
I have no pets- I need a pet-
I am thankful for my family
Brother Campbell and Bishop moon are my special friends.
I love Jesus-

Figure 11.4

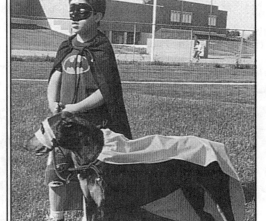

Figure 11.5

write it, they learn to read it. Learning to read cursive enables them to make full use of their ability to read. Any person who cannot read cursive is not fully literate and will be handicapped on many occasions when reading would be most functional and meaningful. Most often, personal notes, cards, and letters are written in cursive. It is important that people with Down syndrome are able to read their personal mail—even if they print their reply. Their reading skills become fully functional, and they avoid embarrassment. Also, some young people with Down syndrome are getting jobs entering data. The ability to read cursive will expand their job opportunities as well.

Learning to write cursive is not necessary for learning to read it. If your child experiences great difficulty and frustration learning to write cursive, teach him to read cursive by the match, select, and name method. In this case, he will match cursive letters and words to printed letters and words—then move on with the selecting and naming of the cursive words and letters. Practice can be provided with lotto and bingo games.

Dear Mrs. Olwein,

3/25/92

I hope you will like this article of me on the front cover of the Advocate paper. It also tells about my life as Down Syndrom and it also tells about how I got involved with school, sports and my social life. So how are you doing? are you enjoying this wonderful weather? What have you been doing? My mom and dad are doing just fine. I will see you soon.

your friend,
Patrick Evezich

P.S. Tell Allison that I said hi and tell her that I love her ok?

Figure 11.6

My goal was being in Peter Pan, and I auditioned for it. I played Nibs, one of the lost boys and every day I studied my lines. I had about 21 lines to memorize and it was hard work. We rehearsed every night for a month. I also had to change the set in the dark At first I was scared. I liked how the director worked with us in Peter Pan, and the choreography was great. I am happy I chose that goal. We performed 3 times a week for two months. We had a cast party at my house and it was a lot of fun. We all loved being in "Peter Pan".

Figure 11.8

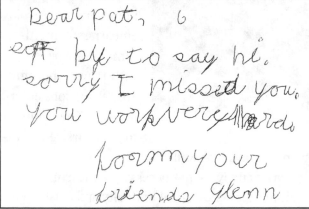

Figure 11.9

12/9/91   MEETING WITH KING COUNTY LEGISLATORS

HI! I AM A DOLPHIN MEMBER WHICH IS A PEOPLE FIRST CHAPTER.
I AM LUPE CANO. WE WANT TO BE OUT THERE, TO STRETCH OUT
ACROSS OUR UNION, AND TO TURN OUR SAD FACES INTO PROUD
HEARTS. WE WANT YOU TO BE ONE OF US, A PEOPLE FIRST MEMBER
AND A SELF-ADVOCATE.

IN PEOPLE FIRST WE TURN INTO OFFICERS. WE LEARN TO BE
INDEPENDENT. WE TAKE OUR OWN CHANCES TO DO WHAT WE THINK.
WE HAVE A SPIRIT AND STRENGTH IN OUR OWN BODIES. WE NEED TO
SAY IT FIERCE AND ACT IT HARD. I'M AN ADVOCATE! I'M AN
ADVOCATE! I WANT ALL THE PEOPLE IN THEIR OWN STATES TO KEEP
SAYING IT - IN TENNESSEE, IN PENNSLYVANIA, IN WASHINGTON,
IN OREGON, IN CALIFORNIA - I'M AN ADVOCATE!

Figure 11.7

Oh, it's in cursive. I can't read it.

When B.J. was in elementary school, she was walking down the hall with her teacher when she noticed a note on a door. She stopped, looked at the note, then said, "Oh, it's in cursive; I can't read it." B.J., an accomplished reader, recognized her limitations—and also recognized the writing as cursive.

Are you speaking in cursive?

When my own son was learning to read, we were at the beach. Near by, there was a Japanese family. The mother was talking to her children in Japanese. My son watched and listened carefully for a while, then he approached the mother and asked, "Are you speaking in cursive?"

We must remember that to those who have not learned to read it, cursive is like a foreign language. Transferring reading skills to reading cursive often has to be taught systematically. We cannot assume that children will just "pick it up."

Let Me Tell You about Glenn

A group of students from Nathan Hale High School, who were participating in a community-based work experience program, came to the University Hospital for their work experience. On Fridays, they had lunch in the cafeteria, and I joined them there when I could. On one occasion, when I was visiting with Glenn, a young man in the program, Rob, who had severe physical impairments and used an electric wheelchair, said, "Ms. Oelwein, let me tell you about Glenn. When it is time to go, Glenn always remembers to get my coat and helps me put it on. He always makes sure that doors are open for me—and stay open until I am through the doorway. And when I roll off the lift into the bus, Glenn is always waiting to strap me in."

Rob did not have to tell me about Dan (the recent graduate). I observed him first hand. Rob's salad had cheese in it, and cheese was a food he had been told to avoid. When Rob said, "Oh, it has cheese in it," Dan spontaneously went to Rob, took Rob's fork, and carefully removed all the cheese. This was a task that Rob, with his limited motor control, was unable to perform himself.

Glenn, as mentioned earlier, is legally blind. Dan has a total hearing loss in his left ear, and the hearing in his right ear is dependent on the current health of that ear. Glenn's impairment is reflected in his handwriting; Dan's in his spelling. In spite of their impairments, both men are able to *communicate effectively with the written word.* In addition, they have the grace and manners that put most of us to shame.

So often, parents become concerned that their child is not as skilled in reading, writing, and spelling as another child the same age. They worry that they are not pushing hard enough, that they have failed their child, or that their child's school program is not as good as someone else's. They become concerned that their child is not reaching his or her "full potential."

There was a time when it was my goal to help children with Down syndrome reach their "full potential." However, after reading a newsletter in which a speech by Ann Turnbull was quoted, I changed my goals. The newsletter stated that Dr. Turnbull invited anyone in the audience who had reached their "full potential" to please introduce themselves to her. She would really like to meet them, as she was unaware of ever having met anyone who had reached their full potential, and would like to have the experience. Dr. Turnbull said that she thought that expecting *anyone* to reach their full potential imposed a great burden on the person. She asked, "What is wrong with an ordinary good life?" (And I ask, "What is wrong with *functional* academic skills that support this ordinary good life?")

Glenn and Dan have the skills to live ordinary good lives, and, at the same time, be extraordinary people. They have much to give and can enrich the lives of many. Rob, with no mental impairment and articulate speech, trapped in a body that does not work very well for him and wise beyond his years, recognized how genuinely caring these young men were, and how valuable their friendship was to him. Rob knows how unimportant academic achievement is; the ability to love and feel loved is what gives real quality to life.

I have no trouble reading either Glenn's or Dan's letters. They communicate well to me. Their writing is very *functional.* With Glenn's impairment, I am impressed that he can write at all; with Dan's impairment, I am impressed that he can spell at all.

(I think I'll wear a costume to Dan's party, and bring my best friend—my husband. We have a very important occasion to celebrate—the twenty-second birthday of a very successful man!)

Writing, for some people with Down syndrome, is not used only for functional communication and creative expression, but some adults with Down syndrome have become published writers as well. Books, essays, and poems written by these adults have had a great impact on social attitudes toward people with Down syndrome. In addition, these authors provide insight on their perspective on a number of issues that can be expressed best in writing. One of Lupita's goals as a young adult is to write a book. I plan to support her in this endeavor. After all, we need a female's point of view. Jason Kingsley and Mitchell Levitz did their part for the males in *Count Us In: Growing Up With Down Syndrome.*

When Do You Begin to Teach Writing?

Because there is such a range of problems and abilities in children with Down syndrome, there is no "magical" or "set" time to start them with writing. Most children with Down syndrome have documented delays in motor development great enough to qualify them for the services of an occupational therapist. The therapist should assess fine motor skills and help determine if your child has the skills needed to start with a writing program. The therapist and/or the teacher can use a formal assessment for writing, such as the one provided in *The Sensi-*

ble Pencil (see below). Parents and teachers should not have to go it alone when making such decisions. The role of the therapist is to team with the teacher and parent and make plans to embed fine motor activities in your child's program throughout the day—whether they are writing activities or non-writing motor activities—that build strength, control, and coordination. Specific objectives should be included in the IEP, and where, when, and how often these objectives are to be worked on should be stated, as well as the person who is going to be responsible for each objective.

In reality, learning to write begins when your child first picks up a pencil, pen, crayon, felt pen, or chalk and makes a mark on a surface. Your encouragement and praise of his efforts—and the continuous availability of writing material (get him a good, sturdy chalkboard and put it in a place where he has easy access to it—as well as providing him with limitless paper, pencils, crayons and felt pens, and ample opportunities for "free form" drawing)—are most important in making it an activity that he wants to continue. Praise him, scribble with him, and do "turn-taking" with him using crayon and paper—first imitating him, and then taking it farther by modeling on your turn. Very likely he will then want to continue with the activity, find it pleasurable, choose to do it often, and improve his fine motor skills. If, however, you start showing him how he can draw something and take his hands and try to force him to draw certain things, he may soon become "turned off" to drawing activities—and you may have a major power struggle on your hands. Remember, it is human nature; we do not like to fail—and it is not all that much fun meeting the goals of others. It is important that your child has the ability and the motivation to do the task. Given the various problems mentioned above, even the simplest tasks, such as copying lines, may be very difficult, and/or very boring and meaningless to your child. Typically, children with Down syndrome attempt to avoid failure by refusing to try to do things that are too hard for them, or in which they have no interest. And, by the way, help him, providing "hand over hand" assistance only if he does not mind. I suggest that you ask him, "Do you want me to help you?" Or, "Tell me when you need help." This puts your child in control and avoids a power struggle.

To help prepare your child for writing, plan *interesting* and *meaningful* art, play, and self-care activities that your child can do, and wants to do. Fine motor skills (in addition to gross motor, communication, cognitive, and social skills) should be embedded in activities that have meaning and interest for your child. For example, if he is learning to cut with scissors, and he is able, at this time, to cut only one-inch strips of paper successfully, with you holding the strips, plan activities, based on his interest and understanding, in which he will need paper cut in these one-inch pieces. If he is interested in snakes, he can cut different colored strips (of his choosing) and paste them on a snake (that you drew) to make a striped snake; if he is interested in fish (perhaps after a field trip to an aquarium), he can cut fins and scales to glue on a fish; if he likes cars, he can cut out windows and glue them on; if he is interested in clowns, he can cut out and paste these pieces of paper on a circle to make a clown with eyes, nose, mouth, etc. In addition, he can help you cut out those snakes, fish, cars, and clowns on which he will paste the parts. When you cut them out, leave one-inch extensions here and there, for him to cut off (on the line—where you goofed—pretend that you made a mistake). After he has practice at this level, and his strength and control are improving, help him to hold the paper himself, and gradually fade out your help. When he is able to cut longer pieces (several consecutive strokes), create a need for these big pieces, and when he can cut on the line, he will, of course, be able to cut out simple shapes for his art projects independently.

Use the same technique when teaching drawing and writing. Rather than asking your child to trace, copy, or imitate drawing lines, circles, and other shapes for no apparent reason to him, embed drawing in the art activities to help him to learn to make purposeful, meaningful, marks on paper. For example, he can draw the stripes on the snake (first, making only one-inch lines, then, later filling them in; you can draw the top of the snake, and he can copy the line, drawing the bottom; he can then draw in the eye (just a dot), and the tongue (just a line sticking out). Draw some scales (little c's on the fish), and encourage him to imitate you (until he can do them all by himself—without your model), and encourage him to draw the eyes, mouth, etc. Draw a circle for the clown's head (or monster, spaceman, cowboy—whatever he's interested in), draw in the nose and mouth, then let him draw circles for the eyes, and each time you draw one, leave out another body part for him to supply. This way, it is fun. He has a reason and desire to do it, he can do it, and he has to really look and decide just where each body part goes. Build on what your child can do, provide him lots of practice at his level, make it fun and meaningful, and encourage him to be creative and draw things on his own. He needs practice, and he needs to learn how to make lines and marks that are purposeful and represent "something."

And then they told me I had to cut on the lines.

Dr. Elizabeth Wiig is a professor of speech pathology at Boston University who has written three textbooks and over 50 research articles and speaks six languages fluently. She graciously shared her experiences as a child with learning disabilities in an essay in *Exceptional Children* (Heward and Orlansky, 1980, First Edition). She told how she struggled and struggled to learn to use scissors. When, at last, she was able to actually cut with them, she felt elated; however, the feeling of elation was short lived. She was then told that she had to cut on the lines.

It is hard for us to imagine how difficult some of these tasks are for children who have motor, coordination, and perception problems. It is no wonder that so many children give up and do all they can to avoid these tasks. Dr. Wiig said that she learned that she could avoid failure by "acting out" in class. When she did, she was sent to the principal's office. She found that sitting there was much more pleasant than staying in the classroom and failing.

It's really hard!

I showed a videotape at a workshop. In the videotape, Kari, six years old at the time, was learning to print her last name, and the teacher offered her help with the *S*, saying, "That *S* is *really a hard one.*" One participant was critical of this comment from the teacher on her evaluation of the workshop. She wrote that children should not be told that tasks are hard; that doing so causes children to be fearful of the tasks and they "clam up" and refuse to try. She added that you should tell them that the task is easy, so they will think that it is easy and that they can do it.

I was sorry that this person did not sign her name, because I could not give her my philosophy about the "easy/hard" issue. Now is my chance. I think that you should tell the child that it is hard. It is *hard* for her, and she *knows* it—she's tried it many times and just can't get that *S* to come out right. Telling her that it is hard validates and justifies her feelings about the task. Telling her that it is easy, discredits her experience and perception of the task; it gives her no empathy or understanding; and it denies that she has impairments that make such tasks difficult. (You *should* be able to do this simple, *easy,* little task—see how well *I* do it. It's so *easy.*). Trying to convince her that it is easy takes away the teacher's credibility. Most students would not cooperate with such a teacher. If, on the other hand, the teacher told her that it is *hard,* a real *challenge,* and that she, the teacher, has faith in her and *thinks* that the student can meet the *challenge* of this *difficult* task, because she is such a *good worker,* the student will be more apt to be cooperative and live up to this self-image of a good worker.

When you tell a child that a task is *hard,* and she fails, then it is okay; she failed at something that is *hard.* If she succeeds, it is a real achievement; she can do something that is *hard*. When you tell a child that the task is *easy,* and she fails, then her failure is really great; she failed at something that was *easy*. If she succeeds, then it was not much of an accomplishment; it was so *easy*.

(Can you imagine how a wife would feel if her husband said to her that he could not understand why her pie crusts were not as flaky as his mother's; after all, making flaky pie crusts is so *easy*. Or, if she did make a nice flaky pie crust, and he said, "Oh, that's so *easy* to do." In either case, such comments should not encourage pie baking on the part of the wife.)

So, when do you start to teach your child writing? *When your child is interested, wants to do it, and is willing to work at it*. Any time he tries to copy or trace his name, or shows any interest in writing any letter or word, build on it. Praise him, and give him lots of opportunities and reasons to write. Strike while the iron is hot. Let him have practice at "free hand" writing on unlined paper. You can help him by providing a model for him to look at, or if he is willing, to trace. You can make him some dot-to-dot games, using the letters in his name—he connects the dots, and when he does so, he writes his name (start with rather large letters). Gradually move on to the lined paper.

If you think that your child has the skills to start writing (can handle a pencil quite well and makes meaningful lines and drawings—imitating, copying, tracing, or spontaneously drawing), but has initiated no interest in writing, start encouraging him to write his name, or the first letter of his name. Tracing is usually the first step (however, if your child tries or wants to do it "freehanded," that's a good way to start). To help him *want* to do it, you may need to give him a *reason* to trace those letters. For example, you can have his name written with a pencil, and let him choose a felt pen (color of his choice) to make it bright and pretty—to "put it in lights." Use your own creativity and think of something that appeals to your child. The "it's cold and it wants you to put a warm blanket on it" story worked well with some children I have had the opportunity to work with—I first used it to encourage children to trace shapes.

"And now the 'O' is cold."

When he was about eight years old, Jordan's mother told me that it was hard to motive him to trace his name. It was hard, and he did not like to do it. His "worksheet" was a page with about five *Jordans* written on it in dotted lines, for tracing. I gave Jordan a red felt pen and told him that the *J* was cold, and that the *J* wanted him to cover him up with a nice red blanket. I spoke for the *J* saying, in a *J* voice (you'll have to guess what that sounds like), "Jordan, please cover me up, I'm so cold, please, I need a blanket." As Jordan seriously started tracing the *J*, I continued to talk for the *J*, saying, "Thank you, Jordan, it feels so good." When he failed to cover the line, I would say, "Brrrrr," and he would immediately correct his mistake. When he finished the *J*, he looked up at me and said, "Now the *o* is cold." He continued tracing all the *Jordans* on the page, announcing the comfort status of each letter as he progressed. It was fun making those letters warm and happy. He had a reason to cover them up. A little novelty goes a long way and accomplishes much.

Teaching Writing

Systematic Program for Teaching Writing

It is not within the scope of this volume to provide a systematic, comprehensive program to teach writing manuscript letters and numbers. That is a volume in itself, and if such a volume is needed, I recommend *The Sensible Pencil* by Linda C. Becht (available from EBSCO Curriculum Materials for $59.95, Part Number 1630, Box 11542, Birmingham, AL 35202, 1–800–633–8623). When *The Sensible Pencil* was published in 1985, Ms. Becht told me that she initially developed it for the children in her class who had Down syndrome. This program is designed to "teach children to write with the highest level of success and a minimum of failure." It moves from the simple to the complex and provides interesting practice sheets and techniques that appeal to young writers. She recommends that the student spend only 10 to 15 minutes on the program each day, and stresses individualizing for each learner. Included in this program is an assessment of skills and pre-writing activities and exercises.

Functional Writing

Systematic writing programs give the writer an excellent background for writing, as your child learns the "language of writing" (go around, down, curve, etc.) as well as all the "technical" aspects of forming letters with a pencil. Some children complete these systematic programs before they start to write words (functional use), others start writing words before they start the program, or while they are still in the program. Some learners, especially if they are older, will not find the systematic writing program meaningful. They need the instant success found in writing words. (This is especially true of learners who have been stuck in pre-writing programs for years because they have not reached "criteria" for moving on to writing.)

Ms. Becht stresses the importance of learning the right way to form letters, so that the writer does not develop bad habits, because these bad habits are hard to correct. For cooperative young learners, I would do all I could to help them to form letters the "correct" way, and give them praise for their efforts. However, if your child does not want to cooperate and do it "your way" (forming letters and staying within the lines) chances are, it will be better to let him do it his way, rather than insisting on "the right way—your way" and starting a power struggle. Such power struggles can cause an unpleasant situation, diverting attention from the goal of learning to write to who is going to "win." Such conflicts can cause writing to become an unpleasant task (for both the student and teacher), and, perhaps result in your child's refusal to write at all. (Most children will "win" one way or the other, and sometimes this means refusal to do the task at all.) If it is "readable" then it is "functional" in sending the message. Some things are negotiable, and how to form letters is one of them. Show your child how you do it, then give him a choice, "Now you know two ways; you can choose the one you like best." Chances are, if the person does much writing, he will use the keyboard anyway.

Materials for Teaching Writing: Purchase appropriate writing materials. The paper should be standard primary writing paper with sets of three lines: a solid top line, broken middle line, and solid bottom line. There should be a space between each set of lines. Pencils with erasers are necessary, so your child can learn to correct errors. If your child needs a primary pencil with a larger circumference that is easier to grasp, provide him with these pencils. For practice and novelty, chalkboards with the three sets of lines painted on them are nice.

Purchase or make a model of the alphabet, and post it on the wall or on your child's desk or work surface for easy reference. (You can make copies of Appendix B-2). The model should have the three guide lines (top, middle, and bottom), and the letters should be placed appropriately between these lines. Arrows, or other markings, should show your child where to start, and the direction the pencil should go to form each part of the letter. Use the script used by your child's school so there will be consistency between home and school.

Where to Begin: I recommend that your child start by learning to write his first name, or initial, if the name is long and difficult to spell and write. What is important is that your child wants to write; that the words that he learns to write are *meaningful* to and *useful* for him; that your child is *successful* in writing readable words; that your child *uses* his writing to communicate. As suggested in Chapter 8, when your child can read his name, then he can start communicating with the written word by placing a label, with his name on it, on his art products. This communicates, "This is mine. I did it." When your child can read *Mommy* and *Daddy,* then he can start communicating who the recipient of this fine art is to be by sticking labels with the names of the recipient (Mommy, Daddy, Grandma, etc.) on his work of art as well. When your child is interested in writing, and is able to make discrete lines, then he can start learning to write his first name and sign his own art work. From there, he can learn to write other words he can use often, such as *to, from, Mommy, Daddy,* etc., rather than relying on stickers.

The general sequence for teaching writing is first tracing the words (or letters), then copying from a model of the word or letter, and finally, writing independently, without a model. This is usually done using the lined primary paper, and, in time when your child can form the letters correctly, standard lined paper can be used.

Adaptations: Use of Mnemonics

Writing is complex, and there is much to remember about all those little lines, curves, slants, circles, and crosses. The writer not only has to remember the name of the letter, the sound that it makes, how each letter is formed, where to start, and how it should be placed between the lines, but he also has to remember which way it is turned. Mnemonics, memory aids often based on vivid imagery, are helpful for most learners, and in some cases, they are necessary for the success of your child.

Mnemonics on Primary Paper Lines: The use of mnemonics on primary writing paper can be very helpful to your child. Several years ago, I saw some primary writing paper on which the lines were color coded: top line green, the middle line yellow, and the bottom line red. At the left margin, there was a traffic light, with the green light on the top line, the yellow on the middle, and the red on the bottom. This type of color coding helps a child remember where to start writing a particular letter, and gives the instructor a means to communicate with the child. Example: "To make an *l*, start up here on the green line, go through the yellow line, and stop on the red." This works well for upper case letters, as most start on the green line, and stop on the red line. However, many lower case letters start on the yellow line, and many go through the red line, so although it still provides a means of communication and association, the start and stop coding does not always apply.

My favorite mnemonic for naming the lines is the little man (figure 11.10). This little man with a hat is drawn in the left margin. The top line is the hat line, the middle the belt line, and the bottom the shoe line. Your child can be cued, "To make the *g*, start on the belt line, go around, then up to the belt line again and down through the foot line

Figure 11.10

and curve up." When your child starts to write a letter, he can consult the model with the little man in the margin and determine which line (the hat, belt, or shoe) to start on and go through and where to stop and curve, etc.

Mnemonics for Holding the Pencil: Some children have trouble remembering how to position the pencil in their hands to write. Mnemonics can help these children as well.

This dog has fleas and wants you to scratch him when you write.

When I was consulting in a classroom, I noticed that the teacher frequently prompted Carmen to hold her pencil correctly. I watched Carmen, and it was obvious that she really wanted to hold it the right way. She was very cooperative and would turn the pencil and try to hold it different ways, but she had difficulty finding the correct position. The teacher, observing this, would go to her and help her position the pencil in her hand. In a short time, the pencil would lose its correct position, and the process of the prompt and help would start over again. (If I've showed her once, I've showed her a thousand times.)

It was obvious that Carmen simply could not remember how to place the pencil correctly in her hand. She needed an imagery. I drew a little dog on her hand, on the space between the index finger and the thumb, and told her that the little dog had fleas. The dog wanted her to scratch him when she wrote, because it would make him feel real good. (Of, course, I got a little dramatic and told her that the dog said, "Please, please, Carmen, scratch me when you write. It feels so good.") Whenever Carmen picked up the pencil, she would first place it on the dog; then it was in the proper position to grasp for writing. After a few days, with the help of the dog, she had enough practice placing the pencil in the correct position, that the dog was no longer necessary. She could remember where to place the pencil, and placing it correctly was becoming automatic.

Mnemonics for Letter Direction and Discrimination: Most young writers reverse letters and some confuse *b* and *d*, *p* and *q*. Mnemonics can be most helpful in providing the writer with associations and imagery that are helpful. The mnemonic needs to be within the writer's experience and understanding and should be individualized for each learner as needed.

She writes Dana with the "a's" going the same direction as the "D."

Figure 11.11

A teacher asked me for help with one of her students, Dana, who the teacher described as having aphasia (i.e., a loss of speech function, usually due to brain lesions). Dana was having difficulty writing her name. She made the *a's* like the *D,* except smaller, turned in the same direction as the *D.* Although the teacher corrected her each time she wrote her name, the next time she wrote it, she made the same mistake. I thought that, perhaps, Dana just needed an image to remember which way the *a's* were to go. I wrote her name on a 3 x 5 index card. On the *a's,* I drew faces in profile and made the straight line into hair (figure 11.11). I told the teacher to tell her that the *a's* said, "Please, please, Dana, let me see the big *D.* Turn me so I can see the big *D* for Dana." The card was to remain on her desk as a model and reminder.

Figure 11.12

This conversation happened after school, and Dana had gone home, so I was unable to observe Dana's response to this mnemonic. Her teacher, however, reported to me that she never had to remind Dana to turn her *a's* around again.)

He has trouble with d, b, and p.

A young man, Sam, was coming to the university for tutoring in reading and writing, because he wanted to learn to drive a car. He needed to learn some good, functional reading in order to achieve this goal. The graduate student who was tutoring him told me that when Sam wrote, he made mistakes with *d, b,* and *p.* He could not remember which was which. They all looked the same to him. I asked the tutor what words Sam read that started with these letters. She said that he knew *dog, bus,* and *people.* I drew the mnemonics (to the left) and told the tutor to tell him to remember that the *d* was for *dog* and that the dog looked away from the tail; the *b* was for *bus,* and the b fits into the front of the bus; the *p* was for *people,* and people's hair hangs down (figure 11.12). These were put on a 3 x 5 index card for Sam to refer to when needed. He very quickly remembered these images and wrote the letters correctly without the use of the card.

Figure 11.13

At that point, Sam was not writing words that started with *q,* so I did not bother him with it. The *q* is easier, because it has a tail that curls up to the *u* that is always there. An imagery could be used with the word *queen*—make the *q* a queen, with the tail on the *q* a hair flip and the rest of the word her train (figure 11.13).

Which is the M and which is the W?

My own son, Walter, confused the upper case *M* and *W,* and would ask, "Which is the *M* and which is the *W?*" I drew a tall "Mommy" with her arms reaching down to a rather short little boy whose arms were reaching up. I told him to remember that *M* was for *Mommy,* and Mommy's arms were like the *M,* reaching down to Walter; and the *W* was for *Walter,* and Walter's arms were reaching up like the *W,* reaching up to Mommy. That was the end of his confusion (figure 11.14).

Figure 11.14

I gave this as an example at a workshop, and a participant said, "But not all little boys are named Walter." The point is that the *instructor* develops mnemonics that apply to the needs and experiences of the individual learner. These examples can be used if your child has the same problem and the mnemonic is within his experience. (The instructor could adapt this mnemonic by telling the child a story about a little boy named Walter, Will, Wally, etc. Use your imagination.)

(By the way, this mnemonic is responsible for this book and my career in the specialty of "Down syndrome." I was Val Dmitriev's student when I developed this mnemonic as a class project. She was so impressed she gave me a job.)

Creative Writing: Journals

Journals are an important part of most elementary curricula; they provide a use for reading and writing skills. In kindergarten classes, and in the beginning of the first grade, until the pupils learn to write, the "journals" usually consist of drawings by the pupils. At journal time, the pupils are told to draw a picture of something they want to talk about, or about something that happened to them. In classes where pupils are learning a "letter of the week" (often, kindergarten classes have a letter of the week, starting with *a* the first week of school and finishing with *z* somewhere around the twenty-sixth week), the teacher may suggest that the students draw something that starts with the letter of the week. Often, there are models—objects and pictures of things that start with that letter—left on display in the classroom, after the class has discussed and practiced the letter and its sound. When pupils finish their drawing, they tell the teacher what it is and why they drew it—what it means to them. The teacher then prints a simple statement about it under the picture, so the child can see it in writing. For example, if the pupil told the teacher that he drew a rabbit because "*R* is for *rabbit*," the teacher may write "*R* is for *rabbit*" under his picture. Or, if the pupil told the teacher he drew Barney because he liked to watch him on TV, the teacher may write, "I watch Barney on TV."

When the pupils are able to copy simple sentences off the chalkboard, the teacher may print a simple "open" sentence for them to copy on primary paper (the kind that has a space for a drawing at the top and lines for writing at the bottom) and then draw a picture of their own experience at the top. For example, when my daughter was in first grade, each Monday, for a period of time, the teacher wrote, "I had fun this weekend" on the chalkboard. The pupils copied it, then drew a picture of something fun they had done over the weekend. We had a wonderful "journal" of her weekends. By looking at the drawings, it was easy to determine the highlight of these weekends. In time, children will be able to write their own experiences, with and without picture illustrations and with and without teacher help.

Journal time is a time for personal growth in expressing oneself with pencil and paper. If your child does not have the opportunity to keep a journal at school, then you can start one at home. As a matter of fact, this whole "language experience approach" should, for the most part, be based on your child's journal—one that you wrote for him and illustrated—or if your child is able to relate his experiences and ideas verbally, one that he dictated to you and you wrote.

If there is a "journal period" in your child's school schedule, specific objectives for this period should be written into his IEP so he can succeed and grow, just as there should be specific objectives for all other periods of the day. His time is valuable and should be well spent with meaningful activities.

Mommy, tell me what I wrote.

Before I started school, I can remember wanting to write when my mother was writing. She would give me pencil and paper, and I would attempt to make my scribbles look like her writing. After filling up the page, I can remember insisting that she read it back to me, as I was sure that I had created a masterpiece and wondered just what I had written.

I did not have the concepts that the writer starts with the information, ideas, or feeling that he wants to express, or that the marks on the paper had to be very specific marks, placed in a very specific order, in order for these marks to form words that could be read, and that had meaning. I could not read, and I had no idea what it was all about.

Her behavior is appropriate; during the journal writing time she is not a problem.

Gail was in an inclusive first-grade classroom. During the journal writing period, she scribbled in her journal, drawing meaningless marks, as I had done. Gail could read, and I felt quite sure that she knew that she was not actually writing in her journal, but was just pretending to, as were some of her peers. When I mentioned this to the teacher, the teacher's response was, "Her behavior is appropriate; during the journal writing time she is not a problem."

Being appropriate isn't enough. Perhaps her IEP objective for the journal period was a social goal—that she would sit at her desk and use pencil and paper and "look" like she was writing in a journal—to look "appropriate." If so, she had met that objective and should have a new one. Gail needed to be learning to write in her journal. She needed to learn, as I eventually learned, that in order to write, first you need to have something to write about, something to communicate on paper, and then, you need to know how to write it down.

After children with Down syndrome have passed the journal picture-drawing stage mentioned above, provide them with adaptations to help them move forward in their ability to communicate on paper.

1. **Dictation:** Perhaps the most common adaptation is dictation. The student dictates what he wants to write to the teacher, the teacher writes it on lined primary paper, and the student copies (or traces) it. If the student articulates well enough, the teacher writes down exactly what he says, and the student copies (or traces) it. If the student is difficult to understand, or just says key words, the teacher helps him put an idea in a simple sentence. For example, when asked what he wanted to write about, the student might say, "John ball." The teacher might ask, "Did you and John play ball?" If the student says "Yes," the teacher may then ask, "Did you have fun?" If the answer is yes, then the teacher might write, "John and I played ball. We had fun." If, however, when asked if he and John played ball, the student says, "No, hit." the teacher might ask, "Did John hit you with the ball?" If the answer is yes, the teacher might ask, "Did it hurt?" If the student answers that it did, the teacher may print for him, "John hit me with the ball. It hurt me." The teacher, or person taking the dictation, should take care that he

writes down what the student intended to express, and then ask the student if it is correct. The student then copies (or traces) what the teacher writes, creating a journal in his own handwriting, or by using a keyboard.

(When students can give dictation clearly enough for a peer to write it for them, peers can team with these students and take the dictation. This usually happens in the upper elementary grades. It is good practice for peers to learn to take dictation as well.)

2. **Fill-in-the-Blank Journals:** Simple, incomplete statements about the day's events can be written, and your child can fill in the blanks. There are three levels for this adaptation: (1) if your child cannot copy words, he communicates by circling the correct word; (2) if your child can copy words, he can circle the correct word and then copy it in the blank; (3) if your child is able to write and spell the words (or knows how to look up the words), no choices are provided, and he writes in the words. (This can also be done on the computer.)

Examples of statements for fill-in-the-blank journals:

Today I came to school by _____ .

bus   car   walking   train   dogsled

The day of the week is_____ .

Sunday Monday Tuesday Wednesday Thursday Friday Saturday

Today the weather is_____ .

cold   hot   stormy   windy   rainy   sunny   cloudy   snowy

In reading we read a story about _____ .

a pet shop   a red bird   a surprise   a cat

At recess I played with _____ .

Anne   Sam   Martha   Jonathan   Cindy   Aaron

For lunch I had_____ .

sandwich   soup   pizza   hamburger   milk   juice

3. **Topics to Write About:** To help the writer to get started, provide some topics to write about. Have a list of topics. The writer can circle the topic he wants to write about, and make a few statements about the topic. Examples:

Things I can write about:

1. The weather (everyone talks about it)

2. What happened in class today (or at school, in gym, in library, at recess)

3. What we had for lunch

4. Friends

5. Feelings—how I am feeling

6. What happened at home

7. What happened on the weekend

8. A TV show

9. A movie

10. Music I like

11. Sports

12. A story

Alternatives for Children Who Have Difficulty Writing

If your child is unable to write letters of the alphabet, or finds it too tedious and becomes frustrated and gives up very quickly, and/or is difficult to motivate to write in general, try teaching him to use a keyboard on a typewriter, computer, or any electronic writing system that seems appropriate. When starting with the keyboard, assure instant success by teaching him to use the "hunt and peck" method to write his name, spell words, and to write simple messages. As your child becomes motivated and interested, if his fingers are long enough, and if he is able and willing, then teach him to use the "touch" method. There are computer programs that teach keyboarding that can be very useful in teaching this skill. Some individuals may find the "touch" method as frustrating and difficult as handwriting. If this is the case with your child, and he is successful using "hunt and peck," then let him continue with this method. You want your child to successfully communicate by writing. The technique used is secondary.

Of course, children who are able to write, or who are able and willing to work on developing writing skills, should be given the opportunity to learn keyboarding as well. They should not be deprived the use of this technology because they are learning to write by hand. The difference is that these children will continue to develop their handwriting skills, writing by hand daily; whereas, children who find writing too difficult will be using the computer or typewriter instead of pencil and paper to do all their writing, at this point. These children (like Danny) may be able to learn to write when they are older and more mature. I would continue to give them opportunities to learn, when and if they are willing, even if it is just writing their name and a few other words that they may find a need to write often. Being able to write is a valuable skill and gives the individual a greater degree of independence.

SPELLING

Introduction

In order to spell, your child needs to know the names of the letters, and have a means of communicating the sequence of specific letters that make a word. This communication can be done: (1) with oral spelling ("c-a-t spells cat"); (2) by writing the word (on any writing surface); (3) by arranging individual letters in correct order (plastic cut-out letters, letter tiles, magnet letters, letters on cardboard, letters on clothespins placed on a hanger, etc.); and (4) by using a keyboard.

Because writing is difficult (and often delayed) in children with Down syndrome, using writing to learn and practice spelling can hinder learning to spell. It may take so much time and concentration on the part of your child to write the letters, that the sequence in which they are to be written is lost in the process. (Of course, he will be writing the words after he learns to spell them—this is learning and practicing spelling.) Also, practicing orally, although it can helpful, should not be the only means used. Your child should be able to see how the word looks. (The only time we need to spell orally is when we are spelling a word for someone else, and most of us need to write the word first, because that is how we use spelling. Remember, too, that most children with Down syndrome are visual learners.) Therefore, it is important to provide an efficient, effective means for your child to progress through the stages of learning to spell (acquisition, practice to fluency, and transfer and generalization). This means depends on the writing skills of your child and the availability of equipment: Is he fluent in writing? Are there keyboards, plastic letters, letter tiles, clothespins, and hangers available?

Spellers with Down Syndrome

As with reading and writing, there is a range in the ability to learn to spell. I have no formal data on spelling and Down syndrome. From informal reports of parents and teachers, however, it appears that spelling is generally consistent with reading. The better readers are generally the better spellers, although this is not always the case. Some good readers are poor spellers (but I know of no cases of poor readers being good spellers).

Some children spell primarily by using their knowledge of phonics and find learning "standard" spelling very difficult. They are communicating by writing, and that's what's important. Teaching these children how to use a word processor and the "spelling check" would be most helpful to them. Of course, the spelling check is helpful to all of us, including better spellers with Down syndrome, but the spelling check, for these learners could be used as an *adaptation*—the primary means of spelling words. Even handwritten notes can first be written on the computer, spelling checked, and then copied by hand, giving it the personal touch.

Another helpful adaptation for these "phonetic spellers" is for the readers of their written communication not to insist on standard spelling. Just as we learn to adapt to their imperfect articulation, we need to learn to adapt to their imperfect spelling. (The phonetic spelling can be very revealing as to how words sound to these children.) Constantly correcting a child's speech will squelch his desire to talk; constantly correcting spelling will squelch his desire to write. We're just pointing out yet another *failure* on the child's part, rather than rewarding his accomplishments. Of course, we want him to speak and write as best he can, and we are going to do what we can to provide opportunities for him to learn to do his best. However, we need to consider that, due to various learning problems, this just may be the best he can do. We run the risk of discouraging him from writing at all, if we are critical of his attempts to communicate by writing. We want him to at least have functional writing, and his "phonetic" spelling may be very functional for him. When he writes a word that you cannot read, you are the one with the problem. You can communicate that the problem is yours by saying, "I need help with this word. Would you please help me?"

Other spellers with Down syndrome learn by rote, with the help of phonics and the rules of phonics and spelling. These children generally pay close attention to the "correct" way to spell words. Some parents have told me that their child with Down syndrome can spell "anything."

Aaron came in a close third, both games.

Aaron's father told me this story: Aaron, a young adult with Down syndrome, played two games of Scrabble with his father, a genetics professor at the University of Washington, and his friend, a visiting genetics professor from Australia, an expatriate Englishman who is a Fellow of the Royal Society. The professor from the University of Washington won one game, with the professor from Australia coming in second, and the professor from Australia won one, with the professor from the University of Washington coming in second. However, in each case Aaron came in a *close* third. Aaron's father said that his friend from Australia was not merely impressed, but astounded by Aaron's close competition with both of them. So am I. But I have been more than merely impressed with Aaron since he was four years old and learned

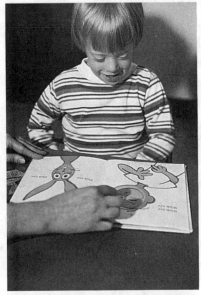

Figure 11.15. Aaron, the third-place Scrabble player, reading his Dr. Seuss book at four years of age.

words so fast that we placed him in the Dr. Seuss early readers series because we were unable to make materials fast enough for him. (Aaron's father added that Aaron had beaten him on a few occasions. In addition to his facility with words, he displays tactical understanding: he goes for the double or triple letter or word squares, and tries to bargain for the Q, X, or Z tiles if his father has one. His victories stem from times when he managed a double or triple Q or other brilliant Scrabble strokes.)

Teaching Spelling

Where to Begin?

The first word that most people learn to read and write is their first name; the first word that most people learn to spell is usually their first name, if the spelling is not too long and difficult. Being able to spell his own name is necessary in order for your child to write his name independently, unless he is able to visualize it and "draw" it, without knowing the names of the letters. Spelling one's own name varies in difficulty, depending on the length of name and the memory of your child. If your child has a long name, and is not able to remember how to spell it, shortening his name may be necessary for him to be able to successfully write it independently. In some cases, the signature may be reduced to initials. Or, if the first name is hard to spell and the last name easy, use the initial of the first name and teach him to spell the last name. Elizabeth Reed may learn to spell and write E. Reed first.

For three years, an IEP goal has been that he will write his name.

When I was consulting in a school, the teacher asked me, "What should I do about Joseph? For the last three years, writing his name has been on his IEP, and he still can't do it. He can trace and copy it, but when you take the model away, he's lost." When I asked her if he could spell his name, she responded that he could not; he could not read and he did not know the alphabet. She had assumed that he would learn how to write his name by tracing and copying it.

At 9 years of age, Joseph did not have the background to spell his name. He did not know the alphabet, the "language" of spelling. He had no way of remembering those symbols, how to make them, and the order in which they needed to be written in order to form a word, yet he was expected to learn how to write his name.

My first suggestion was to make the task easier for him by shortening his name; perhaps he could write "Joe." The teacher responded that his parents were very specific about not wanting him to use "Joe," and he was not to be called "Joe." My next recommendation was that perhaps they could teach him to use his initials, JT. That would be easier. We could use a mnemonic, and he should have no problem with that. The teacher agreed to this compromise.

Now Joseph can, at least, mark his possessions and "sign" his art work. Other solutions could have been: (1) To get him an ID bracelet and let him copy his name from the bracelet, or (2) to get him a rubber stamp with his name on it. The problem with his copying his name each time is that copying was a time-consuming and difficult task for him. I doubt if he would have continued to copy his name willingly for any length of time. The problem with the stamp is, if it is going to be useful, he would have to have it (and the ink pad) with him at any time he needed to write his name. Writing his initials is very likely the most efficient signature for him. It is very functional, and he succeeded, reaching his new IEP objective.

Teaching Your Child to Spell His Name

As always, if your child does not need this careful programming, you can skip a few steps or make adaptations. Here is the "whole thing," just in case you need all the steps.

Materials:

Index cards, 5 x 8 inches, one more than the number of letters in your child's name (for Bob, you need four); and individual alphabet letters (those in his name, B o b, the first letter being upper case, and remaining letters lower case). Individual, cut-out letters are easy for your child to manipulate. (Lakeshore Learning Materials has a "Lakeshore Letters Jar" that includes six of each letter, both upper and lower case, color coded, upper case red, lower case, blue—Item number LC1186, $19.95. Order from Lakeshore Learning Materials, 2695 E. Dominguez St., Carson, CA 90749, 1–800–421–5354).

Or, you may choose to use ruled sentence strips to make both the cards and letters from. (Also available from Lakeshore, Item number NF9763, 100 for $3.45.)

Those wonderful magnetic letters that most people with young children have on their refrigerator can be used as well.

How to Make:

If you are using the 5 x 8 index cards and plastic cut-out letters, take the letters and arrange them on one of the cards, so they spell your child's name. Trace around these letters (your child will be matching the letters to the traced letters). On a second card, make a line where the first letter should go (the width of the letter), and then trace

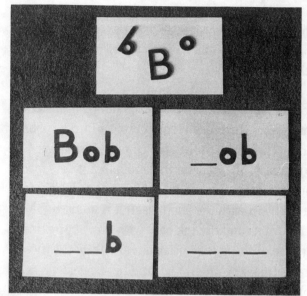

Figure 11.16

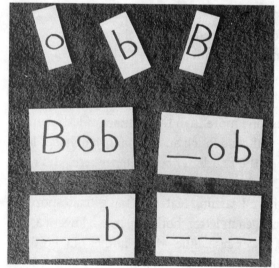

Figure 11.17

the remaining letters. On each remaining card, add another blank for the next letter and trace the other letters. For example, for Bob, the first card would have Bob traced on it; the second card, __ ob; third, __ __ b; and the forth, __ __ __. Number the cards, Bob being number 1, __ ob number 2, etc. (figure 11.16).

If you are using the sentence strips (you can draw the lines and make your own, if you like), print your child's name on the sentence strip (correctly between the lines). Cut the letters out, cutting across the sentence strip between each letter, and leaving the letters on little cards. Then, on the remaining sentence strip, print your child's name and cut across the card, making a card with the name on it. Proceed as described above, writing your child's name, but leaving out one more letter each time. Cut each "name" card out and number them as described above (figure 11.17).

The advantage of using the plastic cut-out letters is that they are easier to pick up and manipulate, and your child may find them more novel and interesting to work with. The advantage of using the sentence strips is that after your child has spelled his name, then he can copy it, and the guide lines are there as a model.

Procedures:

STEP 1: Present the card with your child's name on it (card #1) to your child. Your child should be able to read his name, so ask him to read it to you. He should also know the names of the letters in his name, so after he has read it, spell it with him. Say, "Yes, it says *Bob*. Let's spell it: B-o-b." Point to each letter as you say it. Then show him the cut-out letters and how to match them to the letters in his name. You may want to start by giving them to him, one at a time, saying, "This is a *B,* a big *B* for *Bob* (say the letter sound). Put the big *B* on the big *B* in Bob." This accomplished, say, "This is the *o;* (say the short *o* sound) put the *o* on the *o* in Bob." And then, "This is the little *b;* put the little *b* on the little *b* in Bob." Emphasize the ending *b* sound. After all letters are matched up, say, "Look, you *spelled* your name. *B-o-b,* Bob. You put the letters together to *spell* your name. That is *spelling.* You can *read* it, and you can *spell* it!" (Emphasize what it is called, so he will have the vocabulary along with the concept.)

(In all steps, whenever you can, emphasize the sound the letters make, so your child can learn to use phonetics when spelling.)

STEP 2: Take the letters off the card and mix them up (or ask your child to) and then ask him to match the letters and spell it all by himself. Give him opportunities to hear the spelling, and to orally spell it himself. This is practice. He needs to see the spelling, manipulate the letters to spell, hear the spelling, and say the letters in the correct order.

STEP 3: Present card #2 to your child and say, "Oh, look, something is missing. It's like a puzzle. You fix it. What goes here? What does Bob start with?" If he does not answer, or does not select the big *B* and put it on the blank, show him card #1 and say, "Look at this card and see what comes first." Help him if necessary. After the *B* is in the correct place, cue him to match the other letters to finish spelling Bob. When he can place the *B* in the correct space and match the other letters without assistance, go to the next step. (Remember to provide practice, seeing, hearing, and saying during each step.)

STEP 4: Present card #3 to your child, saying, "Oh, look, this one is really hard. We have two letters to find. What goes here?" (pointing to the *B* space). "And what goes here?" (pointing to the *o* space). If he has trouble putting the letters in place, show him the model to follow, card #1. When he can fill in these blanks and match the remaining letters, unassisted, go to the next step.

(As I mentioned earlier in the chapter, I like telling the child that it is hard, but he can do it. If he gets it right, he has achieved something that is difficult. It is a real accomplishment. If he makes a mistake, then it is okay, it's really hard. He can try again and ask for help, if he needs it.)

STEP 5: Present each of the remaining cards, in order, and follow the same procedures as in step 4, until your child can spell his name by placing all the letters of his name, in order, on the blanks on the last card, independently spelling his name. When your child can do this independently, go to step 6.

STEP 6: To increase the difficulty, put some extra letters (distractors) with the letters that are in your child's name (in Bob's case, you could add a *c, a, t,* and *s*). Mix them up, and cue your child, "Now you take the right letters and spell Bob." Your child selects the correct letters and places them in the correct order on the card with all blanks. When your child is able to do this independently, go to step 7.

STEP 7: Give your child the letters, plus some extra letters (as in step 6), but do not give him a card with the blanks as cues. Tell him, "Spell your name here, on the table." If he does not understand, model for him. When he can do this independently, he can spell his name, without cues (the blanks that tell him how many letters to use).

(You can see the advantage of having a short, simple name. If your child has a long name, and spelling is difficult for him, have a little mercy and shorten it for him. The Elizabeths, Stephanies, Christophers, and Alexanders can spend a long time learning to spell their names.)

The above procedures, for teaching your child to spell his name, provide the teacher with a method that is carefully programmed for children who need these steps. This method can be used to teach your child to spell any word that he needs to learn, if all of these steps are necessary. If spelling is difficult for him, and he needs to go through all the steps to learn each word, then you may need to limit the words taught to those that he writes, or will write, most frequently, and spend some time teaching him how to "look up" words (see "Adaptations for Spelling," below). For most children with Down syndrome, I think that it is a good idea to teach them the first few words they learn to spell using this method, because it is "programmed for success" and they can start by feeling successful as spellers. Spelling is something they can do. (Unlike Joseph who was expected to spell his name by writing it, and had no idea what spelling was.) Also, it will give you some clues as to how carefully you need to "program" the spelling for your child.

Other Teaching Techniques

Copy-Cover-Write-Compare-Correct: Perhaps the most common method used to learn to spell is the Copy-Cover-Write-Compare-Correct method. Your child copies the word; then he covers the word and writes it; then he compares his written word to the model. If it is wrong, he corrects it, then covers and writes it again. This method can be adapted for learners who are not proficient at writing by using plastic letters or a keyboard. Your child "copies" the word from a model using plastic letters. The model is then covered and the letters are mixed up. Your child arranges the letters to spell the word, compares his spelling with the model, and corrects it if it is wrong. This accomplished, distractor letters can be added, and your child selects the correct letters and arranges them in order, and then compares his spelling with the model. If your child has difficulty spelling the word when the whole word is covered, then just part of the word can be covered for each trial Post-its™ are good for covering part of the word, as above (cover the first letter, then the first two letters, etc. until all letters are covered and he can spell the word without the model).

In every method used, take every opportunity to emphasize the letter sounds and to cue your child to use these sounds in spelling.

Use a Tape Recorder: The use of a tape recorder is a good adaptation for students in inclusive classrooms. The teacher puts the words the student needs to practice on a tape recorder. Using earphones, the student practices the words, writing by hand, using plastic letters, or using a keyboard. To determine the pace, the teacher records an actual session with your child. It could go something like this: "Spell *lunch,* l-u-n-c-h (spell it so the child hears the flow of the letters), *lunch.* Now you spell it: *l* — (give him time to write it, arrange the letter, or find it on the keyboard) —u—n—c—h. Is it right? Did you spell l-u-n-c-h? Let's write it again: l—u—n—c—h. Now cover up the words you spelled and spell *lunch* without looking." The tape can include all the words your child is "working" on (perhaps up to five), and can be used for several days. When some of these words are mastered, they are dropped, and a new tape that includes the words not mastered and new words are added.

Use a Computer Program: There are several spelling programs available that allow you to choose the spelling words to be taught. These programs provide practice in drill, unscrambling letters, filling in the missing letters, and using words in sentences. If you have a computer and want to purchase a program for your child, be sure that the program fits his level and interests. Also, you may need to have a voice synthesizer to use some programs. And, as always, a computer program will provide practice for your child, but it will not take the place of instruction and the opportunity to spell, write, and use the words in his daily life.

Spelling Games

Spelling games provide fun and interesting practice and create an additional functional use for the skill. In addition, they provide another option for recreational activities and opportunities for playing interactive games with others.

Spelling Bee

The most traditional spelling game is the spelling bee. Some children with Down syndrome will be able to participate in classroom spelling bees, but care must be taken that they are able to spell most of words, that they enjoy the game, and that they are reasonably successful. Little will be accomplished for a child who is made to wait for his turn, only to fail when he has a chance to spell. For most children with Down syndrome, especially those in inclusive classroom settings, spelling bees require too much waiting time, offer too many opportunities for them to fail, and too many opportunities for others to observe their failures.

Spelling Basketball

A simple "one on one" basketball spelling game has been effective in improving spelling scores in "regular education" classrooms and can easily be adapted to the spelling level of your child with Down syndrome (if adaptations are necessary). It's called "spelling basketball" because the players score two points for each word spelled correctly, as in basketball.

Spelling basketball is a form of "cross peer" tutoring. Cross-peer tutoring differs from "peer tutoring" in that in cross-peer tutoring, the students tutor each other; in peer tutoring, one peer tutors the other, but the tutor does not receive tutoring himself. Usually in cross-peer tutoring, the whole class is divided into small groups and work on skills at the same time. During cross-peer tutoring in inclusive classroom, the child with Down syndrome is on "equal ground" with all the other students in the class—they are all tutoring each other, although there may be some adaptations for the child with Down syndrome.

This is how spelling basketball is usually played: There are two players on each "team." One player, the reader, reads the spelling words (spelling list of the week, usually 10 words—can individualize, adjusting the number of words worked on per week and the words on the list for each speller), and the other player, the speller, spells the words as the reader reads them, either orally, by writing them down, or using cut-out letters. The reader checks the speller's spelling, by checking it against the words on the spelling list, and records his score, giving the speller two points for each work spelled correctly, Next, the reader and the speller change places and repeat the process. As the reader reads the words and checks the spelling of his peer, he is learning to spell the words as well. It maximizes the learning opportunities if both spellers are learning to spell the same words. If a child with Down syndrome is playing with a peer who is learning a different set of words, it would be important for him to be able to read the words on his peer's list; otherwise, an adaptation would be necessary. In this team, it could be peer-to-peer tutoring, with one peer doing all the reading and checking and the other peer (with Down syndrome) doing all the spelling and scoring.

You can adapt this game for playing at home. You and your child can play. You can start out in the speller role, so he can practice reading the words to you, checking your spelling, and giving you a score (you can make mistakes for him to find and not always have a perfect score). You may choose to start with only two words and build up to five words, and then keep it at five, using the "Add-a-Word, Drop-a-Word" list described below.

Scrabble

Learning to play Scrabble can become a recreational activity that can carry over into adulthood, as in Aaron's case. For some children with Down syndrome, a Scrabble game for children will be a good investment. However, your child can use the standard Scrabble boards and letters, if that is what you have on hand. Or, if you have the cut-out letters described previously, you can make a Scrabble board with squares that these letters fit in.

For beginners, ignore the scoring and rules. To start, you want to teach your child how to spell words, placing the letters in the square, and connecting words to other words that have a common letter in them. He can start by spelling his name on the Scrabble board (either with or without a model—if he needs the model, show him how to use it as a guide to spell—which letter is first, second, etc.). On your turn, show him how to find a word that has a letter that is in his name in it, so you can play. Having a few flash cards of the words he can spell, is learning to spell, and/or can read, available and visible, should help to ensure his success as he is learning to play.

For example, if your child's name is Matt, show him how he can spell it on the board, either across or down. Let him choose the way (across or down) and give him the first turn by spelling his name on the board. On your turn, you may choose a flash card with cat on it and say, "Let's try this one. Does cat have any of the same letters as Matt?" If he does not tell you *a* and *t,* or point to one or both of these letters, show him how you can play on either the *a* or a *t.* Let him decide which letter to play on and let him help you. Then, on his turn, (if he needs help), point to the flash cards and ask him, "Are there any words here that start with an *M* like *Matt?*" If he doesn't respond, point to *Mommy* and give him the assistance he needs in spelling *Mommy,* or in following the flash card model. Then, on your turn, you can take the *Daddy* flash card and ask, "Are there any letters free that we can play Daddy on?" You can then, with or without his help, play *Daddy* on the *y* in *Mommy.* At this stage, when he is just learning to play, you can start with as few as two words, and gradually add more. You can also be very flexible and change your mind if either of you see a better "play." In time, if he maintains interest in the game and enjoys it, your child will learn the rules and play real Scrabble.

Crossword Puzzles

Make very simple crossword puzzles, using the words your child can spell—or is learning to spell (you can even "copy" your completed Scrabble game, if you like). The squares should be big enough for Scrabble letters, or for the cut-out letters, so your child can use them if he has trouble writing, and if he can write, the squares will be big enough for him. The definitions, or clues, should be simple and contain words that he can read. However, if your child can't read all the words in the clues, help him, or read the clues to him. It is important that it is a fun game for him, and that he has the opportunity to think, even if you read the clues to him. If he is to write in the words, make several copies of the puzzle, so he can "work" the same puzzle several times. This gives him the opportunity to practice and master a puzzle that he is familiar with—and he should learn to work it independently. If he is using Scrabble or cut-out letters, he can, of course, use the same puzzle over and over.

If you and your child enjoy crossword puzzles, continue to make them for him, adding new words that he is learning to spell. Let him help you. You can use the words put together when he played Scrabble, and he can help you write the clues. When working crossword puzzles, for the beginner, have the words used in the puzzle available (on flash cards or on a list). This way, your child can refer to the list if he can't think of the word when he reads the clue, or if he needs help spelling it. You are teaching him how to look up the answer and problem solve. A crossword puzzle is not a test, but a learning, thinking, problem-solving recreational activity. In addition, it creates another use for spelling, writing, and the use of numbers. (A blank crossword puzzle form is provided in Appendix D-13 and two sample beginning crossword puzzles for Sally are in Appendix D-14 and D-15.)

Regular Spelling Program

If your child is able to participate in the "regular" spelling program with other students, then it would be advisable for him to do so, learning to spell the same words as his classmates in the same sequence. Some adaptations may be needed for practice and testing, and he may not learn to spell the words at the same rate (the same number per week) as his classmates.

Add-a-Word, Drop-a-Word Program

Remember the "probe" for reading, where mastered words are dropped, and new words are added (Chapter 8)? Here is the "probe" for spelling. Start with your child's name, and when he can spell it, add another word, and when he can spell two words, add a third, etc. Each spelling session, after the practice, do the probe, or the spelling test, by asking your child to spell the words independently, using the method that works best for him: the letters as in step 7; writing with a pencil; or writing with a keyboard. The first probe will have only one word (unless you taught two during the first session, or he already knew how to spell some words). When a second word is taught, then two words will be in the probe; when the third word is taught, then three words will be in the probe, and so on, until your child has been taught ten words. When the eleventh word is taught, a word in the original ten that has been mastered (spelled correctly at least 80 percent of the time—4 of 5 times) is dropped from the probe. After ten words have been taught, at each probe, your child will be asked to spell ten words; words will be dropped as mastered, and new words will be added to take their place on the probe list.

Keep a record of responses for each word (or have your child chart it—great math task) so that you will know when a word is mastered and what words your child needs more practice on. (Ten words is the standard number for a probe. However, you may find that a five-word probe may work better for your child if spelling ten words during one session seems too tedious and demanding for him. Always feel free to individualize. These are guidelines.)

What Words Do I Teach?

If you use a "regular" spelling program, then the program will provide the words. However, if you use the Add-a-Word, Drop-a-Word program you will need to make some decisions as to what words will be most functional for your child. These are the words that he will have the most continuous use for in writing, whether it is by handwriting or by using a keyboard. (Remember, what you don't use, you lose.) These words, will, of course vary with each child and his writing skills and needs. To help you decide, here are some suggestions:

(1) If your child is using stickers to determine to whom he wants to give his art work, and it seems feasible that he could start writing rather than using stickers, then teach him to spell *to, from, Mom, Dad,* and *Granny* (or anyone else he typically wants to give things to). He can also use these words when he learns to write simple

messages, either by handwriting or using a keyboard. Other words, such as *Dear, love, you, happy,* and *like* can be added.

(2) If he is giving dictation for his journal, then the words he most often uses in the dictation would be a good start. Or, if he is using the fill-in-the-blank journal format, then he can learn to spell the words that go in the blanks.

(3) "Date" words can be taught. They can be used everyday, and it will reinforce time concepts and give your child a reason to use the calendar. Your child can learn to date his work, write the date in his journal and on messages, and use date words in his creative writing. (It is hot in July. I went swimming Friday.)

(4) If your child goes to the supermarket and writes shopping lists, then "food" words that he uses can be taught.

(5) As your child learns the word families (Chapter 10), teach him to spell the words in each family; this is usually a lot of fun for your child, as he can learn to spell several words very quickly. You may want to help him write stories using these words, or create some fill-in-the-blank stories, so he has a use for spelling these words. If he has a story using these words, print sentences from a story and leave blanks for him to fill in. For example, if you read to him—or he reads *Green Eggs and Ham,* and he is learning the *am* family, you may develop the following exercise for him:

I do not like green eggs and __ __ __.
I do not like them, __ __ __ I __ __.

Adaptations for Spelling

For some children with Down syndrome, spelling is so difficult that they become discouraged and do not want to learn to spell words. They have difficulty using phonics, or letter sounds, to phonetically spell words, and they are not able to spell by rote, to memorize the spelling of words. In order to allow these learners to express themselves in writing, teach them how to look up words.

As described in Chapter 9, each reader should have a dictionary of all the words he can read, and, in addition, a word bank of all the words he can read. Either of these can be used to assist your child in spelling. In addition, your child can be taught to use picture dictionaries for young children such as *My First Dictionary,* which has words with pictures, in alphabetical order, or *The First Word Book Ever,* by Richard Scarry, which has words and pictures by category (household words together, food words together, transportation words together, etc.).

If the dictionary is used, your child will need to look up words and copy them down as they are needed, as most of us do when we consult the dictionary for correct spelling. The advantage of the word bank is that your child can find the words in the word bank, remove them from the file, arrange the words to create the desired sentence or list, and then copy the words, writing the message or list. For example, if your child wanted to write, "Happy birthday, Mommy. Love, Amy," she could find these words, arrange them to express the desired message, and copy it down, thus creating her message independently. If she were making out a grocery list, she could find the words for the desired items, arrange them in categories (produce items together, dairy items together), then copy them down in the desired order.

The words in the word bank should be filed for easy access. This can be done by filing them alphabetically, using a card catalog, Rolodex℗, clothespins, cans, jars, or some other wonderful way that you dreamed up yourself (see chapter 9). To make words easier to find, words in specific categories can be color coded. For example, under *Aa* could be the word *apple,* color coded yellow (on a yellow card, or on a white card with a yellow line across the top, and all foods, regardless of the letter they start with, will be coded yellow), and the name *Amy,* color coded blue, as all names are. Feeling words, such as *love* and *happy* may be color coded pink. At the front of the word bank, the *code* can be available; the word *food* with the yellow line by it; *people* with the blue line; *feelings* with the pink line, etc. Words that do not belong in any specific category that the reader would understand, such as articles and prepositions, may be left white. If, for example, your child wanted to look up *Daddy,* he would first determine that Daddy started with a *D* and look under *Dd,* but he would not have to look at every card under *Dd* until he found *Daddy.* He would look only at cards that were coded blue.

Until your child learns the alphabet, you may want to file the cards in the word bank by categories. Have the name words together, action words together, feeling words together, body part words together, etc. Again, these can be color coded for easy sorting, and the same color code can be carried over when these words are filed alphabetically.

In summary, teach your child to spell words that are functional and useful to him; provide adaptations to compensate for poor writing skills so he can move forward with his spelling; give him the skills and materials to look up words he does not know how to spell; and provide spelling games so he can have fun using his spelling as a means of recreation.

Keeping It Going: Reading Units

Part 3 consists of "reading units" built around themes (action words, household words, self-image, feelings, animals and colors, foods, and time). These units provide models for you as you learn to individualize for your child. Practice with these units will help you learn how to develop units on your own and how to adapt the techniques and choose activities to meet your child's interests and learning style.

After your child has completed the "how to" unit (family names) in Chapter 8, you need to "keep it going" by moving on to another unit, increasing his reading vocabulary, generalization, comprehension, and functional use of reading. New words introduced, as all words taught, should be words that are meaningful to and useful for your child. You can choose units, or develop units that you think will be of most interest to your child, and, at the same time meet your child's needs to expand his functional communication skills. For ex-

ample, if your child needs to learn to say or practice saying certain words, or to say or point to words to communicate, teach him to read these words. You might teach him the names of foods to make specific requests; "all done," to communicate to you when he is finished eating or doing a task; "break," or "I need a break," to communicate to you that he is tired of doing something, etc. A unit of this nature could be called "I Can Tell You What I Want." (This, of course, would be helpful for children who communicate in undesirable ways, such as by squealing, grunting, and sitting down on you.) Generally, for the younger learner, choose units that center around the child, his family, his interests, and his activities. For the older learner, choose units that will help him to function independently at home and in the community.

Chapter 12

ACTION WORDS

Children generally enjoy moving around and being active. Build on this by incorporating the learning of action words with activities that allow your child to be active.

Goal: Your child will increase his reading vocabulary to include action words and additional words used in a book; he will practice reading, generalizing, and comprehending these words by reading them on flash cards, in reading and alphabet books, and while playing games.

The words suggested for this unit should be appropriate for most children, as they are generally within their experiences—these are the things that most children do, and can be incorporated in a story about your child. However, if any of the words suggested do not seem appropriate for your child, feel free to pick and choose. For example, if your child never swims or flies a kite, these words may not be meaningful to him. On the other hand, if you think your child will get carried away with some words, such as stomping, hugging, and kissing, postpone teaching these words (or use picture cards and discourage the activity). Sometimes these activities can be distracting and interfere with reading.

Introducing New Words: Acquisition

Objective 1: Your child will match, select, and name (verbally or by sign) action words using picture cards and flash cards (or two sets of flash cards).

Materials:

Action Word Picture Cards and Flash Cards: Copy flash cards (Appendix C-8) and line drawings (C-9) on white card stock. Cut on the lines to make individual picture cards and flash cards. Materials are pro-

suggestions: hop; clap; swing; stomp; pat; laugh; ride; watch; sing; dance; listen; slide; tip-toe; swim; fly; crawl; climb; drop; play; get; stand; stack; make; splash; say; mark; kiss; hug; and open. Flash cards are provided for these additional words in Appendix C-8. Make two copies so your child can match the words without the picture cards.

Procedures:

Introduce the Action Words: Start by introducing two words, then add new words, one at a time. Example: you may choose to start with *jump* and *run* (or you may show your child the cards and let him choose the words). Show him the picture card and the word, and demonstrate the word: say, "*Jump,* this word is *jump.*" Point to the word, and then get up and jump. Ask him to join you. Repeat with *run.* (When teaching *run,* demonstrate how far you want him to run, depending on the environment; for example, to the couch and back, or to the kitchen and back. If you have a rule of no running in the house, teach another word or use the picture card only (no demonstration) for run, or take the lesson someplace where he can run. After the words have been introduced, give him practice with these words by matching, selecting, and naming, using the picture cards and flash cards, or the two sets of flash cards. After these two words are mastered, and the initial letters have been introduced, then introduce other action words, one or two (or maybe three) at a time.

Demonstrate Action Words: Some words, such as *jump, clap, run,* and *stomp* are simple to demonstrate, but you will need to teach gestures and signs for other words. For example: for *come* and *go* use gestures, hand pulling inward for come, index finger pointing away for go; for *ride,* move as if you are riding a horse or bicycle; for *watch,* hold hands by the side of the eyes, as if to focus your gaze; *listen,* put hands behind ears; *open,* put hands together and open like a book; *swing,* swing your arms; *swim,* move your arms as if you are swimming; *fly,* arms out like a plane. These actions and gestures will be useful when playing games.

Continue with the Alphabet: When you introduce new words to your child, add them to his alphabet books on the appropriate pages (*dance* on the *Dd* page with *Dad; swing, stomp, smile, slide,* and *sing* on the *Ss* page with *Sally; walk* and *watch* on the *Ww* page with *Will*). Make new books to include new letters—the beginning letters of words that have not been introduced previously. For example, the next alphabet book may be the *J R C H Book,* for *jump, run, clap,* and *hop.* Remember, go slowly, if you need to. You don't have to teach it all at once. Give your child time for it to "soak in" before moving on. See Chapter 9.

Word Bank and Probe: Add new words and letters to the word bank and probe, following the procedures in Chapters 8 and 9. Use the probe as a guide to determine the rate for introducing new words. (You may want to color code the "action" words for easy retrieval from the word bank.)

Games and Activities: Practice, Comprehension, and Generalization

Bingo

Objective 2: While playing Alphabet Bingo, your child will: prac-tice saying letter sounds; associate letter sounds (initial position) with words; name upper and lower case letters; and put words in alphabetical categories.

Materials:

Upper and Lower Case Bingo; Word-to-Word Bingo; Picture/Sym-bol-to-Word Bingo; and Word or Symbol-to-Blank (Under letters) Bingo. Add action words that start with the letters on the bingo games that you have already started. Example, for *Sally,* you would add *smile* under the *Ss;* and *walk* under the *Ww.* Make new bingo cards for new alphabet letters introduced by copying the model form provided in Ap-pendix D-4, D-5, and D-6 on card stock (see Alphabet Games in Chapter 9). If you have introduced more words that start with a letter than there are spaces on the game card under that letter, don't be con-cerned. Every word introduced does not have to be in the bingo games; you can use the game card with blank spaces under the letters and ro-tate the flash card words that start with the letters on the card. If, how-ever, you want your child to have more practice with a newly introduced word, and want to use word-to-word or picture-to-word bingo that you have already made, but the spaces are all filled, you can paste the new word over a word that he knows well. If you choose to use symbols in your bingo games, copy the symbols provided for the picture cards in Appendix C-9. You will have to use a copy machine to reduce the size in order for them to fit on the bingo game (unless you choose to make a big bingo game, or to copy or create new drawings by hand).

Procedures:

Follow the procedures for playing bingo described in "Bingo Games," Chapter 9.

Lotto Games

Objective 3: *While playing Action Lotto, your child will: practice reading action words; demonstrate comprehension; and generalize reading skills.*

Materials:

Make Action Lotto Games by copying the forms for lotto games in Appendix D-1, D-2, or D-3 on card stock and supplying the appropriate words or drawings in the spaces provided. If you choose to use drawings, copy the picture cards and reduce the size to fit the spaces on your game cards or disks. For instructions for making lotto games, see "Reading Lotto Games" in Chapter 8. You can name these lotto cards, "Action Lotto." Or, if it seems more appropriate for your child, "I Can." When he finishes a game he can read it, "I can — jump, run, walk, etc."

Procedures:

Follow procedures for playing lotto games in "Reading Lotto Games," Chapter 8.

Charades

Objective 4: *While having a good time playing charades, your child will: practice reading action words; demonstrate comprehension; follow written directions; and remember words after he has read them.*

Materials:

Flash cards with action words; container for words (box, bag, or basket).

How to Play:

Place the flash cards, face down, in a container, or face down on a table. Each player draws a card and reads it silently, keeping the word a secret. Each player takes a turn, placing their card face down on the table, remembering what was on the card and acting out the word he drew (see "Demonstrate Action Words," above). The other players guess what word is on the card. If they guess right (flash card as proof), the "actor" player scores—he communicated the word on the card effectively. (Drop a marble in his jar.)

This game can be played with only two words. As new words are introduced, add them to the game.

Option 1: When four or more action words have been introduced, each player draws two or more words and acts out these words.

Option 2: Use two containers, one for action words, one for names. Players draw a name and an action. The person whose name is drawn has to do the action. The player reads the cards and says, for example,

Figure 12.1. Gini holds onto the table to follow the written direction, "Jump, Gini."

"Mommy jump." More than one card can be drawn from each box; two people can run and jump. (See figure 12.1.)

Option 3: Leave the cards facing up. Let your child select what he wants the players to do. He may arrange the cards to say, "Will jump. Mommy hop. Daddy clap." (This would be a good time to teach the word *and,* so he could arrange the words to say, "Mommy *and* Daddy clap *and* jump.")

Option 4: Introduce the words *hug, kiss,* and *pat* together, and play with just these action words that require interaction of two people. The player draws a name, then an action, then another name. He then puts the cards together in the order drawn, such as "Sally kiss Mommy, Daddy hug Will, Will pat Daddy."

Option 5: Instead of flash cards, use sentence strips with simple phrases or sentences printed on them. The player draws a sentence strip, reads it, and does what it says (Kiss Mommy; pat Butch; jump, hop, and crawl). As new words are introduced (next unit, household words), these sentences can be expanded, such as "run to the door," "tip-toe to the kitchen," "look under the table."

Obstacle Course

Objective 5: *Your child will practice reading, comprehending, and generalizing action words while having fun going through an obstacle course.*

Materials:

Make an obstacle course with signs that tell your child what to do at each station. Stations with some active activities will need to be outside. Examples: Station 1, a balloon hanging from the ceiling (or from a tree or climbing tower), and a sign that says, "jump up" (balloon correct height for the player to jump up and hit); Station 2, a stool, with a sign that says, "jump down"; Station 3, a hula hoop, with a sign inside it that says, "hop in," and a sign by it that says, "hop out"; Station 4, a sign that says, "clap 3 times" (or maybe just "clap"); Station 5, a sign that says, "sing a song"; Station 6, a soccer ball with a sign that says, "kick"; Station 7, a tape deck with three signs by it, "turn on," "listen," and "turn off" (or "push start," "listen," "push stop"); Station 8, a sign on the swing that says, "swing high" (or "swing up 5 times"); Station 9, a balloon on the floor with a sign that says, "stomp." The words used will depend on your child's motor skills and the words in his reading vocabulary. Math concepts, at your child's level, can be embedded in this activity as well.

How to Play:

To introduce this activity to your child, go with him as he goes from station to station and give him help as needed. Encourage him to read the words and follow the "directions" independently (perhaps a marble in the jar for each direction read and followed). Children generally enjoy doing this with other children. It looks like "Follow the Leader," but instead of following the leader, they are following the directions.

Action Word Books: Reading for Pleasure

Objective 6: Your child will: read action words in sentences; generalize reading skills; and experience the joy of reading books.

Do It! Book

If your child is speaking in only one- or two-word utterances, or is learning words slowly, make a simple book with only two or three words per page.

How to Make:

Combine family names and the action words. Each page will have a simple sentence such as, "Mommy, jump!" "Run, Daddy!" "Daddy, kiss Sally." "Will, pat Rex." "Clap, Daddy." "Sally, watch TV." (I am suggesting these "command sentences" rather than phrases such as "Mommy jump," so your child will be practicing correct grammar and normal speech patterns. Besides, children enjoy the opportunity to tell others what to do and this makes the book more fun. This may also be a good time to tell him that the comma means to pause and the exclamation point means to put a little expression in it (model this).

To illustrate the sentences, take photos that depict the activity, and make them interesting. For example: Dad in his jogging suit, sweating and looking beat; Mom jumping rope; and Sally dancing or doing a "trick" with Daddy watching her and clapping. (You may choose to draw the pictures, but most of us will find the photos easier.)

Tape the photos on pages (using tape doughnuts) and print the sentences under the photos. Place a paper flap made of construction paper over each photo, but leave the sentence visible. Tape the flap on the left side, so it opens like a book, or at the top, so it opens like a tablet.

Collate the pages, place a cover over them, and staple. Write the name of the book on the cover.

Procedures:

Teach your child to read the book (see "Reading First Book," Chapter 8); except, this time, after introducing the book to him, have him learn to read it with the flap covering up the photo. After he reads the command, he opens the flap and sees that the person is doing as told. (He reads, "Mommy, jump!", opens up the flap, and sure enough, there is Mommy jumping. What a surprise!)

I Like To Book

This book is for the child who is speaking in more than two-word utterances. It uses the verbs and nouns he is learning, as well as prepositions, pronouns, and adjectives. As always, let your child's interest in the book determine if it is meaningful to him. It should be fun and motivating. If it is not, then it's better to use other materials that interest him.

Materials:

A suggested story in the form of a poem is provided in Appendix E-4. A poem is used to help your child to discriminate rhyming words, to practice saying words in the rhythm of a poem, and to give him clues as to what the words are (it rhymes with ___). The poem has twelve verses. If you choose to use the poem, select verses that apply to your child, take photos of your child doing these activities, and make a book, using photos to illustrate each activity. You may add on to the book, or have several short *I Like To* books. You can, of course, illustrate the book with drawings, if you so desire. Write the title of the book (*I Like To*) on the cover, and staple the pages together.

Procedures:

Introduce one verse at a time. (One, or all, or any combination of verses can be used, in any order.) Choose verses that apply to your child and that contain some words he can read. For each verse, introduce and teach the words your child does not know, using the flash cards and/or the picture cards using the match, select, and name method. Some words, such as *the, like, and,* and *at,* will not have picture cards; use two sets of flash cards as described in "Match, Select, and Name Using Two Sets of Flash Cards" in Chapter 8.

Start by reading the verses to your child, so he will hear the rhythm and flow of the poem. Then read it, pause when you come to a word that he can read, point to the word, and allow him to supply the word. When he learns all the words in the verse, he can read it all by himself.

If the book is too difficult for him now, you may want to simply read it to him for the time being. He will be hearing the words he's learning in the context of simple stories. (He can supply the words he can read—or the rhyming word, if he is willing.)

If he is interested in the first few verses you introduce, but he starts to lose interest, this is an indication that he has had enough of the *I Like To* book. Move on to something else. Twelve verses are a lot; choose the ones that your child can identify with.

Evaluation:

Measure word mastery by probe; comprehension by your child's proficiency at playing games and following directions (charades, lotto, and obstacle course); and fluency by proficiency in reading the books.

Adaptations for the Classroom

These activities can easily be adapted for the classroom and playground. Use classmates' names rather than family names (do not use kiss and hug, if it is not appropriate for the age of the students). Games can be played in small groups, so that children do not have to wait long for a turn.

HOUSEHOLD WORDS

Chapter 13

As with the action word chapter, the activities in this chapter allow your child to move around and experience the words in her natural environment. Labels (flash cards) are taped, at your child's eye level, to common objects that are found in most households, garages, and backyards.

Goal: Your child will increase her reading vocabulary to include household words and additional words used in games and books; she will practice reading, generalizing, and comprehending these words by reading them on flash cards, in reading and alphabet books, and while playing games.

Introducing Household Words: Acquisition

Objective 1: Your child will match, select, and name (verbally or by sign) household words using flash cards and household objects and rooms.

Materials:

Flash cards; masking or Scotch Magic™ tape; the house or apartment and its contents, garage and backyard optional.

How to Make:

Copy Appendix C-10 on card stock. (Make two sets of flash cards for the objects to be labeled—or make two sets of flash cards yourself by printing the words on the cards.) Make a "doughnut" with the tape and tape the flash cards on the objects (one or two objects at a time). (Masking tape, for a short period of time, should not damage most items; however, it may take some paint off the wall or tear wallpaper. If the wall, or other surfaces that masking tape might damage are labeled, choose a surface, such as one with wood, that the tape will not damage and draw an arrow to point to the object. An arrow can also be used to

Figure 13.1. Gini matches household words and practices her stretching exercises.

indicate objects that are out of your child's reach, such as a picture. It is not necessary to damage the house to teach your child to read. Use your good common sense.)

Suggested words: TV, chair, table, floor, rug, wall, door, window, sink, stove, washer, dryer, toys, lamp, computer, refrigerator, mirror, bed, dresser, car (if it is available and easy to get to), kitchen (label on the door), bathroom, powder room (if you call it that), bedroom (could put as many labels up as bedrooms in the house—with the name of the people who sleep there), couch (or sofa), piano, box, cup, teapot, dishes, tape deck, radio, books (or bookcase), bathtub, shower, toilet (or potty), calendar, telephone (or phone), and plant(s).

Procedures:

Use the same sequence of matching, selecting, and naming as with other words, except this time, your child matches the flash card to the label on the actual object, rather than to words on picture cards. Start by labeling two items: Example, TV and chair. Show the labels to your child, saying, "Look, this says *TV,* and this says *chair.*" Then show her a matching card, saying, "This says *TV,* put *TV* on *TV.*" *Repeat with chair.* Hold up the two cards and say, "Point to *TV;* point to *chair.*" Hold up each card, saying, "This says ___, and this says ___." When these words are learned, gradually add other words, labeling the objects as the words are introduced. Let your child's interest and rate of learning be the gauge as to how many of these words you teach.

Figure 13.2. Lupita matches the name of her new class—kindergarten.

Alphabet Book, Bingo, and Alphabet Games

Add the new words and letters to the alphabet books, bingo games, and other alphabet games as described in Chapter 9. Read the books and play the games with your child.

Word Bank and Probe   Add new words and letters to the probe and word bank. Use the probe as a guide to determine the rate for introducing new words.

Games and Activities: Practice, Comprehension, and Generalization

Lotto Game Variation

Objective 2: Your child will practice reading, comprehending, and generalizing reading household words by playing a variation of Household Lotto.

Materials:

Best First Book Ever! by Richard Scarry (Random House) and tokens (colored plastic disks or buttons, one color for each player), or small Post-it™ notes (approximately 2 x 1 inches) with the first letter of the players' names printed on them. (Or you could make Household Lotto Games, if you like. This is to save you some work and to add novelty.)

Procedures:

After your child has become familiar with the book (you and she have read it together several times, and she has been pointing to the pictures and reading some of the words), place the book flat on a surface (table or floor) and open it to the page of household objects. The book, opened to these pages, becomes the lotto card. The players take turns drawing flash cards with household words on them. Each player reads the word on the card she drew, finds it on the page, and places her token on the object (or places the Post-it with her initial printed on it—the advantage of the Post-it is that it stays put, while the tokens may slide around if the book is not flat). When all the flash cards are used up, each player collects her tokens or Post-its and counts them to see how many objects they each found (some math thrown in here).

Treasure Hunt

When your child knows three or four of these words, she can start going on treasure hunts and really use her ability to read these words.

Objective 3: While having fun playing treasure hunt, your child will: practice reading household words; demonstrate comprehension; follow directions; and remember words after she has read them.

Materials:

Clue cards in envelopes and tape: The clue cards can be made of index cards, tag board, card stock, or just plain paper, colored or white. I recommend getting a little fancy and decorating or color coding clue cards so they look different from flash cards and labels. Drawing a border around the clue cards to resemble certificates makes them more game-like and interesting. Any old envelopes to conceal the clues in will do. (You may want to mark the envelopes *Clue 1, Clue 2,* etc. and teach your child the word *clue* if you think she's ready for it.) Tape will be needed to tape the envelopes to the objects.

Labeled Objects: Household objects that are labeled with flash cards (for more "advanced" learners, the labels can be removed). Because there are many walls, doors, floors, chairs, tables, windows, and beds in the house, for this first step, teach your child that the clues are for those that are labeled. Example: if Clue 1 is *chair,* it refers to the chair that you have labeled, not any other chair in the house.

Treasure Box: Use a small box that is easy for your child to carry and open. If "treasure" is not a meaningful word for your child, call it the "surprise box" (and the game can be called Surprise Hunt). Your child could decorate the treasure box by drawing on it, coloring it, or pasting things on it to make it interesting and special. If you happen to have a miniature treasure chest, it would be fun to use.

Treasures: Use what is interesting and meaningful for your child and appropriate for her age and goals. Examples:

Symbolic treasure: If you want to make it easy on yourself, and the game is motivating for your child, use the same treasure for every game (such as an old necklace, or something that looks like treasure). In this case, the treasure is only symbolic and has no real value to her, other than as a prop for a game.

Actual treasure: Or, you can use an actual treasure. This is a good place to incorporate math and money concepts. In the treasure box, each time she plays the game, put a different number of pennies, any number, up to the number to which your child can count. For example, if she counts to 3, put 1, 2, or 3 pennies in the box; if she counts to 10, put in any number up to 10. When she finds the treasure, she counts her pennies and puts them in her bank. (If she doesn't have a bank that is easy to get into, use a jar with her name on it.) Later, after the treasure hunting is over, she puts these pennies in sets of 5's (if she can't count to 5, make a model for her—draw 5 circles on an index card and show her how to place a penny on each circle). Next, she trades each set of pennies for a nickel, which she puts in his bank. When she plays another game, or earns pennies in another way, she puts them in her bank. The next time she counts her pennies and arranges them in sets, she will need to discriminate the pennies from the nickels. In time, when she has enough nickels, she arranges them in sets of 5 and trades each set for a quarter (or sets of 2 and trades each set for a dime). She can then learn the joys of using quarters in machines (such as pop machines and video games), or save the quarters and trade 4 for a dollar, and go shopping, when she has enough money to buy what she wants. And you can keep recycling those coins for more games.

Immediate gratification treasure: If your child is difficult to motivate, you may need to use a treasure that gives her more instant gratification. In this case, you may choose to put a little treat in the box. (Most children get treats, whether or not they learn to read; don't feel guilty). Use treats that you approve of and feel comfortable giving your child, such as cereal, crackers, corn chips, raisins, fruit, etc. These can be put in plastic bags and placed in the box. If you want your child to have something that you can't put in the box, such as yogurt, popsicle, or juice, place the label from the container they came in, or a drawing of the food in the box. Or, better yet, teach her to read these words, then she can read the word and tell you what she gets (you could even have a choice in the box, such as cookies or popsicle). Your child just may have to go on a treasure hunt to find her after-school snack.

Surprise treasure: Put anything in the box that your child may find interesting. Change the items each game. For example, little cars, animals, and dolls, beads, bracelet, spoon, thimble, sticker, audio tape, felt pen, sun glasses, old camera that she can play with, pin-on buttons (such as those with pictures of super heroes or Disney characters on them), etc. (Real surprises, such as birthday presents, can be used in treasure hunts. My own children requested treasure hunts for finding their birthday presents.)

Toy treasure: You may choose not to use a box at all and play "find the teddy bear," "find Barbie," or "find the dinosaur." Hide these items and set up the hunt.

Procedures:

Setting It Up: When your child can read the names of three or four objects, print the name of each object on separate clue cards. For example: On individual clue cards print *TV, chair, table, window,* and place them in the envelopes. With your child out of the room, or hiding her eyes, set up the game: Tape the envelope with the chair clue card in it on the TV (whether you place it in view or out of sight will depend on the age and experience of your child—younger, less experienced children may need it in plain sight; give older children more of a challenge by hiding the clues); tape the envelope with the table clue card on the back of the chair (or under the seat); tape the envelope with the window clue card in it to the leg of the table, or under the top of the table; on the window ledge, seat, or on the floor under the window, place the treasure box, concealed by a cloth, paper, or drapes so your child has to look for it, and is not able to see it before she knows where to look.

Playing the Game: Now that it is set up, give her an envelope that has the first clue card in it, *TV*. Provide the help she needs to learn how to play the game. Tell her that the card tells her where to look for another clue card to find the treasure. Ask her, "What does it say?" She answers, "TV." Tell her to go to the TV and find another clue card. If she can't find it, tell her where to look, or show her where it is, or prompt her to look on all sides of the TV. She's just learning.

When she finds the chair clue card (on the TV), she reads it (it says *chair*) and goes to the chair and looks for the next clue card. Card found, she reads it and goes to the table and finds the next clue card; reads it, and goes to the window; at the window she finds the treasure.

The first time, it may be necessary to model, taking your child with you and showing her what it is all about. It should not take long for her to do the finding all by herself, and, in time, to set the game up for others. This game teaches problem solving, following written directions, and comprehension. It develops memory as well; she reads the clue card and has to remember what it said in order to know where to go next. If she can't remember, let her take the clue card with her to the next clue.

It's really nice when you have siblings or other children play this game with your child. It's a fun game and some children like to play it over and over.

Option: The game described above is for the reader who has only a few words in her reading vocabulary. When she learns more words (or for readers who already know more words), use phrases on the clue cards and hide the clues better. Examples: look in the dryer; in the oven; under the table; on the TV; in the bookshelf; in the bathtub; under Jon's bed; under the kitchen sink; on the dining room door; in Mommy's closet.

Map Treasure Hunt

***Objective 4:** Your child will practice reading, comprehending, and generalizing household words by having fun playing Map Treasure Hunt.*

The map treasure hunt adds another skill to the game. It teaches the reader how to use a map and understand abstract spatial relationships. Map reading will help her reach independence in getting around the neighborhood and finding her way in schools and on work assignments. Start by making a map (floor plan) of one room (perhaps the room where most of the labels are, or a very simple room, such as the bathroom). Print the name of the objects in the room on the map. When your child can find things marked on a map in this room, draw a map of another room; that room mastered, another room; and then, finally a map of the whole house and the yard.

In this game, the place where the treasure is hidden is marked on the map, and the player finds the treasure by using the map.

Materials:

Paper, felt pen, and ruler for drawing the map; Post-its, or pen with washable ink if you choose to laminate the map. Single rooms can be drawn on standard 8½ x 11 paper; you may need a larger size for the floor plan of the house.

How to Make:

Draw the floor plan of the room (does not have to be exact scale). Draw in shapes for the furniture, doors, windows, and closets and label them. Laminate, if you choose to mark on the map; use a pen that has ink that washes off plastic. (For children at this stage, lamination is not usually necessary for protection of the map.) For unlaminated maps, cut a little square of the sticky part of a Post-it and make an *X* on it. This *X* will be stuck on the map to mark the spot where the treasure is. It can be moved around and used over and over again.

Procedures:

Start with one room. Show your child the map. If *map* is not in her vocabulary, label the map, *map,* make a flash card, and have her match it, select it, and name it until she can read and say (or sign) *map.*

Teach your child how to use the map. For example: Stand at the door of the room with her, and show her the door on the map, and say, "We are here—see, it says *door.*" Then ask her to read the labels on the map, one at a time, and point to each object and find it. Example: When she reads a label on the map, say, "Yes, it says *table;* it's to the right, in that direction (pointing right). We need to walk this way to find the table." (If she does not know left and right, this would be a good time to teach it. See instructions on next page.) Walk over to the table with her, then ask her to find where you are on the map. Continue with other objects until she understands the concept.

Now that she has an idea of what it is all about, have her leave the room, hide a treasure or a surprise, mark where it is on the map, using the pen, if you laminated your map, or the Post-it *X* if you didn't. Invite her in, give her the map, and let her find that hidden treasure.

Activities for Learning Left and Right

Start by teaching your child to read *left* and *right*. Print *left* and *right* on blank stickers. Stick them on the top side of her hand—*left* on her left hand, *right* on her right hand, so that they are right side up for her to read. Make matching flash cards. Teach her to read *left* and *right* by matching the flash cards to the stickers on her hands, then selecting, and naming.

Play games: Leave the stickers on (or put new ones on each time you need them).

(1) Give your child something to hold in each hand, and ask her what is in her left hand; her right? Or, ask her which hand the car is in; the pencil? (Encourage her to read the sticker to answer.)

(2) Play "Simon Says." "Simon says, pick up the pencil with your left hand; pick up the crayon with your right hand." This done correctly, drop a penny in the jar.

(3) When she is seated next to others, ask her, "Who is on your left? Your right?" Or make a statement, such as, "I'm on your left; Daddy is on your _____" and let her fill in the blank.

(4) Blindfold yourself and have your child direct you to go somewhere by telling you to turn left, turn right, go straight ahead. Then blindfold her and you tell her how to get there.

(5) Without the blindfold, give her verbal directions on how to find the treasure: "Go straight ahead, now turn right, stop."

(6) Play "Hokey Pokey" putting your right and left everything in and out.

(7) Write instructions for setting the table: "Forks on the left; knife, spoon, and glass on the right."

If your child wears an ID bracelet or a watch, place a small sticker on it, with an *L* or an *R*, to indicate which side it is on.

Option 1: Let her hide the treasure, mark it on the map, and you (or other players) come in and find it.

Option 2: Hide more than one thing, or several of one thing, and have several *X's* on the map. The Easter bunny might even leave a map for her to help her find the eggs.

Option 3: Hide her after-school snack, mark the spot on the map, and let her find it. (It could be in the refrigerator, oven, dishwasher, dryer, cupboard—wherever your imagination takes you.)

Evaluation

Measure mastery of words by the probe; comprehension by proficiency in playing games, and fluency by reading books.

Reading for Pleasure

Objective 5: Your child will: read household words in sentences, generalize reading skills, and experience the joy of reading a book.

Materials:

Materials for making a book, *Treasure Hunt,* are provided in Appendix E-5. Copy and staple the pages together to form a book. Color it if you like.

Procedures:

Introduce one verse at a time. For each verse, introduce and teach the words your child does not know, such as *the, and, even, under, what,* and *at,* using two sets of flash cards using the match, select, and name method without picture cards. See "Match, Select, and Name Using Two Sets of Flash Cards" in Chapter 8.

Start by reading the verses to your child, so she will hear the rhythm and flow of the poem. Then read it, pause when you come to a word she can read, point to the word, and allow her to supply the word. When she learns the words in the verse, she can read it all by herself.

If the book is too difficult for her now, you may want to read it to her for the time being. She will be hearing words she's learning in the context of simple stories. (She can supply the words she can read, or the rhyming word, if she is willing.)

Adaptations for the Classroom

Label classroom objects and play treasure hunt in small groups. For the Map Treasure Hunt, start with a map of the classroom and expand it to the school and playground. Send students on errands around the school, using the map. For example: The teacher may ask a student to take a note to Ms. Hope's room. She would show the student the map with the room marked on it. She can draw the route that the child is to take and explain how to get there. She may say, "Go out the door. Turn right. Ms. Hope's door is the third door on the left, number 102. Look on the door and find the number before knocking." The teacher could, of course, give these directions in writing.

Chapter 14

SELF-IMAGE

Reading and communicating information about ourselves is something most of us do all the time. We fill out medical histories at the doctor's office, and information about our work experience when applying for a job. We browse the drug store aisles looking for a shampoo or conditioner that is right for our hair color and type, or a medication that will ease whatever discomfort we might be experiencing. Individuals with Down syndrome, too, should have the opportunity to learn to read and write words that describe themselves, their activities, and their interests.

This chapter expands on the family names unit in Chapter 8, which explains how to teach your child to read his name, the names of family members, and simple stories about himself and his family. It includes activities designed to help your child learn to read words related to body parts, gender, health, and other personal issues. The adaptations for school emphasize teaching your child about his school, his classmates, and his schedule. As in other chapters, the books and reading content will need to be individualized for your child. Books about your child, with important information about himself that he should know, understand, and have access to, should be added over the years.

Goal: *Your child will: increase his reading vocabulary to include body parts and gender words; read a book about himself; and increase his awareness of his body and self-image.*

Introducing Self-Image Words: Acquisition

Objective 1: Your child will match, select, and name 12 body parts words and the words boy and girl using picture cards and flash cards.

Materials:

Flash cards and picture cards for boy, girl, and body parts (any body parts you want your child to read—hair, eyes, nose, mouth, ears, neck, body, hands, arms, tummy, legs, feet; and, if you want to get into sex education, vocabulary that will help him to communicate about private parts. Picture cards and flash cards are provided for copying on card stock in Appendix C-11 and C-12.

Procedures:

Teach body-part and gender words using the match, select, and name method, using picture cards and flash cards, or two sets of flash cards.

Add new words to the alphabet books, bingo games, and other alphabet games, as described in Chapter 9. Also add new words and letters to the word bank, and probe, following procedures in Chapters 8 and 9. Use the probe as a guide to determine the rate for introducing new words and letters.

Games and Activities: Practice, Comprehension, and Generalization

Body Part Lotto

Figure 14.1. Jeff reads and matches body-part words on a chart in the classroom.

Objective 2: Your child will practice reading body-part words and demonstrate comprehension by matching body-part symbols to words.

Materials:

Make the lotto game and matching disks or cards by copying and reducing the drawings provided for the picture cards in Appendix C-12, or make your own drawings. You can draw just the body part on the card or disk.

Procedures:

Give your child opportunities to play lotto, with others and alone.

Boy/Girl Bingo

Objective 3: Your child will practice reading, comprehending, and generalizing gender words by sorting names by gender, placing the names of females under the "girls" column, and males under the "boys" column. (If your child is older, teach him "male" and "female.")

Materials:

Copy the forms you need for bingo games in Appendix D-4, on card stock. At the top of this two-column form, print "boys" (or males) above one column and "girls" (or females) above the other. Leave the spaces below these titles blank. Use flash cards of family names, names of pets, and names of others that the child can read.

Procedures:

Show your child how to sort the cards, putting the names of females in the spaces under the "girl" column and males under the "boy" column. As your child draws the cards, he places them under the correct gender. Use all the names that your child can read, including pets, grandma, grandpa, friends, etc. After the card is filled, or all the names are used up, your child reads the cards: Example: "Boys—Dad, Chad, Spot, and Grandpa; girls—Mommy, Sally, Kitty, Grandma."

Human Model

Objective 4: *Your child will practice reading, comprehending, and generalizing body-part words by sticking Post-its™, with body part words printed on them, on or near the body parts of a person, poster, or large doll, matching the words with the body parts.*

Materials:

Post-its (or other removable stick-on label) with the name of a body part printed on each; a person willing to have his or her body labeled (you?), a poster with a person on it, or a large doll.

Procedures:

Demonstrate to your child how he can put the stickers on you to label your body parts (or on a poster or doll). Let your child stick them on your body parts (hair in your hair, neck on your neck, etc.), on a poster of a person, or on a doll. For mouth and eyes, draw arrows on the label, so the Post-it can be placed by the body part. Manage this game in a way that is comfortable for you and is fun for the child. I'm sure your child would find it funny if you walked around all labeled saying something like, "I am a walking book."

> **Option 1:** Print the word on the Post-it and ask, "What does it say?" Your child says, "Nose." Then you say, "Put it on my nose."

> **Option 2:** Print the words in a "book" of Post-its. Let your child tear them off and "label" your body parts, as he takes each label out of the book.

Option 3: Ask your child to name or point to a body part. Print the body part on the label, give it to your child, and say, "This says hand. Put it on my hand."

Playing Doctor

Objective 4: *Your child will practice reading, comprehending, and generalizing body-part and gender words by filling out a "medical chart."*

Materials:

Doctor kit; mat for "examining" table; sign, "Doctor Is In"; name tag (Dr. James, Sally, or Joe—use first or last name); clipboard, or other means to hold the "chart" and copies of chart, provided in Appendix D-16; prescription forms (Appendix D-17). Make several copies of the chart and form so you can play often. Generally, children with Down syndrome like to play doctor. They usually have lots of experience with doctors.

Procedures:

(1) Set up a "doctor office" with an examining table and the sign that says "Doctor Is In." Have your child wear the "Dr.____" name tag.

(2) Show your child the medical chart and how to use it. You may demonstrate by playing the part of the doctor first, or guide your child by helping him check things off the chart. Tell him that doctors need to fill out the chart, and they need to know whose chart it is. Show the "doctor": where to place the name (either with a name label, or if your child can and wants to, have him copy or write it); where to check "boy" or "girl" to indicate the gender of the patient; and how to check the chart to indicate the status of each body part. (The doctor "examines" each body part and asks the patient, "Head hurt? Ears hurt? Eyes hurt? Neck hurt? Feet hurt?" The patient responds with pretend complaints about some body parts, and says that others are okay.) After the "examination," show the "doctor" how to write a "prescription" for the patient (circle what the patient needs: a shot, pills, or liquid medicine).

(3) Teach him to play this game with his friends and/or siblings.

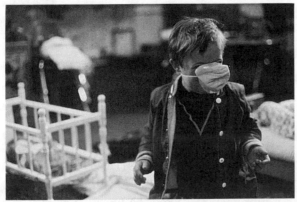

Figure 14.2. Dr. Roger prepares for surgery.

All about Me: Reading for Pleasure and Information

Objective 5: *Your child will practice reading sentences by reading a book about himself that includes the names of body parts and information about them.*

Materials:

Make an individualized book, using sample pages in Appendix E-6, and adding personal information about your child. Change the drawings when necessary—or do your own or use photos.

Typical examples of the pages in the book are:

I am a girl (or boy).

My name is _____.

I am ____ years old.

My eyes are brown (or blue or green—color in correct color).

My hair is (short, long, curly, black—color and draw in hair similar to your child's).

I have one nose, two ears and many teeth.

My neck connects my head to my body.

My foot is this big. (Trace your child's foot.)

My hand is this big. (Trace your child's hand.)

Procedures:

Teach your child to read the book. For words that he does not know, teach them using the match, select, and name method.

Evaluation:

Measure your child's word mastery by using a probe, as described in Chapter 8; his comprehension and generalization by responses when playing games and reading the book.

Adaptations for the Classroom

Units on self-image and self-esteem should be a part of the curriculum in every classroom. In the inclusive classroom, when other students are writing their autobiographies, help the child with Down syndrome to make a book about himself, at his level of understanding and comprehension, and teach him to read it. A simple notebook could be started and expanded throughout the child's life.

Adaptations for Older Learners and Learners with More Extensive Vocabulary

As your child with Down syndrome grows older, he should have important information about himself written in a notebook, or another form of a book that is designed to accommodate additions and changes. Having access to this information builds his independence and competence and puts him in control. The information should be written simply, so he can read and understand it. It should be organized so that he can easily find needed information, making it useful to him. Notebook dividers serve this purpose well. If he has easy access to this information, he does not have to remember it. He can look it up when needed.

Examples of information in the **All about Me** Notebook:

Basic information often needed to fill out forms:

My name is: _____

My birthday is: _____

My social security number is: _____

My address is: _____

My phone number is: _____

My parents are: _____

My parents' address is: _____

My parents' phone number is: _____

My legal guardian is: _____

My guardian's address is: _____

My guardian's phone number is: _____

My brothers are: _____

My sisters are: _____

My school is: _____

I work at: _____

My work address is: _____

My work phone number is: _____

Personal information:

My favorite things: _____

My favorite kind of music is (rock and roll, country-western, classical, show tunes). _____

My favorite band (or performer) is_____

My favorite song is _____

My favorite color is _____

My favorite flower is _____

My favorite foods are _____

My favorite clothes are _____

My favorite TV show is _____

My favorite video tape is_____

My favorite candy is _____

Sizes:

I weigh _____ pounds.

I am _____ high.

My shirt size is _____

My pants size is_____

My dress size is_____

My shoe size is _____

What I like to do:

I like to cook pizza. It's my specialty.

I like to swim. I go swimming on Tuesdays and Thursdays.

I like to go to Special Olympics. I swim and run. I won two blue ribbons.

I like to: watch TV; play Nintendo; go to parties; have friends over; dance; ride my bike.

Medical Information:

I was born at _____ Hospital in the city of _____.

The day I was born was
(date of birth, may add day of week):_____

I was (full term or premature—"I came 1 month early, or I came on time.") _____

I have Down syndrome. My kind of Down syndrome is called Trisomy 21.

Health record: (A list of hospitalizations, dates, and surgeries)

Shots I have had and the dates: (immunizations) _____

My blood type is _____

My health insurance company is: _____

I take one heart pill two times a day. At breakfast and at bedtime. These pills are called: (name of medication)_____

Allergies:

I am allergic to eggs. I get bumps all over when I eat them.

Personal Family Information:

This section should give information about your child's family members and friends. This builds his independence in developing and maintaining relationships.

Examples of information about family members:

Names of family member and friends (can be listed in categories—parents, grandparents, siblings, aunts, uncles, nephews, nieces).

Their address and phone numbers.

Their birthday (at the beginning of each year, he can look in the notebook and write birthdays on his calendar, so he can plan on it—buy cards or gifts.)

Other special days to remember the person (such as Mother's Day, Father's Day, Valentine's Day, parents' and siblings' anniversaries).

The person's favorite color, flower, candy, and music, and special things they like or dislike (Aunt Martha collects frogs; grandpa likes country-western music and hates rock and roll).

The person's sweater size (or whatever may be appropriate).

(It would be a good project for your child to call these people and get this information from them. Learning and having this information helps him to know about those who mean so much to him. It gives him the tools to reciprocate and take some of the responsibility for his relationships.)

I'd better take my notebook.

Christopher, who is 18 years old and takes two different medications, was invited to spend the night with a friend. Before he left, he said to his mother, "I'd better take my notebook." With the help of his notebook, he could take responsibility for taking his medication, and giving his hostess any other information she might need. He liked the security and independence that his notebook gave him.

Chapter 15

FEELINGS

When children do not have the expressive language skills to talk about their feelings, they may resort to "inappropriate" behavior to express their emotions. They may bite or throw a tantrum, shriek or squeal, stiffen their bodies or flop like rag dolls. Teaching your child words related to emotions is therefore not only important in improving her reading vocabulary, but also in helping her learn to identify her feelings and express them appropriately. This chapter is designed to facilitate learning about feelings and strategies to deal with them.

Goal: Your child will increase her reading vocabulary to include feeling words and words related to feelings; increase her awareness of feelings; and learn strategies for expressing feelings.

Introducing Feeling Words: Acquisition

Objective 1: Your child will match, select, and name feeling words using flash cards and picture cards.

Materials:

Picture cards (line drawings) and flash cards of the words *happy, sad, angry, lonely, afraid, sick, tired, hot,* and *cold.* Copy flash cards provided in Appendix C-13 and drawings in Appendix C-14 on card stock. Cut out to make flash cards and picture cards.

Procedures:

Introduce and teach these words using the match, select, and name method for the acquisition stage, adding new words gradually. As you introduce the words, talk about these feelings, act them out, and encourage your child to do the same. Talk about and demonstrate what you do when you have these feelings. (See "Charades," below, if you need help.)

Add new words and letters to the alphabet books, bingo games, and other alphabet games, as described in Chapter 9. Also add new words and letters to the word bank and probe, following the procedures in

Chapters 8 and 9. Use the probe as a guide to determine the rate for introducing new words and letters.

Games and Activities: Practice, Comprehension, and Generalization

Feelings Lotto Game

Objective 2: *Your child will practice reading and comprehending "feeling" words by matching the line drawings with the words.*

Materials:

Make the lotto game using the form in Appendix D-3 (or make your own). Copy Appendix C-14 on card stock; cut out the faces and paste them in the lids. Print the words on the lotto form. Name it "Feelings Lotto."

Procedures:

Teach your child to play Feelings Lotto, and give her opportunities to play with others and alone.

Charades

Objective 3: *Your child will practice reading and comprehending feeling words by "acting out" feelings and how to express them by playing charades.*

Materials:

Two boxes or baskets: one with cards with line drawing of feelings in it; the other with "feeling" flash cards in it.

Procedures:

Show your child how to play charades with feeling words: The players draw from either box, the one with line drawings in it, or the one with flash cards (you may alternate the use of symbols or words, or may flip a coin, to add another dimension to the game; heads, draw from line drawings box; tails, from words). The players "act out" the feeling, and/or what to do when you feel the emotion that is on the card. Suggestions for gestures you can teach your child: for *angry,* stamp feet, or clap hands against legs (what you feel comfortable with— your child needs a way to express this other than throwing a tantrum, running away, or refusing to comply with your wishes); *lonely,* pretending to pick up a phone and call someone, or motion for others to come to her; *happy,* a big smile, and clapping hands; *sad,* a sad face, mouth curving down and wiping eyes as if crying; *sick,* put hands together and lean head on them, as if you want to lie down; *cold,* hug and rub self as if trying to get warm and pretend to shiver, or pretend to put on coat or wrap up in a blanket; *hot,* wipe hands across face as if wiping off sweat, fan self with hands, pretend to take off clothes; *afraid,* eyes and mouth open as if screaming, hands held up, palms out for protection, moving backward as if trying to escape; *tired,* take a deep breath, a deep sigh, and slump.

Feeling Book: Reading for Pleasure and Information

Objective 4: *Your child will read a book about feelings and ways to express feelings. (Or, your child will listen and attend to the story when an adult reads it to her.)*

Materials:

I Know What To Do Book: Make a book about feelings. You will have to illustrate this one yourself using drawings or photographs. Suggestion: On the page that has the feeling, you could use the same line drawing used for the picture cards; on the page that says what to do, use a photo of your child doing the action.

I Know What To Do (Suggested text):

When I feel happy, I know what to do: (happy face line drawing)
I sing and clap and smile at you. (photo of child clapping and smiling)
When I feel lonely, I know what to do: (lonely line drawing)
I call a friend and say, "I want to play with you." (photo of child on phone)
When I feel angry, I know what to do: (angry drawing)
I take a deep breath and say, "I feel angry! Are you angry too?" (photo of child talking)
When I feel tired, I know what to do: (line drawing of tired)
I say, "I need a break, and a rest too." (photo of child resting)
When I feel sick, I know what to do: (line drawing of sick)
I lie down and say, "I need help from you." (photo of child lying down)
When I feel sad, I know what to do: (sad drawing)
I cry a tear and say, "I'm sad, boo-hoo." (photo of child pretending to cry)
When I feel afraid, I know what to do: (drawing of afraid)
I run to Mom and Dad and say, "I want to be near you." (photo of child in parent's arms)
When I feel cold, I know what to do: (cold drawing)
I put on a coat and snuggle up to you. (photo of child snuggling and warm)
When I feel hot, I know what to do: (drawing for hot)

I take a dip and cool off too. (photo of child in swimming suit or in bathtub or wading pool)

Procedures:

As with all units, you can choose the words and pages to use with your child. Teach your child to read the words she does not know, and help her read the book. Or, read it to your child, and let her supply the words she knows.

Additional Activities

Talk about Your Feelings: When you are with your child, help her to become aware of feelings by talking with her about how you are feeling. For example: I feel *tired,* I've been working hard. I need a rest (or a break); I feel so *happy* when you hug me; I feel *afraid* when you run in the street; I feel *sad* because you are sick; I feel *angry* because I spilled the juice; I feel *lonely*—come play with me; I feel *sick*—I'm going to bed.

Talk about the Feelings of Others: When you are reading a story to your child, ask her how she thinks the characters are feeling or comment on how they must be feeling. Examples: How did the little bear feel when he found his porridge eaten up? His chair broken? Someone else sleeping in his bed? How did Goldilocks feel when she woke up and saw three bears looking at her? How did the little pigs feel when the wolf was blowing their house down? How did the wolf feel when he fell in the hot water? How did Little Red Riding Hood feel when she saw that it was a wolf instead of her grandma?

When your child is watching TV, ask her how she thinks the people in stories are feeling, or comment on how you think they feel. Also, talk about the choices the characters are making. When a character hits or hurts another character, make comments such as, "Bad choice—that hurts him."

Sing about Feelings: Sing the song, "If You're Happy and You Know It," with your child. Make adaptations for concepts you want to teach. For example:

If you're lonely and you know it, call a friend.
If you're tired and you know it, take a break.
If you're angry and you know it, take a deep breath.
If you're happy and you know it, clap your hands (or smile and smile).
If you're sad and you know it, cry a tear.
If you're cold and you know it, put on your coat.
If you're hot and you know it, take a dip.
If you're afraid and you know it, go to Mom (or Dad)
If you're sick and you know it, go to bed.

As you sing this song, do the motions that demonstrate these feelings, as described above.

Your child can choose the emotion she wants to sing about by naming a feeling or selecting the symbol (line drawing) or the word for the feeling.

You could also make an audio tape recording of you singing the song with your child. To go with the tape, write down the feelings in the sequence in which they appear on the tape. As your child listens to the recording, she will be able to anticipate what comes next.

Evaluation:

Add the feeling words to the probe, and use the probe and the feelings book to determine your child's proficiency in reading words; determine comprehension by her accuracy in matching words with symbols (line drawings) and acting out feelings.

Adaptations for the Classroom and Older Learners

Primary children act out Peter, Peter, Pumpkin Eater. "How did Peter's wife feel when he put her in that pumpkin shell?"

Lotto and Charades: Play the same games, lotto and charades, as described above in the classroom.

Role-play: Role-play situations in which people experience feelings and show good ways to express these feelings. For example, the class can act out nursery rhymes and stories. *Jack and Jill* fell down the hill (they were hurt—which one had the worse injury?); *Little Miss Muffit* (she was frightened); *The Three Bears* (little bear was angry; Goldilocks frightened).

Art Project: During the unit, write "feeling" words on poster boards, such as *happy* on one and *sad* on another. The students look through newspapers and magazines and find pictures of people who they think feel happy or sad. They cut out these pictures and paste them on the appropriate paper. They can do the same with pictures that make *them* feel happy or sad. An ad for a pizza may make them feel happy, just thinking about it. A picture of an accident or disaster may make them feel sad.

Sing: Sing "If You're Happy and You Know It," either with or without adaptations.

Add New Feeling Words: Expand the "feelings" vocabulary to include other feeling words: frustrated, confident, guilty, hurt, satisfied, shocked, surprised, ecstatic, envious (or jealous), disgusted, bored, anxious. There are an infinite number. Give the children the vocabulary they need to learn to express themselves well.

Chapter 16

ANIMALS AND COLORS

Most children are generally quite interested in animals, so learning animal words is usually motivating and fun. Learning these words also gives them a vocabulary that leads to recreational reading, since many children's stories are about animals. Color words, which are functional and basic, are easy to teach in conjunction with animal words.

Goal: *Your child will: increase her reading vocabulary to include animal and color words; practice reading and comprehending words by playing games; and read the book,* Brown Bear, *independently.*

Introducing Color Words: Acquisition

Objective 1: *Your child will match, select, and name nine color words using picture cards and flash cards.*

Materials:

Color cards, with splashes of color instead of pictures (can use felt pens or crayons—your child can make these). Cards with color words are in Appendix C-16 for you to copy on card stock, color, and cut out. Color-word flash cards are provided in Appendix C-15 (copy on card stock and cut out). Color words suggested for this unit are: brown, red, yellow, blue, green, purple, white, black, and gold. (You may want to substitute orange for gold, but this unit incorporates a book that uses the word *gold*.)

The book *Brown Bear,* by Bill Martin, Jr. (Henry Holt & Company, NY) will be used throughout this chapter. Check the book out of the library or purchase a copy. It is readily available where children's books are sold.

Procedures:

Teach color words using the match, select, and name method, gradually increasing the number of words. To stimulate interest in colors and the book, read *Brown Bear* to your child either before or after the session, or anytime you and your child want to read it.

Continue to add new words and letters to the alphabet books, bingo games, and other alphabet games described in Chapter 9. Also add new words and letters to the word bank and probe, following procedures in Chapters 8 and 9. Use the probe as a guide to determine the rate for introducing new words and letters.

Games and Activities: Practice, Comprehension, and Generalization

Color Lotto

Objective 2: *Your child will practice reading and comprehending color words by matching the color words with colors.*

Materials:

Make a word-to-color lotto game. You will need nine spaces for this one, so you may want to adapt the bingo form in D-6 or make one up on your own. Copy the form you choose on white card stock. Color the spaces on the lotto card brown, red, yellow, blue, green, purple, white, black and gold (or orange)—the same order these colors appear in *Brown Bear*. Use felt pens, crayons, or paste in colored construction paper. Print the color words on the disks.

Procedures:

Teach your child how to play color lotto and give him opportunities to play with others and alone.

Color Hunt

Objective 3: *Your child will practice reading, comprehending, and generalizing color words by finding objects of specific colors and labeling these objects with the correct color words.*

Materials:

Post-its™ with the names of colors printed on them. Objects in the environment.

Procedures:

Go color hunting, looking for objects that are the color of the word on the Post-it. (Use color words that have been introduced to your child). When he finds an object that color, he sticks the Post-it with the name of the color on the object. Example: your child has been introduced to the color word *brown*. Walk through the house, looking for brown things with your child. When he finds something brown, he tears off a Post-it that has "brown" printed on it, and sticks it on the object (these "objects" can include clothing that people are wearing, or clothing and other objects in the closets and cupboards—we are, after all, "hunting"). As additional color words are introduced, go on hunting trips looking for these colors.

Fine Motor and Math Bonus:

When you or your child take down the Post-its, have your child sort them out, placing same words together. Then count the number of each thing he found of each color and record the number on a graph. Your child can color in the correct colors, making a color-coded bar graph.

Color Basketball

Objective 4: Your child will practice reading, comprehending, and generalizing color words by playing color basketball.

Materials:

Colored paper taped to baskets and/or buckets; beanbags or soft balls.

Procedures:

The players "draw" a flash card of a color word, and then toss the bean bag or ball into the basket of the matching color. (Your child draws the word *red* and tosses the bean bag in the basket with red on it). When the player gets the bean bag or ball in the correct basket, he scores.

Math and Fine Motor Bonus:

Give your child an opportunity to practice math and fine motor skills as well. Each time he tosses a beanbag into a color-coded basket or bucket, place a penny or chip in a color-coded jar, can, or box that "matches" the basket or bucket. When the game is over, help your child to count his score for each color; write down the number of chips for each color; make a simple graph with numbers up the side, and color words across the bottom. Help your child to draw in the bars to the correct number for each color. Your child then colors in the bars, using the correct color. (The problem with counting the bags in the baskets—instead of the pennies—at the end of the game is that players don't score if the bag goes in the wrong basket. Also, if someone else is playing, how do you know which bags are yours?)

Color Relay

Objective 5: *Your child will practice reading, comprehending, and generalizing color words through playing color relay.*

Materials:

Objects of different colors (or color cards) and flash cards with color words written on them.

Two "stations" and space for running back and forth.

Procedures:

Place flash cards with color words at station A; objects or color cards at station B. Your child draws a flash card, reads it, and runs to station B, picks up the object or card of the correct color and returns to station A, where he leaves the colored object or card and draws another card, and repeats the task. Your child repeats the procedure until all the objects or color cards are at station A. Remember to start with only the colors your child has been introduced to and add additional colors to the game as he learns to read the names of the colors.

Adaptations for the Classroom

Besides adapting the above activities for the classroom, students may take a survey of their classmates. (This is especially good for interaction in an inclusive classroom.) Have the child ask each classmate what his/her favorite color is, or ask the classmate to point to his or her favorite color. The child then places a mark, recording the "vote" of each classmate by the correct color word on his survey sheet. The next step is for the child, with the help of peers in the cooperative learning group, to count the tally and make a large graph showing the vote. This graph is then displayed in the classroom for all to ponder: the color that is the favorite of most classmates; the fewest; and maybe some colors are no one's favorite.

Introducing Animal Words: Acquisition

Objective 6: *Your child will match, select, and name nine animal words using picture cards with animal symbols (line drawings) and flash cards.*

Materials:

Picture cards with animals and matching flash cards with animal words: bear, bird, duck, horse, frog, cat, dog, sheep, and fish. For picture cards, copy Appendix C-17 on card stock; for flash cards, copy C-15. (You most likely already have these, as they are with the color flash cards.)

Procedures:

Teach animal words using the match, select, and name method, gradually increasing the number of words. Continue to read *Brown Bear* whenever you and your child feel like it, allowing him to fill in the words he can read.

Continue to add new words and letters to the alphabet books, bingo games, and other alphabet games described in Chapter 9. Also add new words and letters to the word bank and probe, following procedures in Chapters 8 and 9. Use the probe as a guide to determine the rate for introducing new words and letters.

Games and Activities: Practice, Comprehension, and Generalization

Animal Lotto

Objective 7: *Your child will practice reading and comprehending animal words by matching the words to symbols (line drawings) of animals.*

Materials:

Make an animal lotto game card by copying and adapting the form in Appendix D-6. Print the names of the animals in the circles; paste reduced drawings of the animals (Appendix C-17) on the disks. Color the animals on the disks the same as they are colored in *Brown Bear*.

Procedures:

Show your child how to play animal lotto and give him opportunities to play animal lotto with others and alone. When playing with others, more than one lotto game can be used (or your child can play using two or more cards). For example: one player has the color card; the other player has the animal card. The disks with the drawings and color words are placed face down on the table. The players take turns drawing disks, determining whose card it belongs to, and playing it. (See "Playing Lotto," Chapter 8.)

You can also combine the color and animal lotto games. Use the color lotto card you made for color lotto. Have your child match the animal (colored the same as the animals in the book) with the color on the color lotto game card. For example, match the bear with *brown;* the frog with *green*. When all disks are matched, the animals are in the correct sequence. Your child can now tell you the story of *Brown Bear* using the lotto game as a guide.

Animal Charades

Objective 8: *Your child will practice reading, comprehending, and generalizing animal words by playing charades, "acting like" animals.*

Materials:

Flash cards with the names of animals printed on them.

Procedures:

Play charades with your child as described in Chapter 12. The players take turns drawing a flash card with the name of an animal on it, acting like that animal, and saying the animal sound. Other players guess what animal the person has drawn. Suggestions for "acting" like animals: *bear,* growl, walking slowly, waving "claws"; *bird,* "flap" arms like wings, saying, "tweet, tweet"; *duck,* squat and waddle, saying, "quack, quack"; *horse,* gallop, saying, "nay, nay"; *frog,* hop, saying "croak, croak"; *cat,* creep on all fours, saying, "meow, meow"; *dog,* walk on all fours, barking; *sheep,* walk on all fours, saying, "baaa, baaa"; *fish,* move arms as if "swimming."

Animal Relay

Objective 9: *Your child will practice reading, comprehending, and generalizing animal words by playing animal relay.*

Materials:

Toy animals, or animal cards (cards with pictures of animals on them), flash cards with animal words printed on them. Two "stations" and space for running back and forth between them.

Procedures:

Same as for Color Relay, except the player draws an animal flash card and goes for the toy animal or animal picture card.

Animal Basketball

Objective 10: *Your child will practice reading, comprehending and generalizing animal words by playing animal basketball.*

Materials:

Pictures of animals (or animal words) taped to baskets or buckets; flash cards with animal words on them; beanbags or soft balls.

Procedures:

The player draws an animal flash card and tosses the beanbag into the basket with the picture of the same animal on it. Or, if the names of animals are taped to the baskets, the player tosses the beanbag into a basket and reads the word on the basket that he "made."

Math and Fine Motor Bonus:

Same as for Color Basketball, except substitute animals for colors.

Sing "Old MacDonald"

Objective 11: *Your child will practice reading, comprehending, and generalizing animal words by drawing or selecting flash cards to determine which animal will be sung about.*

Materials:

Animal flash cards.

Procedures:

Sing "Old MacDonald" with your child. Before each stanza, ask your child to "draw" an animal card and read it, to determine which animal to sing about next. Or, have the animal cards displayed, word up. Ask your child to select the animal that he wants to sing about next. Your child takes a card, reads it, and tells you what to sing about next.

Adaptations for the Classroom:

Students can take turns drawing cards; class sings "Old MacDonald."

Brown Bear: Reading for Pleasure

Objective 12: *Your child will read the book* Brown Bear, *transferring and generalizing reading skills.*

Materials:

The book *Brown Bear*, two sets of flash cards for words that are in the book, but have not been introduced to your child (such as, perhaps, *what, do, at, children, that's, us,* and *we;* flash cards for *gold, fish, red,* and *bird.* Cut these cards so that there is no space after the *d* in *gold* and *red* and before the *f* in *fish* and the *b* in *bird.* (Just cut *goldfish* and *redbird* to make four words—your child will put them together again.)

Procedures:

For words that your child does not know that are in the book (other than color and animal words), teach using the match, select, and name sequence, using two flash cards for each word (without picture cards; see Chapter 8).

Teach your child how to read the compound words *redbird* and *goldfish.* After he has learned *red, bird, gold,* and *fish,* place the *red* and *bird* flash cards before your child. Ask him to read *red* and *bird.* Then move the two words together to make one compound word. Ask him, "Now what does it say?" as you point to each word. If your child does not read the compound word, demonstrate again, reading it to your child, first as two words, then as one word. Another activity: Place the

Figure 16.1. Kari, eight years old, reads children's literature.

red and *gold* flash cards to the left of your child and the *bird* and *fish* to the right. Ask your child to put the words together to say *redbird* and *goldfish*.

Help your child read the book. Provide extra practice by matching, selecting, and naming words that your child needs help with.

Evaluation:

Add new words to the probe to determine fluency and mastery. Make notations of words your child has trouble with in the book. Provide extra practice with these words. Decide when to introduce new words, based on data collected from the probe.

Adaptations for the Classroom

Students can take a survey of their classmates, asking each if they have a pet at home. If the classmate does, then the child asks him/her to tell what their pet is, and places a tally beside the animal word on the survey sheet. If some classmates live on farms, the student can ask what animals live on the farm, and tally those as well. The students can then take the information and put it on a large graph. Display the graph for all to see and discuss. If the *Brown Bear* animals are used, discuss what animals make good pets, what animals are farm animals, and what animals are "wild" animals and not used as pets or kept on farms.

Chapter 17

FOODS (MENUS, GROCERY LISTS, AND RECIPES)

Food is a necessity of life and will be important throughout your child's lifetime. Being able to read menus, market lists, recipes, and directions on packages and cans will greatly increase her independence and competence. Food words are therefore good functional words to learn.

Goal: *Your child will increase her independence and competence by reading the names of foods and descriptive words on: menus (ordering her own food); shopping lists (selecting foods on a list in the supermarket); and recipes and directions (following simple recipes and directions on packages).*

Introducing Menu Words: Acquisition

Objective 1: *Your child will match, select, and name her favorite menu items.*

Materials:

Two sets of flash cards with favorite menu items (such as hamburger, cheeseburger, pizza, fries, ice cream, yogurt, milk, chicken nuggets, salad, cereals, fruits, juice) and other menu words (such as small, medium, large, low fat, diet, etc.); or, if your child needs the pictures, a set of picture cards and flash cards. McDonald's has picture menus available. Items can be cut from these to make picture cards. Your child can also make her own picture cards by finding these items in ads in newspapers and magazines, cutting them out, and pasting them on cards. Start with the words that your child has the greatest opportunity to use.

Procedures:

Teach the menu words you have chosen for the greatest opportunity to use, using the match, select, and name method, gradually increasing the number of words.

Add new words and letters to the alphabet books, bingo games, and other alphabet games, as described in Chapter 9. Also add new words and letters to the word bank and probe, following procedures in Chapters 8 and 9. Use the probe as a guide to determine the rate for introducing new words and letters.

Games and Activities: Practice, Comprehension, and Generalization

Menu Lotto

Objective 2: *Your child will practice reading, comprehending, and generalizing words through playing lotto.*

Materials:

Make a game card with menu words and disks with pictures of menu items (or help your child make them). Use pictures of menu items from picture menus or from pictures of foods in ads.

Procedures:

Show your child how to play menu lotto and give her opportunities to play Menu Lotto with others and alone.

Home Menus

Objective 3: *Your child will practice reading, comprehending, and generalizing menu words by reading home menus and ordering food at home.*

Materials:

Menus: For meals when your child has choices as to what she can have to eat, make menus with these choices on them. For example, for breakfast, if there are choices for beverages, cereals, jams, bread (toast, light or dark bread, or muffin), make a simple menu for these things. Put choices on the menu that you know your child would not choose (just like a restaurant menu), as well as choices you know she will choose. For example, if you have orange juice, cranberry juice, and prune juice, but know that your child will drink only apple juice, put at least some of the other choices on the menu. Leave off items that you are not willing to serve her or that you are out of, or put a line through the item to communicate to your child that that is not a choice for that day. For example, if you run out of Cheerios, draw a line through it, or if you do not have time to make pancakes, cross it out or leave it off the menu. If, however, your child has a choice between pancakes and French toast, then give her this choice. You may develop several menus, each with different choices (perhaps a weekend breakfast menu and a school-day breakfast menu). Also, you can start with a very simple menu and expand on it as your child's reading vocabulary of menu words expands.

How you want your child to communicate menu choices will determine how you make the menu. If you want her to simply read the menu and tell you what she wants, then you can use the same menu over and over without giving it any special treatment. Because a child can verbally give her choices without actually reading the menu (she knows what the choices are), I like to make the menu so that your child makes a choice by checking off or circling the items she wants. This makes it more of a "workbook" activity that is meaningful. It gives your child practice communicating on paper and a chance to practice "writing" skills in a functional way. If you want your child to mark her choices, make copies of the menu or laminate the menu and give your child a "wash-off" pen to use. (A sample menu is in Appendix D-18.)

Procedures:

Show your child the menu and help her read it. If you want your child to communicate choices by writing on the menu, show her how to do this. Teach her your limits for ordering. For example, if she can choose only one beverage at a time, teach her the rule. Return a menu that has more than one beverage marked on it and tell your child that she must make only one choice. Ask her to read her choice, either verbally or by pointing, whether or not she has marked it on the menu. Allow your child to make choices using the menus whenever possible (a snack menu would be nice). Follow through and serve what is ordered.

Eating Out

Objective 4: *Your child will generalize reading food words by ordering her own food in a restaurant, by reading from the menu, pointing to desired items on the menu, reading items of choice from a list, or by giving a written list to the person taking the order.*

Materials:

Restaurant menu; pen and paper or flash cards.

Procedures:

The most important aspect of this activity is that your child communicates her choice of food directly to the person taking the order, rather than relying on others to do it for her. Actually using the skill in a *real* situation. This is to build your child's confidence and independence, so it is important that the interaction is set up for success. If your child's articulation is such that strangers often have trouble understanding her, be sure that your child has another way to communicate, to "back up" the verbal communication. In a restaurant where the waiter comes to the table and takes the order, perhaps you can teach your child to point to the desired items in the menu as she orders them. If orders are given at a counter, as in most fast food restaurants, and the menu is posted on the wall, ask your child to look at the menu and decide. Print, on paper, the items your child tells you she wants (or if she can, have her print it). Or, have your child decide before going to the restaurant and have her select flash cards with the items she wants written on them (if she can print or use the computer, have her copy the names of the items herself). She can take the list or the flash cards up to the counter and read the names of the desired items to the person taking orders (like from a shopping list—cheeseburger, small French fries, low fat milk). If the person taking the order does not understand what your child is saying, your child can point to the words on the list or flash cards, communicating directly to the person taking the order.

Adaptations for the Classroom

Classroom Menus: If there are any choices of foods or beverages when food is served to children at school, teach them to read the choices and make a choice by checking off what they want, or by circling desired items.

School Lunch Menus: Teach the student to read items that most often appear on the school lunch menu. She can then go to the office or cafeteria and get the menu and return to the classroom and read it to the class. (A very useful service; she can be learning independence, navigating through the building, and interacting and communicating with others as well.)

Worksheets: Make a "worksheet" that has "What I Had for Lunch Today" printed across the top. Below, in categories, print the most common items served at lunch (or that the student brings in her lunch). For example: Entree—chicken, macaroni and cheese, pizza, spaghetti, hamburgers; Fruits and Vegetables—apple sauce, fruit salad, vegetable salad, peaches; Desserts—cookies, cake, pudding; Breads—rolls, biscuits, sliced wheat bread, sliced white bread; Beverages—milk, apple juice, orange juice. After lunch, she can circle the items that she had for lunch that day, take it home, and read it to her parents. This page becomes part of her "journal" and gives her "notes" to help her remember information that she can share with her parents. (She can also put the date on it, and print in who she sat by at lunch. We want her to remember experiences and share them, *and* we want her to *use* her reading skills to help her remember and share.)

In time, the child can expand on this; she can rate the food, giving her opinion as to how good it was that day. The words *not good, good,* and *delicious* can be written by each category. The child circles the words that apply to the food served in that category. This should increase her awareness and give her more to share with those at home.

Introducing Shopping List Words: Acquisition

Objective 5: *Your child will match, select, and name the names of favorite foods that appear on the family shopping list.*

Materials:

Two sets of flash cards with the names of the food on them, or one set of flash cards and a set of picture cards, if picture cards are needed.

Procedures:

Teach your child to read the names of these food items using the match, select, and name method.

Add new words and letters to the alphabet books, bingo games, and other alphabet games, as described in Chapter 9. Also add new words and letters to the word bank and probe, following procedures in Chapters 8 and 9. Use the probe as a guide to determine the rate for introducing new words and letters.

Games and Activities: Practice, Comprehension, and Generalization

Objective 6: *Your child will generalize reading food words by selecting specific items in the supermarket using a shopping list.*

Materials:

Shopping list containing items that your child is interested in buying. The first shopping lists should be very simple, such as *ice cream, pizza,* and *yogurt* (whatever those first words taught were). As your child becomes more advanced, descriptive words should be added, such as *non-fat chocolate ice cream, pepperoni pizza, strawberry yogurt.*

Procedures:

When your child can read the words, print them on a shopping list, or, if your child can copy them, either by hand or on the computer, have her make the list, or she can use the flash cards with the names of the desired items on them. In time, as the list becomes longer, help her put the items in categories (such as produce, dairy products, frozen foods, canned goods, pasta, etc.), and teach her to use the signs in the store to find these sections.

Take your child to the supermarket with you. Ask her what is on her list. As she reads it, ask her, "Do you know where to find it? Do you want to find it by yourself, or do you need help?" If she needs help say, "Ice cream—let's see if we can find it on the signs." (Or, "Let's find the frozen food section.") In doing so, you are not just teaching her how to find things, but also how to think and problem solve. If your child is younger and not ready for such independence, take her to the correct section, right where the item is, and let her find it. Play it by ear, staying at your child's level, maintaining her interest, and encouraging as much independence as you can. Remember to start with only a few items that your child really likes, and build on this over time.

"Shopping games" can also be played to practice reading skills. Your child can match flash cards (with the name of the item) with the item, or an empty container that the food came in; or, your child can draw a flash card and "go hunting" in the kitchen to find the food that is on the card.

Introducing Recipe Words: Acquisition

Objective 7: *Your child will match, select, and name words used in recipes.*

Materials:

Two sets of flash cards (for teaching words without pictures), or one set of flash cards and one set of picture cards, of words used in recipes your child will use: *chocolate, milk, glass, cup, pour, push, beat, stir, dip, teaspoon, tablespoon, cup, bowl, microwave, timer.*

Procedures:

Teach recipe words using the match, select, and name method, starting with the words used in the simplest recipe and gradually adding new words.

Add new words and letters to the alphabet books, bingo games, and other alphabet games, as described in Chapter 9. Also add new words and letters to the word bank and probe, following procedures in Chapters 8 and 9. Use the probe as a guide to determine the rate for introducing new words and letters.

Games and Activities: Practice, Comprehension, and Generalization

Recipe Charades

Objective 8: *Your child will practice reading, comprehending, and generalizing "direction" recipe words by playing charades.*

Materials:

Flash cards for *pour, push* (as in *push* the numbers on the microwave), *beat, dip, turn,* and *stir.*

Procedures:

Play charades, taking turns drawing these words, acting them out, and guessing the word the player drew.

Recipe Lotto

Objective 9: *Your child will practice reading, comprehending, and generalizing recipe measurement words.*

Materials:

Large lotto card: Make a lotto card big enough to place measuring equipment on it (approximately 12" x 16"). Divide the card into sections that will accommodate specific measuring equipment. In the sections print in: *¼ cup, ⅓ cup, ½ cup, 1 cup; ¼ teaspoon, ½ teaspoon, 1 teaspoon, 1 tablespoon. (See figure 17.1). Measurement equipment listed above (the measuring cups and spoons).*

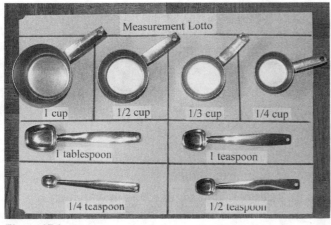

Figure 17.1

Procedures:

Take your child to the kitchen with the lotto board. Show your child where the measurement equipment is stored, how to find the numbers on the spoons and cups, and how to match them up with the measurements on the lotto card. Allow her to practice by going into the kitchen and putting the equipment on the board. Before cooking, she can assemble the measuring equipment needed by placing cups and spoons in the proper place on the board, making the correct size easy to find.

Following a Simple Recipe

Objective 10: *Your child will generalize reading recipe words by following a simple recipe with supervision.*

Materials:

Flash cards of words not previously taught (two sets, or one set of flash cards and one set of picture cards). A simple recipe, typed or written in print that your child can read. The recipe should be written in steps. For example:

Chocolate Milk

1. Pour milk in a glass
2. Add 3 teaspoons Nestle Quick
3. Stir

Hot Chocolate

1. Put 1 mug of milk in microwave
2. Push *time cook*
3. Push 2–0–0 (2:00)
4. Push *start*
5. Take out when timer goes off
6. Add 3 teaspoons Nestle Quick
7. Stir

French Toast

1. Turn electric frying pan to 300
2. Put in a bowl:

   2 eggs

   ½ cup milk

   ¼ teaspoon salt

   ¼ teaspoon cinnamon

   1 teaspoon sugar
3. Beat
4. Put 1 teaspoon butter in fry pan.
5. Cut 6 slices bread in half (easier to handle)
6. Use a fork and dip both sides of half slices of bread in egg mixture
7. Put in fry pan
8. Brown on both sides
9. Serve hot with syrup or jelly (can sift powdered sugar on it, if your child wants to get fancy)

Procedures:

Start with the simplest recipe (such as chocolate milk), teaching words new to your child that are in the recipe using the match, select, and name method. Read the recipe with your child, giving as little help as possible. Next, let your child read it and follow the directions with your help and supervision. Allow her to do as much independently as possible. Teach her to clean up after herself. You may want to expand on the recipes and add the "cleaning up." For example, the recipe may say:

1. Pour 1 glass of milk
2. Put milk back in refrigerator
3. Put in 3 teaspoons Nestles Quick
4. Stir
5. Put spoon in sink
6. Put Nestles Quick away
7. Enjoy your chocolate milk
8. Rinse glass and put in dishwasher

We want reading to build independence and competence; learning to read recipes and directions is a good place to start. Be sure to start with recipes of things that your child really likes. For some children, you may want to start with directions for cooking frozen pizza.

Give your child a recipe file for her recipes, or make a recipe book for her, adding pages as new recipes are learned. Your child should eventually be able to go to the kitchen, select a recipe, fix the food, and clean up.

Market List Using Recipes

***Objective 11:** Your child will generalize and use reading skills by compiling a market list by checking recipes and food supply.*

Materials:

Recipes of foods your child likes.

Procedures:

Before going to the supermarket, ask your child what she plans to prepare during the next week—what recipes she plans to use. You may need to prompt her, "Go look in your cookbook (or recipe file) and see if there is anything you would like to cook. See if there is anything we need to buy." Or, "If you plan to make chocolate milk next week, check the recipe and see if we need anything." If your child needs help, demonstrate how to find the recipe; check the cupboards and refrigerator; and see what ingredients you are out of. Help her put these items on a list. That list becomes her shopping list.

Evaluation:

Add new words to the word bank (coded as food words) and continue with the probe. Note the words that your child has trouble reading while following recipes, and whether she comprehends the directions and follows them. Give her extra practice with troublesome words and help with directions, until she can follow recipes unassisted.

Lupita had her teacher for dinner, and she cooked the whole meal herself!

When Lupita was 14 years old, her mother told me that Lupita invited her teacher to dinner, and she (Lupita) cooked the whole meal. This was a real accomplishment for Lupita, as it would be for any 14–year-old. I am sure that her teacher was most impressed.

Chapter 18

TIME: SCHEDULES AND CALENDARS

When we wake up in the morning, the first information we usually seek is, "What time is it?" and "What day of the week is it?" This information is absolutely necessary for us to know what to do next. If we look at the clock and discover that it's hours before getting-up time, we can turn over and go back to sleep. If it is our usual getting-up time, but we become aware that it is Saturday, then we may decide that we can snuggle in a little longer. It is time, and our knowledge of what we need to accomplish (our goals) within time periods, on specific days, that is the driving force that motivates us to do what we need to do at any moment. When we are able to achieve these goals, we feel in control, and our self-esteem is generally good. When things happen (often out of our control) that interfere with meeting our goals, we are apt to be upset or frustrated, and feel like failures. Our self-esteem dips.

We have the past, the present, and the future to guide us. For example, we may know from past experience that if we do not leave by a certain time, we will be late to work; thus, we know that we need to manage our present well to leave on time, for our future, at work, may be in danger if we are often late. The rest of our day is structured by the clock as well. As long as we are able to meet our schedule, and achieve what we need to within each time period, we feel in control, and usually all goes well for us.

Children need an understanding of the past, present, and future as well. They need to remember past experiences and learn from them; to understand what is expected and required of them in the present; and to know that what they do in the present affects their future. This gives them the advantage of being able to anticipate what is going to happen in the future. All of us need this anticipation to "gear up" and prepare for what is going to happen next. The only time most of us do not have the opportunity to prepare for the next event is during an emergency or a fire drill. Many children with Down syndrome do not have the tools to anticipate and "gear up" for the next event. Other people are generally in control, constantly telling them what to do and when and how to do it. This is not unlike having a fire drill several times a day at unpredictable times; regardless of your own agenda, you must do what someone else has decided. Most of us would rebel against such frequent intrusions, just as some children with Down syndrome do.

As discussed in Chapter 4, children with Down syndrome generally have difficulty processing and remembering auditory information, and that is the way most of us communicate information about time and schedules to children: "It's time to get ready—hurry, you'll be late. . . . Now it's time for dinner." Time is a very abstract concept, and we need to make it tangible, visible, and comprehensible for children with Down syndrome. This chapter focuses on how to do this.

Teaching children to read, follow schedules, and keep a calendar gives them the tools to be in control, to anticipate what will happen next, and to prepare for the next event. In addition, their past, present, and future is right there, tangible and visible, in the form of a schedule, for easy referral. Having these tools makes it possible for children to learn to set goals and achieve them, building independence, competence, and self-esteem.

He really has trouble with transitions.

Trevor was in an inclusive first-grade classroom. During transitions he frequently caused a disturbance. He would refuse to put away his materials, sit down on the floor, and refuse to move. There was no schedule posted, and he had no schedule at his desk. He was totally reliant on his teachers to tell him what to do next, and he often was not prepared for their agenda and communicated this to them through his behavior.

His teacher made a schedule for him, using symbols, words, and numbers for the sequence of activities, and the number of minutes allowed for the activity. At the beginning of each activity period, Trevor put a circle around the activity on the schedule and set a small electronic timer (available at Radio Shack) using the number of minutes stated on his schedule. He clipped the timer to his clothes and participated in the activities. When the timer went off, he consulted his schedule, put an "X" over the activity just completed, circled the next activity, and announced to the class what the next activity was. He was the leader, the person in charge and in control. He was also learning reading, math, writing (communicating with circles and X's), fine motor (using the timer), and communication skills (he had important information to relay to the other students).

His teacher reported to me that he is doing *very well.*

Where are we going tonight?

Tina's mother said that she told Tina in the morning that they were going to a skating show that evening. Her mother reported that Tina asked several times during the day where they were going that evening. Her mother found this annoying, and could not understand why Tina kept asking. Of course, it could be that Tina had learned a good way to "push her mother's buttons," but I believe that Tina had trouble remembering. The information was given orally, and Tina may have had relatively few memory channels. She would understand at the time, but as soon as new information entered her short-term memory, she lost the skating information. And although she may have known what skating is, she may not have had a "file" on skating, or perhaps could not retrieve the information she had to help her remember. Plus, she may not have been able to visualize a *skating show,* although she knew what skating was. (See Chapter 4.)

I suggested to her mother that she put events on a calendar in a way that Tina could understand them. For Tina, who was just learning to read, I suggested both the written word and a simple drawing (for example, of a skater or a skate). Whenever Tina asked her mother where they were going, her mother could say, "You tell me; go look at the calendar." The symbol and word on the calendar would be there, *tangible* and *visible,* and Tina could look at them for as long as she needed in order to comprehend their meaning and to rehearse the information. Unlike the spoken word, which vanishes immediately, the visual words and symbols are available for as long as necessary.

Goal: *Your child will increase his competence and understanding of the past, present, and future by learning to read and use schedules and calendars.*

Introducing Schedule Words: Acquisition

Objective 1: *Your child will match, select and name schedule words used in his school schedule.*

Note: It's important to team with the teacher on this and other activities in the chapter.

Materials:

Picture cards with symbols (line drawings) of activities in the schedule and matching flash cards. On the picture card, put the number of the sequence (or time period) for that activity. Example: If "group" or "sharing" is the first activity, put a "1" on the picture card for group; if reading is the second activity, put a "2" on the picture card

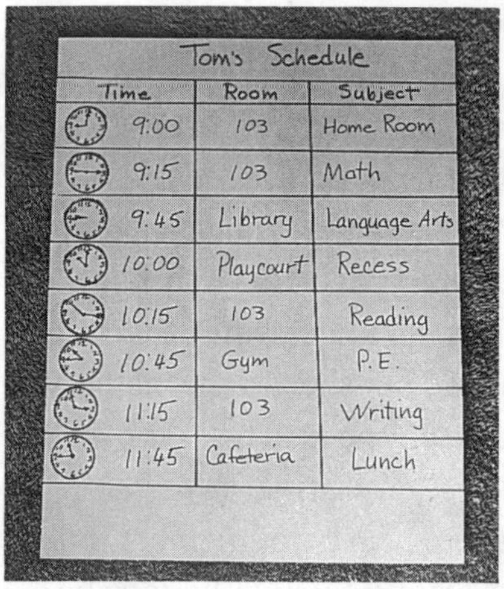

Figure 18.1

for reading. The specific schedule words will depend on what the teacher calls the activities during each time period; your child's schedule and involvement in resource room, self-contained classroom, and community-based activities; and the grade level of your child. Schedule words used as examples in this unit are: *schedule, group, reading, spelling, journal, writing, math, social studies, lunch, recess, activities, library, P.E., and dismissal.* (Appendix D-19 is a sample schedule for preschool or kindergarten.)

Figure 18.1 is a sample of a schedule using clocks to indicate time.

Procedures:

Teach the schedule words using the match, select, and name method, starting with the word *schedule,* or *My Day* (if the word *schedule* is a little difficult for your child), and gradually increase the number of words.

Add new words and letters to the alphabet books, bingo games, and other alphabet games, as described in Chapter 9. Also add new words and letters to the word bank and probe, following procedures in Chapters 8 and 9. Use the probe as a guide to determine the rate for introducing new words and letters.

Games and Activities: Practice, Comprehension, and Generalization

Schedule Lotto

Objective 2: *Your child will practice reading, comprehending, and generalizing schedule words by playing Schedule Lotto.*

Materials:

Make a one-column, word-to-symbol lotto game with symbols for schedule words on the game card, arranged in the usual sequence that the activities occur; flash cards with the schedule words on them. Figure 18.2 is a schedule lotto game made from Appendix D-19.

Procedures:

Show your child how to play Schedule Lotto and give him opportunities to play with others and alone.

Figure 18.2

Following the Daily School Schedule

Objective 3: *Your child will circle the current activity on the schedule and cross out the activity when it is finished.*

Materials:

Several copies of schedules with symbols and words. Make a schedule for each day of the week, if your child's schedule varies from day to day (such as, "library" on Monday, Wednesday, and Friday; "P.E." on Tuesday and Thursday). At the top of each schedule print the day that it is for (*Schedule for Monday*). Determine the number of periods in the school day and divide the remainder of the page up according to that number. Draw horizontal lines across the page, leaving a space for each time period. Draw vertical lines forming four columns (if your child is learning to tell time) or three columns (if he is not yet learning to tell time), making the first two columns narrower (if four columns are used; one column narrower if three columns are used). In the first column write down the number of the period; in the second column (if 4 columns are used), draw a clock showing the time the period starts, with the time written under it; in the third column, draw the symbol for the activity for that time period, and print the name of the activity under it; leave the last column blank for now.

Procedures:

Show your child the schedule and read it with him (he is learning to read the words and symbols). Point to the current activity and say, "Look, it is group time; draw a circle around group time. That is what is happening now." Give your child assistance only if it is needed. When the period is over, ring a bell (or if you are using a timer, when timer goes off), ask your child, "What comes next?" Cue him to consult his schedule, cross out the previous period, and circle the next. Continue throughout the day. Each day, as the schedule is given to your child, point to the day of the week that is at the top and say, "Today is *Monday;* this is your *Monday* schedule. You go to the library on *Monday*."

The Daily Report (Or Adaptive Journal)

Objective 4: *Your child will record, by circling symbols or words, or by copying words, something that happened during each period in the schedule.*

Materials:

The schedule (for Objective 3) with choices in the last column. Adapt the schedules to the level of your child:

> **Phase 1:** For learners who do not have the reading vocabulary: draw symbols (three or four) in the last column of each time period that represent activities that may have taken place during that period. Under each symbol, print the word.

Examples: for *group time,* there may be a symbol for a calendar, a book, songs (music notes or tape deck), money (for lunch money); for *reading,* a symbol for book, flash card, lotto game, computer; for *recess,* symbols for various playground activities, such as a ball, swing, climbing equipment; for *lunch,* milk, pizza, hamburger (or the usual school or brown bag lunch that the child typically eats).

Phase 2: For learners who can read the words, but have difficulty copying and writing words: print, in the last column, words that represent activities that may have taken place during each time period. Example: for *group time* you may print, if you sing these songs during this period: This Land is Your Land, Wheels on the Bus, There Was an Old Lady; for *reading,* the titles of stories.

Phase 3: For learners who can copy words, print open-ended statements on primary paper, or on the computer, leaving space and lines big enough for the student to copy in his activities. Examples:

In group today we sang _____

In reading we read about _____

At recess I played _____. I played with _____

At lunch we had _____. I sat next to _____

Today I felt _____

The most special thing we did today was_____

Phase 4: For learners who can write, primary paper and pencil.

Procedures:

Phase 1: Toward the end of the day (or after each activity to start out with, if it works out for you), show the child how to use the last column. Guide him, saying, "Look, here are things we do in group time. Circle the things we did today, and cross out the things we did not do." Pointing to the symbol say, "This means money for lunches; did we take up lunch money today?" Help him either cross out or circle the money symbol. At lunch you may say, "This means hamburger; did you have hamburger for lunch today?" Give as little assistance as possible, and, in time, expect him to complete his report independently. If he cannot remember, and it is possible for him to "look it up," show him how to do it. For example, if the lunch menu is posted, he could go and look on the menu (he may have to have the teacher read it, or he could look for "hamburger" written under the symbol).

The "homework" assignment for this student is to take his "report" or "journal" home and use it to inform his parents what went on at school. If he has trouble talking, he can point to the things circled, or the parent can "read" it saying, "You took up lunch money in group." Or, "Did you really have pizza at school today?" The important concept is for him to learn to use his marks on paper to remember and to communicate with others.

Phase 2: Use Phase 2 materials, words without symbols. Change the choices often, expanding on the choices. Proceed as in Phase 1, except teach the child to read the choices and circle the correct ones. This report also goes home and the child is responsible for sharing his day with his parents, using this report that he completed.

Phase 3: Help the student copy in words that complete the sentences. If the words exist in print and are readily available, as on the menu, or in the reading book, or student names on desks, or in the student's word bank, the student can copy from the source. If it is not, he "dictates" to the teacher what he wants to put in the space. The teacher writes it down, and the student copies it in the correct space. If the student is not willing to try to copy, or if his copying is not legible, using the computer is a good option. The form can be kept in the computer; the student completes the statements, using the computer. He can print it out and take the journal home.

Phase 4: The student writes his own journal. The teacher provides help needed. Options for adaptations to help with spelling and provide models for forming letters: (1) The student can arrange flash cards from his word bank to say what he wants to, and copy or type them. (2) The student can dictate his journal to another person, and copy or type it. The journal is shared with parents as before.

You know, we have several children in here who could benefit from this. I'm going to use it with them too.

Tammy, who was six years old, was included in a first-grade class. She was doing well with her reading, in the same reading program as her first-grade peers. Writing was difficult for her, and after a few attempts at tracing and copying letters and words, she would give up. During the journal period, she sat at her desk, drawing little marks that had no meaning, pretending to "write" like the other children. She looked very "appropriate," as it looked as though she was doing the same as her classmates. However, just looking appropriate is not good enough. She needs to be learning as well. To help her to learn how to communicate on paper, and to give her the concept of recording things that happened, and to use "notes" to communicate and remember what happened during the day, I recommended using the schedule, starting with Phase 2. Her teacher had the schedule in the computer, and changed the choices in the last column each day, to be sure that the choices were appropriate for that day (if pizza was for lunch, she typed in *pizza;* if the story in reading was *The Shop,* then she typed it in). During the journal period, Tammy circled the correct choices. She took her "journal" home and read it to her parents, reporting to them all the important events of the day. She soon moved on to Phase 3.

Her teacher was delighted with the adaptation. Her comment was: "We have several children in here who could benefit from this. I'm going to use it with them too."

(Appendix D-20 contains actual reports that a student filled out to evaluate his own behavior. This, too, is an adaptation of a journal and can be helpful in communicating to parents about the kind of day a student had.)

Daily Home Schedule

If your child is dependent on you to prompt him to complete tasks necessary for getting off to school in the morning, he can learn independence by following a schedule at home as well. Make a schedule of the morning routine that you want your child to follow. Include the amount of time allowed for each task (bathing, dressing, eating, brushing teeth, grooming). Your child sets a timer for the amount of time allowed for each task and plays "Beat the Clock," working to finish the task before the timer goes off. When this goal is reached, your child checks the task off; when the task is not finished before the timer goes off, he draws a circle around the task. When he is all dressed and ready to go out the door, he places a dime (or token) on each check, and then puts them in his jar (earning money for something important, such as a new tape, movie rental, or a trip to McDonalds).

Introducing Weekly Schedule Words: Acquisition

The weekly schedule described here is a schedule for the school week. Saturday and Sunday can be added after the student has learned to follow the school-week schedule.

Objective 5: *Your child will match, select, and name the days of the week.*

Materials:

Two sets of flash cards with the days of the week.

Procedures:

Teach the days of the week using the match, select, and name sequence, using two sets of flash cards. Show your child the days of the week on the calendar. (He has already been exposed to these words on the daily schedule, and may be reading these words already. As always, adjust your instruction to your child.)

Add new words and letters to the alphabet books, bingo games, and other alphabet games, as described in Chapter 9. Also add new words and letters to the word bank and probe, following procedures in Chapters 8 and 9. Use the probe as a guide to determine the rate for introducing new words and letters.

Games and Activities: Practice, Comprehension, and Generalization

Days-of-the-Week Lotto

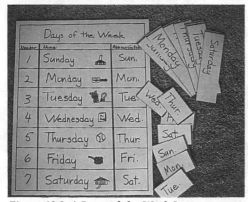

Figure 18.3. A Days-of-the-Week Lotto.

Objective 6: *Your child will practice reading abbreviations of the days of the week and match abbreviations with the word.*

Materials:

Make a lotto card with the days of the week; flash cards with the abbreviations of the days of the week; flash card with the word *day* on it. (See figure 18.3.)

Procedures:

Show your child a calendar that has the abbreviated days of the week and tell him, "See, this is the short word for *Monday, Tuesday,* etc. Short words fit better on the calendar and are faster to write." Then show him the flash card with *day* on it, saying, "This word says *day*." Show him that the word *day* is on the end of each day of the week, reading the words, emphasizing the *day*. Ask him to match the *day* flash card with the *day* in the days of the week. Show him how to play Days-of-the-Week Lotto, matching abbreviations with the whole word. Give him opportunities to play the game.

Following a Weekly Schedule

Objective 7: *Your child will follow a weekly schedule.*

Materials:

Make a weekly school schedule with six columns, the first one for the time period, and the remaining five for the school days. Under each day, print in the student's schedule, transferring the information from the daily schedules, using words only, if the student has learned the words.

Procedures:

Show the student how to follow the schedule, circling the current period/activities and crossing out activities as they are finished. At the beginning of each day, ask him to tell you what the day of the week is, using his schedule. If he has trouble with this, show him how the previous day is marked off, finished, therefore, it must be the next "unused" day. When the student is absent, print "absent" across the periods of the days absent. Tell the student what the word says, and say, pointing to the schedule, "Look, yesterday was Wednesday and you were absent. You missed all of these things that happened on Wednesday because you were sick. What day is it today?"

Introducing the Months of the Year: Acquisition

Objective 8: *Your child will read the current month and year using a calendar.*

Materials:

A calendar with the name of the month printed plainly across the top, and with squares for the days big enough to write in events, or to draw a symbol of events; felt pen, for writing in events or drawing symbols; flash cards for the months of the year; flash card of the year (1995); an alarm clock or a clock radio.

Procedures:

Introduce the calendar to your child. Say, "This is your very own calendar. We use the calendar so that we know when important days are coming. Days like birthdays, Halloween, and Valentine's Day. The calendar also helps us know when to go to school, to work, and on vacations." Place the calendar on the wall, at your child's level, and attach it so that it can be taken down and put up again easily.

At the beginning of each month, introduce the month to your child. For example: Pointing to the word on the calendar say, "The name of this month is *January.*" Then show him the *January* flash card and ask him to find it on the calendar and match it. (Repeat this each day until your child can read the word spontaneously, telling you that the month is January, reading it on the calendar.) Also introduce the year. Say, as you give him the flash card, "The *year* is *1995*. Find it on the calendar." Ask him to match it. You can then hold up the two cards and say, "Which card says *January? 1995?*" There is no hurry, he has a lot of days to practice 1995.

Objective 9: *Your child will use the calendar to anticipate upcoming events.*

After introducing the month to your child, help him "fill out" the calendar, so he can anticipate what will be happening. Print in the events, if your child can read the words (or teach him to read them); or, if your child likes to put labels on things, print or type the events on labels, cut them to fit the calendar, and show him where to put them. For holidays and birthdays, draw in little symbols to make the calendar more interesting and appealing; or, if you can find appropriate stickers, use sticker symbols. If your child has not been taught most of the words, you can use symbols for every event.

Examples: On January 1, write in *Happy New Year* and add a symbol, such as a baby, or a party hat; or, you may use just a symbol. On January 18, write in *M.L.K. Day* (for Martin Luther King Day) and a little drawing, or paste in a little picture of M.L.K., or a drawing of a birthday cake, indicating that it is M.L.K.'s birthday. On the days that your child stays home from school, print in *home* (or the label), or draw a symbol for a house. For school days, print in *school*. Add any other events that are important for your child: examples: favorite TV shows that come on just once a week; church or Grandma's on Sundays; dance on Saturdays. At the beginning of the year, help him fill in family birthdays (or the date of important events, such as the due date of a baby expected by a family member or teacher; or the last or first day of school; or family vacations). Using his calendar, he can look ahead to the future and see what events are coming up.

At the end of each day, as a part of the bedtime ritual, help your child to cross off the day just finished. Then ask him to tell you what day tomorrow is, and what is going to happen. ("It's Friday. I go to school; It's Saturday and I stay home and go swimming; It's Martin Luther King Day. I stay home; It's Daddy's birthday. I go to school. We have a party at night.") Based on events marked on the calendar, help him make decisions, such as what to wear the next day, or whether he needs to turn on his alarm. You may ask, after marking off the day and noting what tomorrow will bring, "Do you need to turn on your alarm clock for tomorrow?" Or, "It's picture day at school. Do you want to wear your blue shirt or your red sweater?"

When you greet your child in the morning, or any time during the day, use calendar words, such as "Happy *Tuesday* to you!" Or, "How are you this snowy (cold, rainy, foggy, or sunny) *January* morning?"

Holidays

On the month of each holiday, teach your child to read the name of the holiday and words associated with the holiday. Plan a unit to teach him to read simple greeting cards for the holiday, using greeting cards for books. Call his attention to signs in stores that use holiday and greeting words. Point out these words in the newspaper and magazines. When he is anticipating a birthday, teach him to read *happy birthday,* so he can read his own birthday greeting. Put a *Happy Birthday Mike* banner up for him to see and enjoy. Help him select greeting cards to send to others.

Lotto

Months-of-the-Year Lotto can be made and played, matching month to month, or abbreviation to month. Wait until your child has been introduced to about four months and make a four-month lotto, with space for adding other months, as he learns them.

You can also make Holiday Lotto. A symbol for the holiday can be matched to the word. Examples: the baby or party hat to New Year's Day; heart to Valentine's day; Jack-o-lantern to Halloween; flag to 4th of July; profile of Washington or Lincoln for President's Day; a birthday cake for your child's own birthday.

References

Blaha, R. (1988). Functional communication activities and strategies that work for severely involved students, presentation, Workshop in Special Education. Seattle: University of Washington.

Brigance, A.H. (1978). *Brigance diagnostic inventory of early development.* Woburn, MA: Curriculum Associates.

Buckley, S. (1985). Attaining basic educational skills: reading, writing, and number. In D. Lane and B. Stratford (Eds.), *Current approaches to Down's syndrome,* (pp. 323–330). Westport, CT: Praeger.

Buckley, S. (1984) *Reading & language development in children with Down's syndrome: A guide for parents and teachers.* Portsmouth: Down's Syndrome Project.

Carr, E.G. and Durand, V.M. (1985). Reducing behavior problems through functional communication training. *Journal of Applied Behavior Analysis,* 18, 111–126.

Carr, J. (1988). Six weeks to twenty-one years old: A longitudinal study of children with Down's syndrome and their families. *Journal of Child Psychology and Psychiatry,* 29, 407–431.

Coleman, M. (1988). Medical care of children and adults with Down syndrome. In V. Dmitriev and P.L. Oelwein (Eds.), *Advances in Down syndrome* (pp. 7–18). Austin, TX: Pro-Ed.

Conners, F.A. (1992). Reading instruction for students with moderate mental retardation: Review and analysis of research. *American Journal of Mental Deficiency,* 96, 577–597.

Connolly, J.A. (1973). Intelligence levels of Down's syndrome children. *American Journal of Mental Deficiency,* 83, 193–196.

Downs, M.P. and Balkany, T.J. (1988). Otologic problems and hearing impairment in Down syndrome. In V. Dmitriev and P.L. Oelwein (Eds.), *Advances in Down syndrome* (pp. 19–34). Austin, TX: Pro-Ed.

Dunn, L.M. (1959). *Peabody picture vocabulary test (PPVT).* Circle Pines, MN: American Guidance Service.

DuVerglas, G. (1984). A comparative follow-up study of Down's syndrome children who attended the Model Preschool Program. Doctoral dissertation. Seattle: University of Washington.

Durling, D. & Benda, C.E. (1952). Growth curves in untreated institutionalized mongoloid patients. *American Journal of Mental Deficiency,* 56, 578–588.

Dykens, E.M., Hodapp, R.M., & Evans, D.W. (1994). Profiles and development of adaptive behavior in children with Down syndrome. *American Journal on Mental Retardation,* 98, 580–587.

Edwards, J. & Dawson, D. (1983). *My friend, David.* Austin, TX: Pro-Ed.

Engelmann, S.E. (1977). Sequencing cognitive and academic tasks. In R.D. Kneedler & S.G. Tarver (Eds.), *Changing perspectives in special education.* Columbus, OH: Charles E. Merrill. As cited in Heward, W.L. & Orlansky, M.D. (1984). *Exceptional children: Second Edition.* (p.124). Columbus, OH: Charles E. Merrill.

Fredricks, H.D., Mushlitz, J. Jr., & DeRoest, C. (1987). Integration of children with Down syndrome at the elementary school level: a pilot study. In S.F. Pueschel, C. Tingey, J.E. Rynders, A.C. Crocker, and D.M. Crutcher (Eds.), *New perspectives on Down syndrome*. Baltimore: Paul H. Brookes.

Fowler, A. (1988). Determinants of rate of language growth in children with Down syndrome. In L. Nadel (Ed.), *The psychobiology of Down syndrome* (pp. 217–245). Cambridge, MA: MIT Press.

Franken, A. (1992). *I'm good enough, I'm smart enough, and doggone it, people like me!* New York: Dell Publishing.

Gibson, D. (1966). Early developmental staging as a prophesy index in Down's syndrome. *American Journal of Mental Deficiency,* 70, 825–828.

Golden, D. (1994). Building a better brain. *Life* (July), 63–70.

Grieser, D.L. & Kuhl, P.K. (1988). Maternal speech to infants in a tonal language: support for universal prosodic features in motherese. *Developmental Psychology,* 24:1, 14–20.

Hayden, A.H. and Dmitriev, V. (1975). The multidisciplinary preschool program for Down's syndrome children at the University of Washington Model Preschool Center. In B.Z. Friedlander, G.M. Sterritt, and G.E. Kirk, (Eds.), *Exceptional infant,* vol. 3, (pp.193–221). New York: Brunner/Mazel.

Hunt, N. (1966). *The world of Nigel Hunt.* London: Darwen Finlayson.

Kessler, M.E., and Randolph K. (1979). The effects of early middle ear disease on the auditory abilities of third grade children. *Journal of Academic and Rehabilitation Audiology,* 12:6–20.

Korenberg, J.R., Pulst, S.M., and Gerwehr, S. (1992). Advances in the understanding of chromosome 21 and Down syndrome. In I.T. Lott & E.E. McCoy, (Eds.), *Down syndrome: Advances in medical care* (pp. 3–12). New York: Wiley-Liss.

Kumin, L. (1993). *Communication skills in children with Down syndrome: A guide for parents and teachers.* Bethesda, MD: Woodbine House.

LaVeck, B. & LaVeck, G. (1977). Sex differences in development among young children with Down's syndrome. *Journal of Pediatrics* 91: 767–769.

Loveland, K.A. & Kelley, M.L. (1988). Development of adaptive behavior in adolescents and young adults with autism and Down syndrome. *American Journal on Mental Retardation,* 93, 84–92.

Loveland, K.A. & Kelley, M.L. (1991). Development of adaptive behavior in preschoolers with autism or Down syndrome. *American Journal on Mental Retardation,* 96, 13–20.

McCreary, A. (1992). Study shows early influence of language on infants. *CDMRC Outlook,* 5:2.

Miller, G.A. (1956). The magical number seven, plus or minus two: Some limits on our capacity for processing information. *Psychological Review,* 63, 81–97. (Cited in: Myers, D.G., 1986, *Psychology.* New York: Worth Publishers.)

Oelwein, P.L. (1988). Preschool and kindergarten programs: strategies for meeting objectives. In V. Dmitriev and P.L. Oelwein (Eds.), *Advances in Down syndrome* (pp.131–157). Austin, TX: Pro-Ed.

Pieterse, M., & Treloar, R. (1981). The Down's Syndrome Program: Progress report. North Ryde, Australia: Macquarie University.

Rhodes, L., Gooch, B., Siegelman, E.Y., Behrms, C., and Metzger, R. (1969). *A language stimulation and reading program for severely retarded mongoloid children.* California Mental Health Research Monograph No. 11. Sacramento, CA: State Department of Mental Hygiene.

Sandall, S.R. (1988). Learning to take turns. In V. Dmitriev & P.L. Oelwein (Eds.), *Advances in Down syndrome* (pp. 261–269). Austin, TX: Pro-Ed.

Wiig, E. (1980). And then they told me I had to cut on the lines. In W.L. Heward & M.D. Orlansky, *Exceptional children: First edition.* Columbus, OH: Charles E. Merrill.

Wishart, J.G. (1988). Early learning in infants and young children with Down syndrome. In L. Nadel (Ed.), *The psychobiology of Down syndrome* (pp.7–50). London & Cambridge, MA: A Bradford Book, the MIT Press.

Wishart, J.G. (1989). Learning to learn: The difficulties faced by infants and young children with Down's syndrome. In W.I. Frazier (Ed.), *Key issues in mental retardation.* (pp. 249–261). London: Routledge.

Zadig, J.M. (1987). Elementary education for children with Down syndrome. In S.F. Pueschel, C. Tingey, J.E. Rynders, A.C. Crocker, and D.M. Crutcher (Eds.), *New perspectives on Down syndrome.* Baltimore: Paul H. Brookes.

Appendix A–1

READING APPROACHES, PROGRAMS, AND MATERIALS

Reading as an area of study is too vast to be comprehensibly covered in one book, so the following list of approaches/materials is not totally complete. These approaches/materials can be used to provide a systematic instructional process for teaching reading to children with Down syndrome, as well as "typical" children. Adaptations in teaching using these processes are needed according to the functional level of each individual child.

Reading Approaches

The five major approaches to teaching reading are the basal reading approach; the language experience approach (used in the program described in this book); the individualized reading approach; the linguistic approach; and the psycholinguistic approach. There are also numerous combinations of the above approaches, as well as many other teaching methods, strategies, approaches, and techniques, including: programmed instruction, Distar, the phonics method, the Fernald method, and the Orton-Gillingham-Stillman approach. Only the five major approaches are described below.

The Basal Reading Approach

The majority of elementary schools (89–95 percent) use a basal reading approach. This approach uses a series of books of stories written on different levels of difficulty. Beginning at the pre-primer level, most programs progress through upper elementary levels. Workbooks and worksheets usually accompany the basal readers and are used for reinforcing and practicing skill development, as well as for providing valuable diagnostic data on the students' level of mastery of specific skills.

Comprehensive teacher manuals accompany the basal reading approach. These manuals are normally highly structured and written in detail. Each lesson is outlined, and skill objectives, specific questions, vocabulary words, and suggested motivational activities are provided.

The Language Experience Approach

The language experience approach is a highly individualized approach which reflects the belief that a child can learn to read if reading is presented in such a way that the following thinking process is followed:

1. What I am thinking, I can talk about.

2. What I talk about, I can write (or someone else can write for me).

3. What is written, I can read, and so can others.

4. I can read what I have written and what others have written for me to read.

Research indicates that the language experience approach is based on three assumptions:

1. Children have had and will continue to have experiences.

2. Children are able to talk about their experiences.

3. If children can learn to write down what they say, this may be used as an instructional tool to teach them to read.

The experiences that a child brings to this approach is of primary importance since these experiences will provide the basis for the child's reading material. The role of the teacher is to enrich and broaden the child's experiences so that she will have a wide base of experiences from which to think, speak, and write.

Going on field trips, creating art work, seeing films, discussing interesting topics and items all lead to multifaceted experiences.

The Individualized Reading Approach

The individualized reading approach requires a teacher who is extremely familiar with, and has a comprehensive knowledge of, reading goals and objectives and is able to teach without the step-by-step structure found in the basal reading approach.

To use this approach, the teacher must have access to a large supply of books written on various reading levels and reflecting a wide variety of interests. The idea is that there should be books available that are appropriate for every student's readiness level, reading abilities, and individual needs. Students are encouraged to choose their own reading materials. The individualized approach also includes group activities, checklists of skills for the teacher, and interaction between students.

The Linguistic Approach

With the linguistic approach, students are asked to learn word patterns. The emphasis is on decoding and mastering a limited number of consistent spelling patterns, with a gradual introduction of less consistent patterns. The earliest programs did not use pictures so as to avoid distracting the reader. Newer programs may include pictures, introduce high-frequency words or some other word identification skills, or place greater emphasis on comprehension.

Usually, programs based on this approach include basic reading books, workbooks, and teachers' manuals. Some are aimed at specific groups of readers, such as children who are learning English as a second language.

The Psycholinguistic Approach

The psycholinguistic approach to teaching reading is a combination of the contributions of the disciplines of communication theory, sociology, and anthropology with the fields of linguistics and psychology. In this approach, reading is considered a psycholinguistic process in which thought and language interact as the reader builds meaning. As students read, they maintain a sense of what is being read and may "guess" where their reading is going and what sentence structure, words, or phrases are coming next.

According to Rhodes and Shannon, teachers must be willing to rethink many traditional assumptions about teaching reading to use this approach:

1. Rather than assuming that reading and writing are taught by teacher-initiated sets of drills, teachers must believe that students learn reading and writing by doing them.

2. Rather than assuming that oral language is a prerequisite skill for reading or writing, teachers must believe that engaging in speaking, reading, and writing leads to new learning in all areas.

3. Rather than assuming that letter and word recognition is a prerequisite for comprehension, teachers must believe that because of what they already know about oral language, students gain meaning from print.

4. Rather than assuming that for students to express their ideas in writing they must first learn letter formation, conventional punctuation systems, and spelling, teachers must believe that all of these develop as they are used.

5. Rather than assuming that mistakes in reading and writing are to be eliminated, teachers must use them as clues to the student's current levels of understanding. They are part of the strategy of learning.

Reading Programs and Materials

Ball - Stick - Bird (Fuller, 1975)

P.O. Box 592

Story Brook, NY 11790

This approach has been found to be effective in teaching reading to children with severe mental retardation. All letter forms are derived from combinations of balls (0), sticks (1), and birds (<).

Edmark Associates, 2nd Edition

P.O. Box 3218

Redmond, WA 98073–2318

Phone: 1–800–362–2890

This is a beginning reading program, specifically for students who have not succeeded with other reading methods. Word recognition and comprehension are taught using 350 commonly used words. The approach is multisensory and students interact through seeing, hearing, saying, and touching. The program consists of cards, manipulatives, and story books, designed for Grades K-1.

Computer software materials are available. Useful for students with developmental delays or learning disabilities or in Chapter I and ESL programs.

Supplementary materials for home or school practice are a strong component of the program.

Happily Ever After

Dale Seymore: Palo Alto, CA

Uses a whole language approach with "Big Books" and audiotapes for Pre-K through first grade.

Love and Learning

P.O. Box 4088

Dearborn, MI 48126–4088

This program uses no-pressure teaching techniques that are programmed for success. The early learning kit focuses on early vocabulary words and over 100 phonetic components.

Mott Semi-Programmed Series

Allied Education Council

Galiem, MI 49113

This program consists of a series of workbook texts programmed for self-pacing with immediate feedback. Behavioral objectives are provided for each unit. Areas of study include beginning phonics, elementary comprehension, and word-attack skills. Cursive writing is also covered. Excellent for intermediate through high-school level students.

The Multisensory Teaching Approach (MTA)

Margaret Taylor Smith

Educators Publishing Service, Inc.

75 Moulton Street

Cambridge, Massachusetts 02238–9101

This is a multisensory, process-oriented ungraded curriculum based on the philosophy and techniques of Orton-Gillingham and Alphabetic Phonics. It covers reading, spelling, cursive handwriting, alphabet and dictionary skills for both regular and remedial instruction. Can be used as basic instruction for primary-age students, as a supplement to a basal reading program, or as a remedial program for students of any age. Materials are nonconsumable and may be reused by one or more teachers year after year.

Palo-Alto Reading Program: Sequential Steps in Reading (Glim, 1973)

Harcourt, Brace and Jovanovich
757 Third Avenue
New York, NY 10017

This is a linguistic-slanted reading program for readiness through third grade. Materials and interest levels cover primary and intermediate age ranges.

Peabody Rebus Program

American Guidance Service
4201 Woodland Road
P.O. Box 99
Circle Pines, MN 55014–1796

Appropriate for remedial instruction using workbooks with pictured words (rebuses) as a transition to spelled words.

Phonovisual Products, Inc.

18761 N. Frederick Ave.
Rockville, MD 20852

This is an organized system of phonics-based instruction, based on phonetically arranged pictorial charts. The reading program based on the charts presents instruction in three primary steps: initial consonants, final consonants, and vowels and blends. In addition to the phonics charts, workbooks, word lists, and games are also available as supplementary aids.

Recommended as a developmental program for beginning readers as well as a remedial program for older children.

Reading Mastery Distar K-6

Science Research Associates
P. O. Box 543
Blacklick, OH 43004–0543

Suitable for the classroom as a basal reading program using a direct instruction approach.

Remedial Reading Drills (Heggs, Kirk, and Kirk, 1940, 1969)

George Warh Publishing
Ann Arbor, Michigan 48108

These materials consist of over fifty drills and exercises which can serve as daily instructional lessons. The drills begin with short vowel sounds using simple word families (i.e., fat, cat, pat). Successive lessons cover phonetically similar families of words that increase in difficulty to sound combinations and polysyllabic words. When used with students for whom it is found to be appropriate, the drills initially represent a complete or total program of instruction. As progress is made throughout the program, other instruction such as nonphonetical word recognition skills and comprehension skills must be combined with the drills. Supplementary materials such as basal readers or high-interest, low-vocabulary books could be used.

Sing, Spell, Read and Write
2220 Paramont; Suite 105
Chesapeake, VA 23320
Phone: 1–800–321–TEAC

This program introduces reading skills with a song; practices with a game; reinforces with consummable textbooks; applies the skill in a storybook, linked sequentially to the next step. There are two programs provided: Primary Age - Pre-K, K, Level 1 and Level 2; Preteens and Adults (Winning Program, described below).

Specific Skills Series
(Barnett Loft Publishers)
Order from: SRA
P. O. Box 543
Blacklick, OH 43004

A self-paced reading lab useful as a supplement to a basal text. Includes grades 1–6. Individual books cover comprehension skills, including getting the main idea, drawing conclusions, following directions, using the context, locating the answer, getting the facts. Available as a kit levels 1–8.

Stevenson Program
Stevenson Learning Skills, Inc.
85 Upland Rd.
Attleboro, MA 02703
1–800–343–1211

This language skills program is a total approach that covers reading, spelling, vocabulary building, comprehension, and more. The skills are strategically coordinated. The materials are thoroughly organized and sequenced for the teacher. The key to the Stevenson Program is learning by association—a well-documented technique for enhancing a student's ability to remember information. Clues, also called mnemonics, are used to unlock the decoding process with a specific word attack strategy. This procedure stimulates the student to make images in her mind, a process which engages the right hemisphere of the brain. Involving the right hemisphere can be helpful to students with learning disabilities, whose left hemisphere functions are often weak. The program is suitable for younger readers and readers with disabilities of all ages.

Stick-on-Story Books
Science Research Associates
P.O. Box 543
Blacklick, OH 43004–0543

Utilizes a language experience approach. The books provide visual stimulation while the student provides the text.

Superkids
(Addison-Wesley Publishing Company)
Route 128

Reading, MA 01867

1–800–552–2259

Superkids is a phonics-based program designed to give children reading independence with stories that help them relate the written word to the spoken language they use every day. Superkids features four levels: Pre-primer through Grade 1.

The Winning Literacy Program (Sue Dickson, 1989)

Sing, Spell, Read, and Write

Virginia Beach, VA 23463

This is a systematic how-to-read program that coordinates the teaching of reading, writing, phonics, spelling, and speaking (English) for students from pre-teens to adults of all ages. Can be used on its own or as a supplement and booster to basal reading programs in schools (upper elementary through college).

Zoo Phonics

P.O. Box 1219

Groveland, CA 95321

Zoo-Phonics is a tactile, kinesthetic, whole-brain approach for teaching reading and spelling. Each letter sound is introduced by animal names (such as Allie Alligator says "a"). After teaching the basic shapes and sounds of the alphabet, the program moves through the blends, digraphs, and diphthongs. The program is most suitable for grades K-3, and children with mild mental retardation, Down syndrome, or autism.

Computer Programs/Software

Most computer companies will allow you to preview programs for 30 days. This gives you the chance to assess the usefulness of a particular program for your child. Inquire about previewing policies before you order.

Broderbund's Living Books

Educational Resources

1550 Executive Dr.

Elgin, IL 60123

Uses CD-ROM. Child interacts by activating sounds or actions, using a mouse.

Intellikeys

Unicorn Engineering, Inc.

5221 Central Ave., Ste. 205

Richmond, CA 94804

Keyboard overlays that simplify using the computer for younger or lower-functioning students (K-2). These are available for Apple, MacIntosh, and IBM.

Kid Words 2

Davidson and Associates

P.O. Box 2961

Florrance, CA 90509

An interactive reading program that targets writing skills, designed for four- to ten-year-olds. Available for Apple/MacIntosh and IBM.

Phonics Skills Series

Steck-Vaughn
P.O. Box 26015
Austin, TX 78755

Uses workbooks to remediate phonic skills for grade levels 1–5.

Power Words Programs

Steck Vaughn
P.O. Box 26015
Austin, TX 78755

Workbooks aimed at remediating students with low vocabulary skills in grades 2–6; written on a first-through third-grade level.

Reader Rabbit 1 and 2

Educational Resources
1550 Executive Dr.
Elgin, IL 60123

Designed for use with Pre-K to grade 2 students, using a game format. Available for Apple, MacIntosh, and IBM.

Sticky Bear Alphabet Weekly Reader

Educational Resources
1550 Executive Dr.
Elgin, IL 60123

Uses a game format to drill alphabet identification for ages 3–6. Apple, MacIntosh, and IBM.

Supplementary Reading Materials

Alphabet Books

Story House Corp.
Bindery Lane
Charlottesville, NY 12036

Facts about large birds and sea animals are used to reinforce alphabet skills.

Alley Alligator Series

Benefic Press
Westchester, IL 60153

Stories center around three rangers and a baby alligator.

Breakthrough Series

Allyn and Bacon

470 Atlantic Ave.
Boston, MA 02210
   Reading levels, 2–6; interest level, junior and senior high.

Checkered Flag Series
Field Education Publications
2400 Hanover St.
Palo Alto, CA 94002
   Stories appropriate for high school students, but written on grade levels 2–5.

Deep Sea Adventure Series
Harry Wagner Publishing
609 Mission St.
San Francisco, CA
   High-interest, controlled low vocabulary stories, written at grade level 2–6.

First Start Easy Readers, Grade K-2
Troll Instructional Materials
Troll Associates
100 Corporate Dr.
Mahway, NJ 07430
   Simple text uses comical approach to add interest.

First Start Adventures, Grade K-2
Troll Instructional Materials
Troll Associates
100 Corporate Dr.
Mahway, NJ 07430
   Available with cassette tape. Uses simple vocabulary to expand beginning readers' independent skills.

The Monster Books
Bowman
Glendale, CA 91201
   Appealing to young children beginning to read.

Mystery Adventure Series
Benefic Press
Westchester, IL 60153
   Reading level 2–6; appropriate for grades 5–12. Mystery stories involving a teenaged boy and girl.

Appendix A-2

GUIDELINES: TYPICAL SEQUENCE FOR TEACHING READING

The guidelines given here are intended to help those who wish to use the language experience approach introduced in this book to teach higher-level reading concepts (prefixes, suffixes, word endings, compound words, etc.). Remember, however, these are only guidelines. Not all concepts have to be taught in the sequence given here, and not all concepts have to be taught. If your child has a hard time learning phonics and applying rules, continue to teach sight words and use these guidelines to give you ideas as to the types of words and concepts to work into his program.

Pre-primer Level

1. Sight words: 50 in reading vocabulary

2. Word analysis: Can match words as described in Chapter 8; can hear rhyming words and select words that rhyme

Primer Level

1. Sight words: 100 in reading vocabulary

2. Uses context and picture clues to read words

3. Begins using structural analysis (sees sight words in other words, as *in* and *to* in *into*)

4. Supplies rhymes in rhyming sentences

5. Recognizes common endings (*s, ed,* and *ing*)

First Reader Level

1. Sight words: 200 in reading vocabulary (See Appendix B–1 for basic sight word list)

2. Matches, selects, and names both upper and lower case letters (i.e., *A* and *a* are the same letter)

3. Groups words by beginning letters (sorts or files words by beginning letters)

4. Recognizes similarities in words (words starting with the same letters, words having the same endings, and words belonging to the same "word family," such as *bat, mat, hat,* and *sat.*)

5. Recognizes and uses consonant sounds, except for *v, x,* and *z.*

6. Recognizes and uses only hard sound of *c* and *g*

7. Recognizes the sounds of digraphs—*ch, sh, th,* and *wh*—but does not call them by name

Second Reader Level

1. Sight words: 300 in reading vocabulary

2. Supplies initial and final consonants in words used in a sentence, such as, "Dick can pull the _ago_."

3. Recognizes consonant blends, used as the initial sound of a word, or used elsewhere in a word:

bl cr fr pl sc sl sp st thr br dr gl pr scr sm spr str tr cl fl
gr qu sk sn qu sw tw

4. Changes beginning consonant and makes new words (*same* and *came; make* and *cake*)

5. Learns vowel sounds, short vowel sounds first, then long vowels.

6. Learns to use rules that make vowels long in one-syllable words, such as, "When two vowels go walking, the first one does the talking" (as in *boat, rain, coat,* etc.); and "An *e* on the end makes the vowel say its own name" (as in *came, bake, like,* etc.)

7. Learns and uses soft sounds of *c* and *g*

Third Reader Level

1. Sight words: 500 in reading vocabulary

2. Learns vowel combinations - *oo* and *ee*, and diphthongs, *oi, oy, au, aw, ou, ow.*

3. Learns common prefixes - *com, con, de, dis, en, ex, in, pre, pro, re,* and *un*

4. Learns common endings - *able, al, less, ness, y,* and *lie*

5. Learns and uses *v, x,* and *z* sounds

6. Learns to hear the syllables in words and tell how many there are

Rules to Help in Teaching Hard and Soft Sounds of C and G

1. *C* has no sound of its own.
   - A hard *c* uses the sound of *k* and is usually followed by the vowels *a, o,* or *u,* as in *cat, cot,* and *cut.*
   - A soft *c* uses the sound of *s* and is usually followed by the vowels *e, i,* or *y,* as in *cent, city,* and *bicycle.*

2. *G* uses its hard sound *g* or borrows the sound of *j* for a soft sound.
   - A hard *g* is usually followed by the vowels *a, o,* or *u,* as in *gave, got,* and *gun.*
   - A soft *g* is usually followed by the vowels *e, i,* or *y,* as in *give* and *get,* but this rule has many exceptions, as in *gentle, engine,* and *gypsy.*

Rules of Syllabication

Knowing the rules of syllabication are important in sounding out words. If you do not know where a word breaks, you do not know what pronunciation rules apply or which syllable to accent. (Pi-lot sounds different from pil-ot.)

1. Every syllable has a vowel sound. There are as many syllables in a word as there are sounded vowels - ga-la, boil-er, and bean.

2. Prefixes and suffixes usually form separate syllables. These parts are actually units by themselves and not just a part of a long word or root. Examples: re-call-ing, pre-view, help-less.

3. Double consonants are usually split; one goes with each of the two adjoining syllables. Examples: pil-low, mur-mur, and grem-lin.

Never break a consonant blend in dividing words into syllables. Examples: In pic-ture, the two sounds are pronounced separately; in pock-et, the *ck* is one sound; in dis-tress, *tr* is a consonant blend.

4. A consonant between two vowels usually goes with the vowel following it. Examples: pi-lot, and po-lite.

A syllable ending with a vowel, as *pi* in pilot, is called an open syllable, and the vowel sound is usually long. In contrast, a closed syllable is one ending with a consonant, and the vowel sound is usually short as in dad-dy and moth-er.

5. In words ending with *le,* the final *le* forms a separate syllable with its preceding consonant. Examples: a-ble, lit-tle, ta-ble, and crum-ple.

Appendix B-1

A BASIC SIGHT VOCABULARY OF 200 WORDS

These words comprise 50–70 percent of the words in material used by elementary school students.

a	could	help	new
about	cut	her	no
after	did	here	not
again	do	him	now
all	does	his	of
always	done	hold	old
am	don't	hot	on
an	down	how	once
and	draw	hurt	only
any	drink	I	open
are	eat	if	or
around	eight	in	our
as	fall	into	out
ask	far	is	over
at	fast	it	own
ate	find	its	pick
away	first	jump	play
be	five	just	please
because	fly	keep	pretty
been	for	kind	pull
before	found	know	put
best	four	laugh	ran
better	from	let	read
big	full	light	red
black	funny	like	ride
blue	gave	little	right
both	get	live	round
bring	give	long	run
brown	go	look	said
but	goes	made	saw
buy	going	make	say
by	good	many	see
call	got	may	seven
came	green	me	shall
can	grow	much	she
carry	had	must	show
clean	has	my	sign
cold	have	myself	sit
come	he	never	six

sleep
small
so
some
soon
start
stop
take
tell
ten
thank
that
the
their
them
then
there
they
think
this
those
three
to
today
together
too
try
two
under
up
upon
us
use
walk
want
warm
was
wash
we
well
went
where

which
white
who
why
will
wish
with
work
would
write
yellow
yes
you
your

MODELS FOR PRINTING AND WRITING

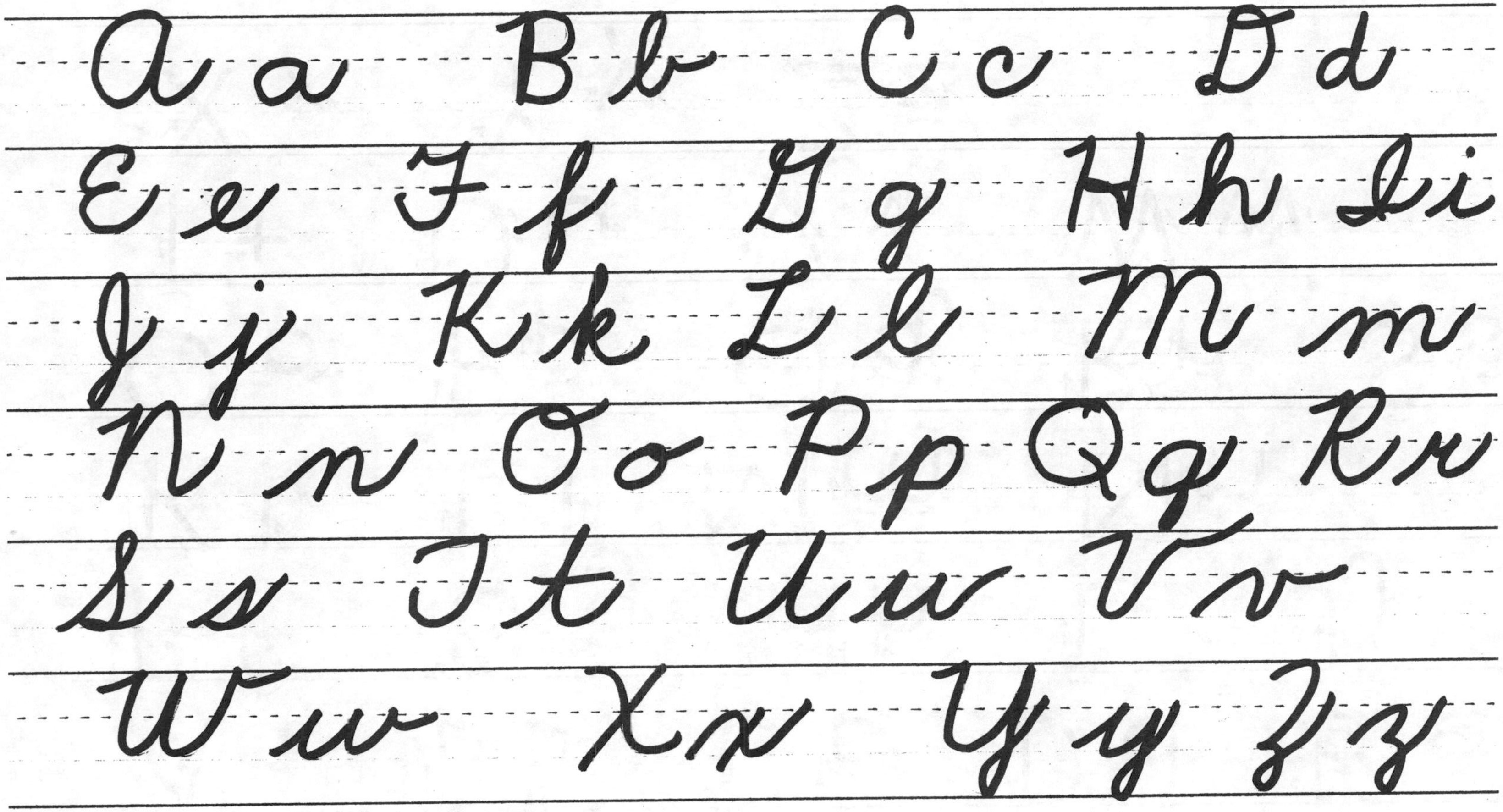

A a a

B b b

C c c

D d d

E e e

F f f

G g g

H h h

I i i

J j j

K k k

L l l

M m m

N n n

O o o

P p p

Q q q

R r r

S s s

T t t

U u u

V v v

W w w

X x x

Y y y

Z z z

Aa Bb Cc Dd Ee
Ff Gg Hh Ii Jj
Kk Ll Mm Nn
Oo Pp Qq Rr Ss
Tt Uu Vv Ww
Xx Yy Zz

at	b	c	f
h	m	N	v
P	r	s	
an	c	D	

f	J	m	p
r	t	en	B
d	h	K	
m	p	t	

ig	b	d	f
j	p	r	w
b	h	j	l
m	p		

cat	tan
bat	van
sat	Dan
rat	Jan
vat	fan
mat	ran
hat	pan
man	

big	bug
fig	lug
dig	pug
pig	rug
wig	tug
rig	hug
mug	jug

hen

ten

men

pen

cat

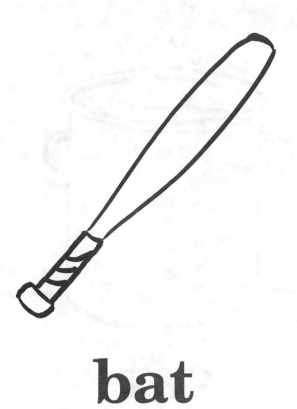

bat

sat

rat

vat

mat

hat

man

tan

van

Dan

Jan

fan

pan

ran

can

lug

pug

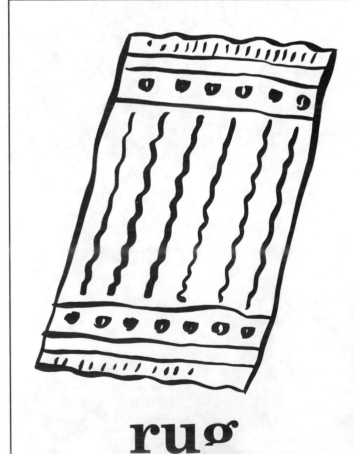

rug

tug

bug

hug

mug

jug

hen

men

pen

ten

big

dig

fig

wig

pig

rig

run	
walk	
jump	
kick	
eat	
smile	
go	
come	

hop	sing
clap	dance
swing	listen
stomp	slide
pat	tip-toe
laugh	swim
ride	fly
watch	crawl

drop	mark
play	kiss
get	hug
stand	open
stack	throw
make	win
splash	take
say	

eat

smile

go

come

run

walk

jump

kick

mirror	box
bed	cup
dresser	teapot
kitchen	dishes
bathroom	tape deck
bedroom	radio
couch	books
piano	bathtub

TV	chair
table	floor
rug	wall
door	window
sink	stove
washer	dryer
toys	lamp
computer	refrigerator

shower	
toilet	
potty	
calendar	
telephone	
plant	

boy	chest
girl	tummy
hair	hands
eyes	arms
nose	legs
mouth	feet
ears	teeth
neck	back

boy

girl

hair

eyes

nose

mouth

ears

neck

chest

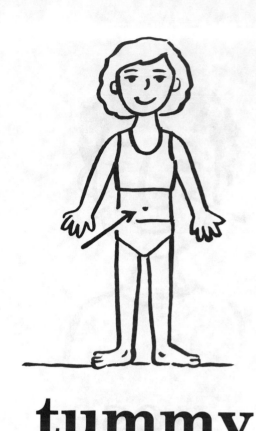

tummy

hands

arms

legs

feet

teeth

back

happy	
sad	
angry	
afraid	
sick	
tired	
hot	
cold	

happy

sad

angry

afraid

sick

tired

hot

cold

brown	**gold**
red	**bear**
yellow	**bird**
blue	**duck**
green	**horse**
purple	**frog**
white	**cat**
black	**dog**

sleep

fish

brown

red

yellow

blue

green

purple

white

black

gold

bear

bird

duck

horse

frog

cat

dog

sheep

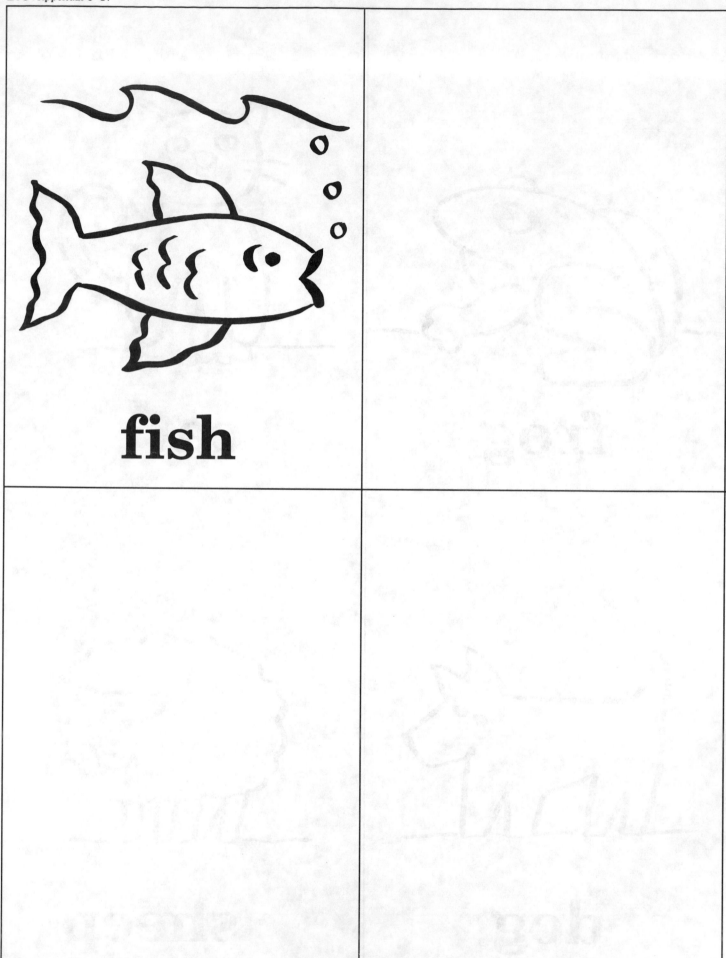

fish

Family Lotto

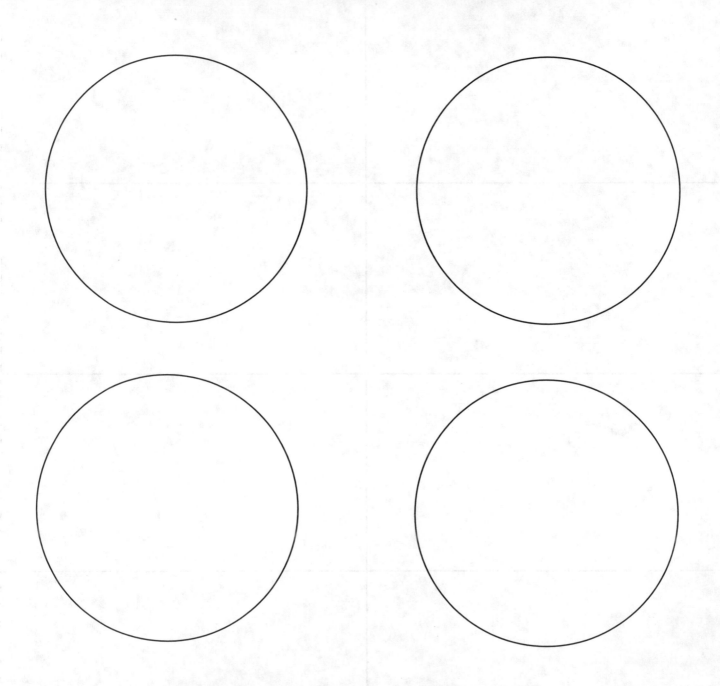

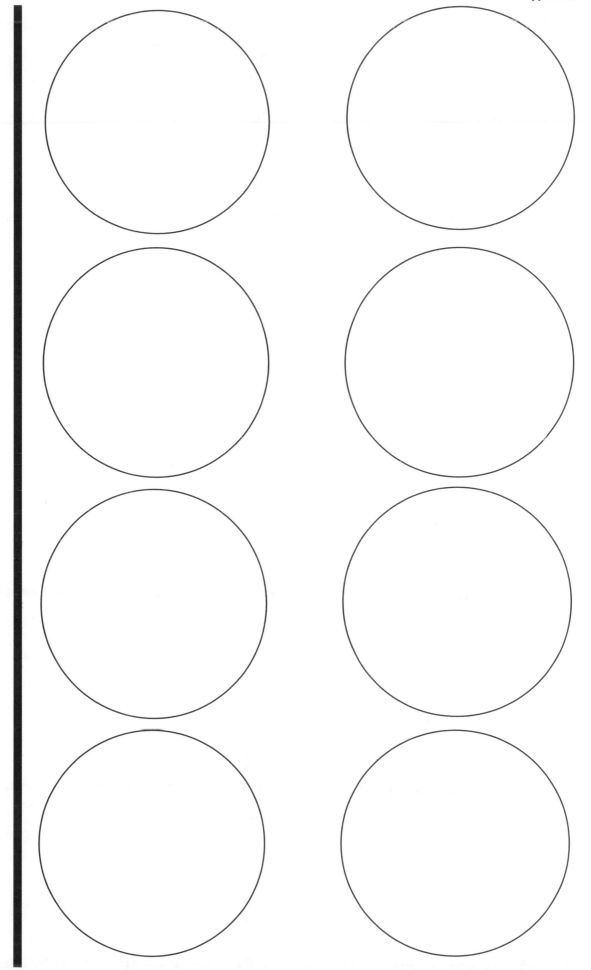

BINGO

BINGO

BINGO

b
c
f
h
m
N
P
r
s
v

_____ **at**

Photocopy page. Cut out pieces and cut on the dotted line. Slide letters through the cut-out to make different words.

c
D
f
J
m
p
r
t

an

**B
d
h
K
m
p
t**

_ _ _ _ _ _ _ _ _

en

_ _ _ _ _ _ _ _ _

b
d
f
j
p
r
w

_____ **ig**

b
h
j
l
m
p

_____
_____ **ug**

en **ug**	**h**
at **en** **ug**	**m**
at **an** **at**	**r**

ug at en an ig	
	b ---------- ----------
at an an	c ---------- ----------

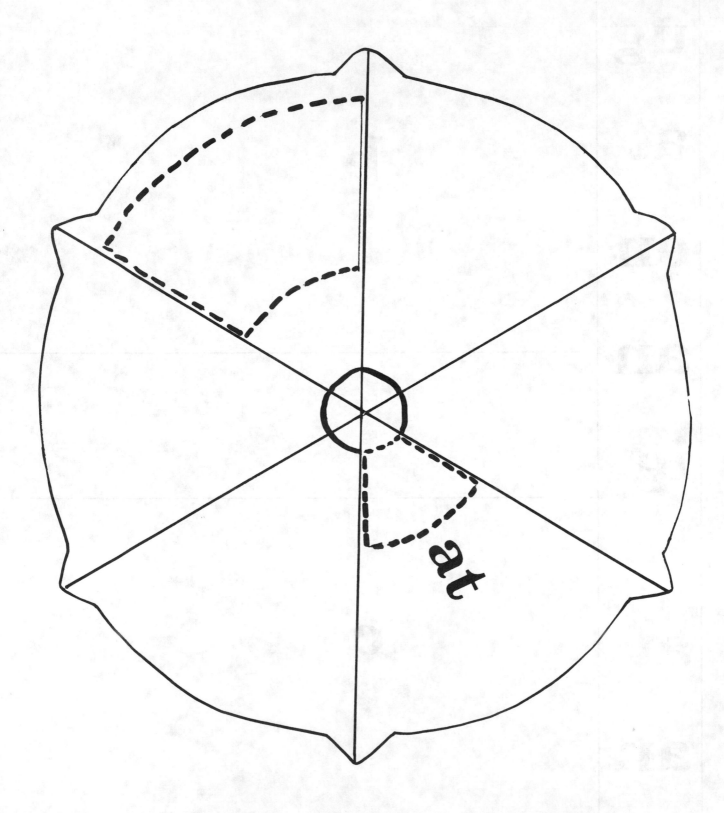

at

Cut along dotted lines

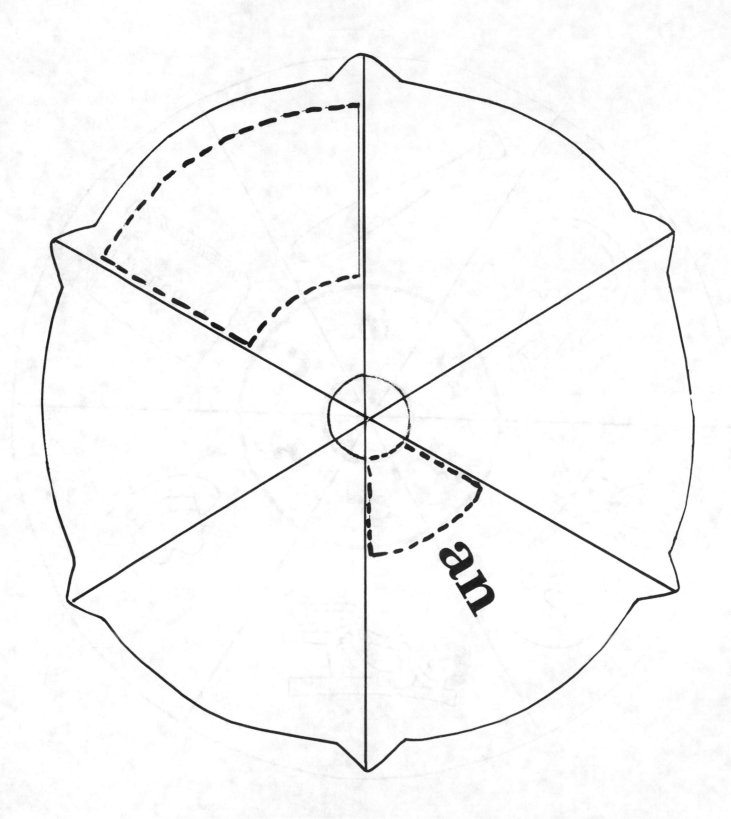

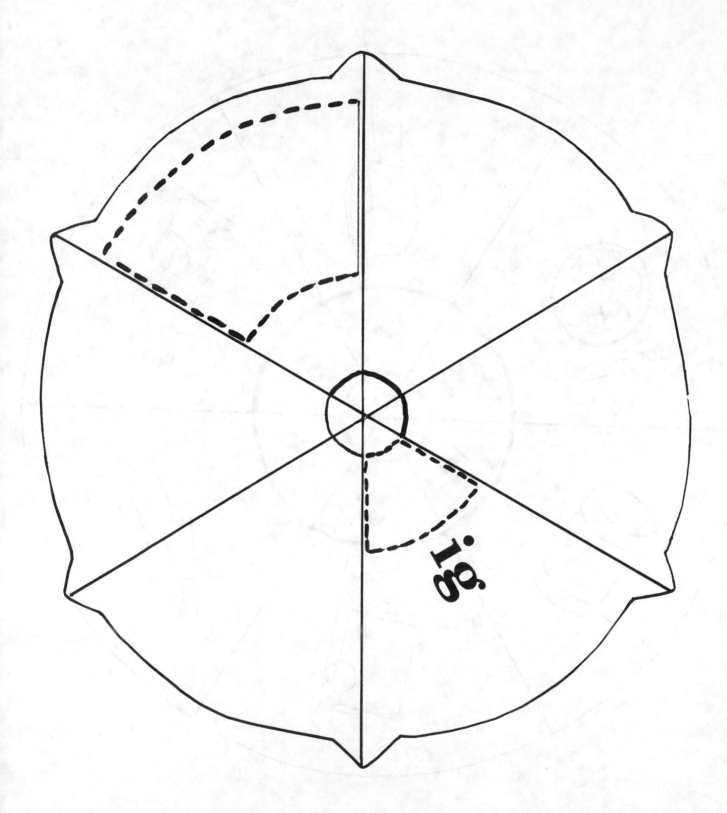

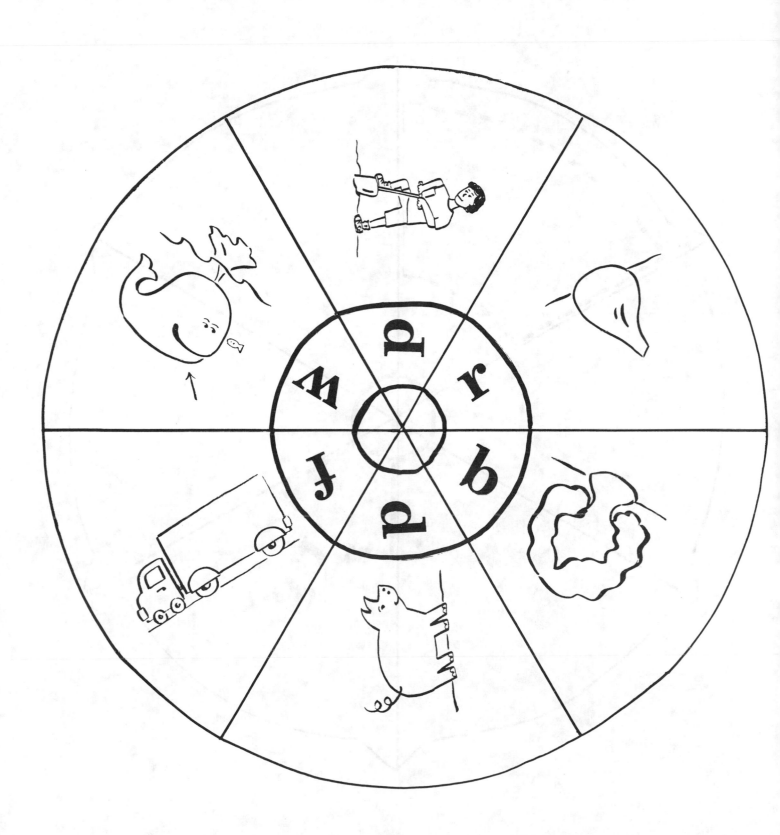

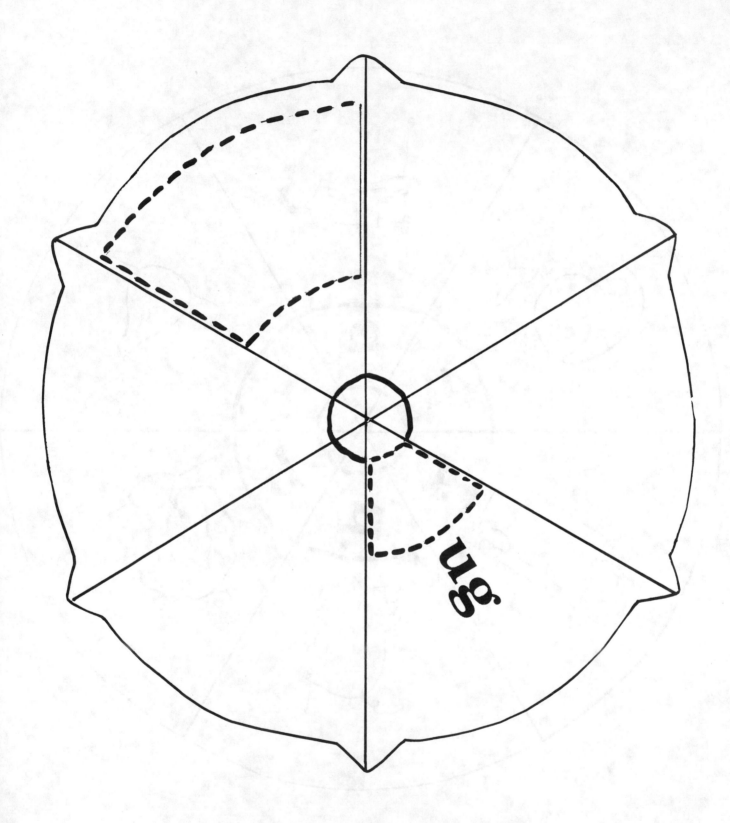

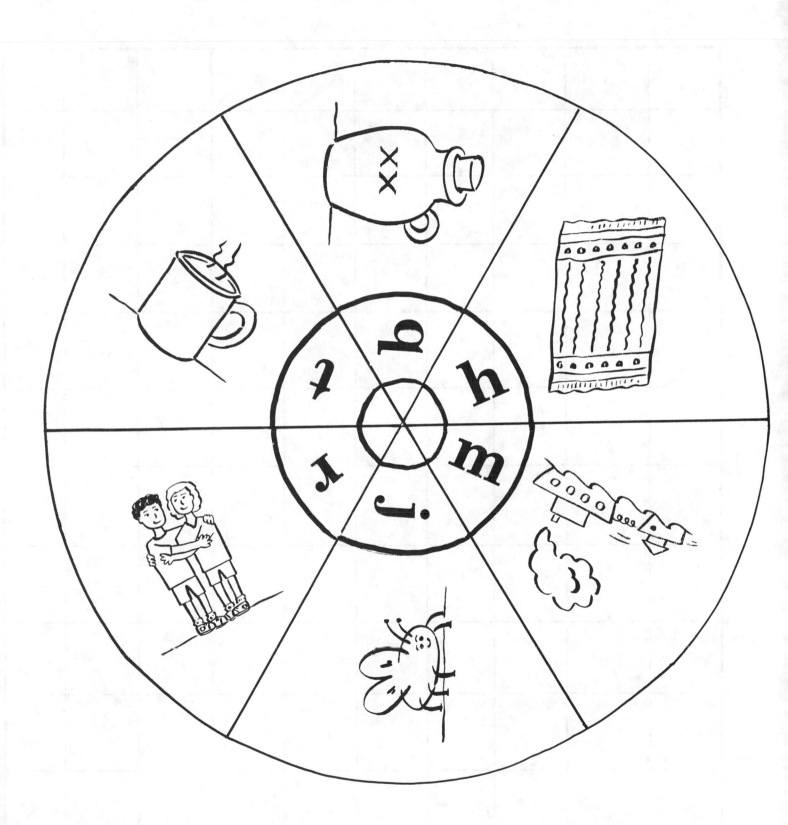

Crossword Puzzle No. 1

Crossword Puzzle: No. 1

Across:

3. I like to read a _____.
5. I shop at the _____.
7. My name is _____.
8. No means I don't want it; _____ means I want it.

Down:

1. Daddy and _____.
2. My brother's name is _____.
4. Mommy and _____.
6. I _____ you.
9. I _____ with my eyes.

Crossword Puzzle No. 1
Answers

				M¹			W²	
	B³	O	O	K			I	
				O			L	
	D⁴			M⁵	A	L⁶	L	
S⁷	A	L	L	Y		O		
	D					V		
	D					E		
	Y⁸	E	S⁹					
			E					
			E					

Crossword Puzzle No. 2

Crossword Puzzle: No. 2

Across:
1. The cat chases the _____.
3. I _____ with my eyes.
4. I love Daddy and _____.
7. It says meow, meow.
9. My _____ is Sally.
11. When I talk, I _____ words.
13. My name is _____.
15. You hit balls with it.

Down:
2. Also: I want to go _____.
3. I will not eat green eggs and ham; I will not eat them _____ I am.
5. Daddy is not a woman, but a _____.
6. When I don't want it, I say no; when I want it, I say _____.
8. A big family that cat, hat, bat, sat, and rat belong to.
10. This is _____ puzzle; it's mine.
12. When there is no more it is _____ gone.
13. Little Miss Muffit, _____ on her tuffet.
14. I _____ Mommy and Daddy.

Crossword Puzzle No. 2
Answers

	R¹	A	T²		S³	E	E		
			O						
		M⁴	O	M⁵	M	Y			
				A			Y⁶		
C⁷	A⁸	T		N⁹	A	M	E		M¹⁰
	T						S¹¹	A¹²	Y
								L	
					S¹³	A	L¹⁴	L	Y
					A		O		
			B¹⁵	A	T		V		
							E		

Doctor's Chart

Name_____ girl _____ boy _____

eyes hurt?	yes / no	tummy hurt?	yes / no
nose hurt?	yes / no	hands hurt?	yes / no
ears hurt?	yes / no	arms hurt?	yes / no
mouth hurt?	yes / no	legs hurt?	yes / no
neck hurt?	yes / no	feet hurt?	yes / no
chest hurt?	yes / no	back hurt?	yes / no

Dr _____

Rx for _____

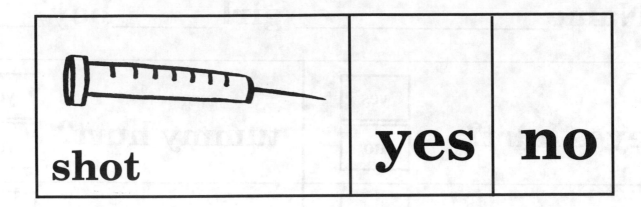

shot | **yes** | **no**

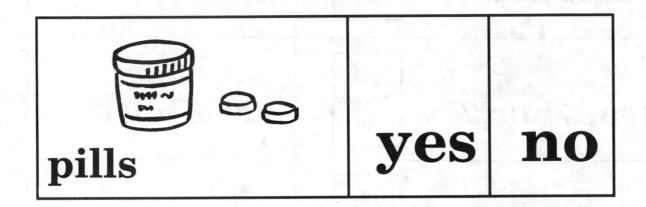

pills | **yes** | **no**

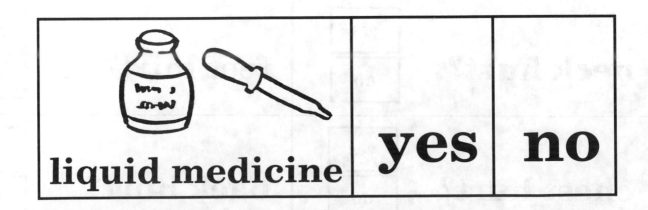

liquid medicine | **yes** | **no**

BREAKFAST MENU

Beverages

_____ apple juice
_____ orange juice
_____ cranberry juice
_____ milk
_____ hot chocolate

Cereals

_____ corn flakes
_____ Cheerios
_____ Rice Krispies
_____ oatmeal
_____ cream of wheat

Breads

_____ toast
_____ English muffin
_____ bagel
_____ muffin

Main Dishes

_____ omelet
_____ scrambled egg
_____ fried egg
_____ poached egg
_____ French toast
_____ pancakes
_____ waffles

DAILY PROGRESS REPORT
for

_____

Date 3-10-94

1) I worked hard in Mrs. Ault's class.

2) I worked hard with other teachers.

3) I was a good listener during group times.

4) I played nicely on the playground.

DAILY PROGRESS REPORT
for
_____

1) I listened to my teachers in first grade.

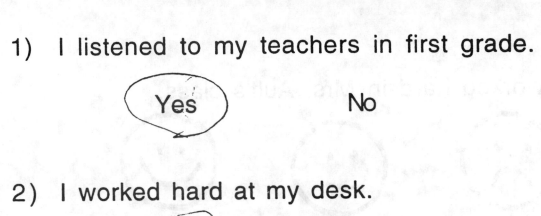

Yes   No

2) I worked hard at my desk.

Yes   No

3) I worked hard on the rug.

Yes   No

4) I played nicely on the playground.

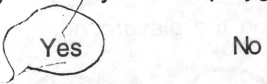

Yes   No

5) I worked hard in John's class.

Yes   No

The "AT" Family

PAT, THE FAT CAT

Pat, the fat cat, sat on the mat.

Nat, the rat, ran under the hat.

Pat, the fat cat, sat on the mat.

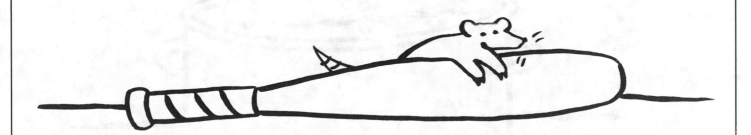

Nat, the rat, jumped onto the bat.

Pat, the fat cat, sat on the mat.

Nat, the rat, jumped into the vat.

Pat, the fat cat, left the mat.

Nat, the rat, sat on the mat.

Pat, the fat cat, sat on the rat on the mat.

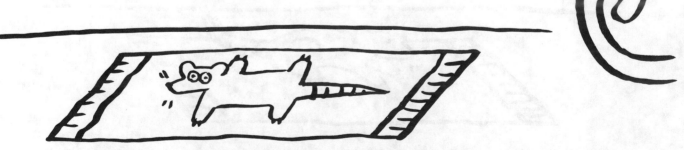

Now Nat, the rat, is flat on the mat.

The "AN" Family

MOVING DAY FOR JAN AND DAN

It is moving day for Jan and Dan.
"May we ride in the van with the man?" asked Jan.

"Yes, you may! Ask the man in the van!"

Dan ran to the man in the van.

"May we ride with you in the tan van?" asked Dan.

"Yes, you may," said the man in the van.

"Bring juice in the can and snacks in a pan."

Dan and Jan ran to the van with juice in the can and snacks in a pan.

"It is hot in the van," said Dan.

"Turn on the fan," said the man.

Jan turned on the fan in the van.

Jan and Dan and the man felt cool in the van,

**under the fan, drinking juice from the can
and eating snacks from a pan.**

Good-bye, Jan. Good-bye, Dan.

Write when you can!

Appendix E–3

DOUG THE BUG

Doug the bug lived on a tug.
The tug had rugs to lug.

Doug the bug was lonely on the tug.
Doug said, "I need a bug to hug."

Doug the bug went to look for a bug to hug.
Doug looked in a jug and found a pug.
"No pug in a jug!" said Doug,
"I need a *bug* to hug!"

Doug the bug looked in a mug and found a slug.
"No slug in a mug!" said Doug,
"I need a *bug* to hug!"

Doug the bug looked at the lug.
Doug said, "There must be a bug in a rug on that lug."

Doug left the tug and went to the lug
and found a bug in a rug.

"Just what I need," said Doug,
"A bug in a rug to hug."

Doug the bug is very smug
in the rug with a bug to hug.

BEN AND KEN AND THE HEN

Ben and Ken, two men, had a hen in their den.
"We need a pen for our hen," said Ben.

"How many posts do we need for the pen?" asked Ken.
"We need ten," said Ben, "Ten posts for the pen."

The men, Ben and Ken, built a pen for the hen.

"We need a house for the hen," said Ben.
"How many boards for the house?" asked Ken.
"We need ten," said Ben.

The men, Ben and Ken, built a house for the hen in the pen.

The hen laid eggs in the house in the pen.
"How many eggs?" asked Ken.
"Ten eggs under the hen," said Ben.

The men, Ben and Ken, left the eggs under the hen.

The hen in the pen sat on the eggs, and then,
the eggs cracked open.
And then there are chicks in the pen with the hen.
"How many chicks in the pen?" asked Ken.
"Ten chicks in the pen with the hen," said Ben.

The men, Ben and Ken, are happy in the pen
with ten chicks and the hen.

Now no one is in the den,
not the the men, the chicks, or the hen.
They like it in the pen.

The End

SIG AND MIG JIG

A pig named Sig
wanted to jig.
He called his friend Mig
and said, "Let's go to the gig."

"Okay," said Mig,
"but I need a wig for this gig.
I have just a twig."

"My pants are too big to jig," said Sig.
"These do not fit this pig."

Sig and Mig got in Sig's rig
and went to buy pants and a wig.

"I want the big wig," said Mig.
"I want the fancy pants," said Sig.

"I dig this big wig," said Mig.
"I dig these fancy pants," said Sig.

"Are you ready to jig?"

"No, I want a fig," said Mig.
"Make mine small," said Sig.
"Make mine tall," said Mig.

Sig and Mig got in Sig's rig
and went to the gig.

Mig went zag
and Sig went zig;
Sig in fancy pants
and Mig in the wig.

"I dig this gig," said Sig.
"I dig this pig," said Mig.

ROY, THE COY BOY

Roy was a boy who was very coy.
He played with a toy But not with joy.

Roy watched Ray play
by the bay with clay and in the hay.

He wanted a way that he could say
that he wanted to play with Ray.

And then one day along came Jay and Fay
and took Roy's toy away
and threw it in the bay.

"Ahoy! ahoy! There goes my toy!"
shouted Roy.

Ray heard Roy
and came to save the toy.

"Hold my hand," said Ray.
"It's the safe way
to get the toy out of the bay."

Ray gave the toy back to Roy.

"Thanks for saving my toy," said Roy.
"It's okay," said Ray,
"Want to play?"

Roy and Ray played by the bay,
in the hay, with the clay,
with Roy's toy
and felt lots of joy.

Now Roy is not coy but a happy boy.
He can say, "Ray, want to play?"
And Roy and Ray play every day.

Roy knows the way to ask Ray to play.

TAD, THE LAD, HAD A FAD

There was a lad named Tad,
who liked to wear the latest fad.

This lad named Tad had a silly fad.
For a hat he wore a pad.

His dad was mad
Because of this fad.
He didn't like the pad Tad had.

Dad said, "Tad, that pad looks bad.
You look like a cad."
Tad said, "Dad, I *like* my pad.
It is the fad."
Dad said, "The pad looks bad, Tad."

Tad, the lad, was sad.
He did not want to look bad, like a cad.
He did not want his dad mad.

His dad gave him a hat he had.
Dad said, "Wear it this way.
It is the fad."

Now Tad is glad.
He has a fad.

He likes the hat his dad had.

His dad is glad, not mad.
He likes the hat fad on Tad the lad.

Appendix E–4

I LIKE TO

I like to jump up
    and jump down;
Sit on the floor
    and crawl around.

I like to listen to music
    and stomp my feet;
Clap my hands
    and keep the beat.

I like to kick a ball
    and throw it high;
Ride my bike
    and say, "Bye, bye!"

I like to climb up
    and drop down;
Swing up high
    and ride the merry-go-round.

I like to walk outside
    and hop back in;
Play bingo
    and *win, win, win!*

I like to get dressed up
    and look my best;
Watch TV
    and take a rest.

I like to run fast
    and fly my kite;
Watch the birds
    fly out of sight.

I like to tip-toe
    and stand up tall;
Stack up blocks
    and make them fall.

I like to swim
    and make a splash;
Go down the slide
    in a dash.

I like to read a book
    and sing a song;
And make Mommy happy
    all day long.

I like to laugh at cartoons
    and smile at friends;
Open the door
    and say, "Come in!"

I like to go to McDonald's
    and eat a lot;
Play treasure hunt
    and mark the spot.

I like to kiss my Mom
    and hug my Dad;
Pat my dog
    and go to bed.

Good night!

TREASURE HUNTS
(OR I LOOK AND LOOK AND LOOK)

I go on treasure hunts.

and look and look and look;

in the sink,

in the dryer,

and even in a book.

I look on the table,

on the lamp,

and on the wall;

I read my clues and follow them all.

I look under the bed,

under the desk,

and under the chair.

I look and look and look *everywhere*.

I look in the mirror, and what do I see?

I see the treasure looking back at me!

ALL ABOUT ME

I am a girl.

I am a boy.

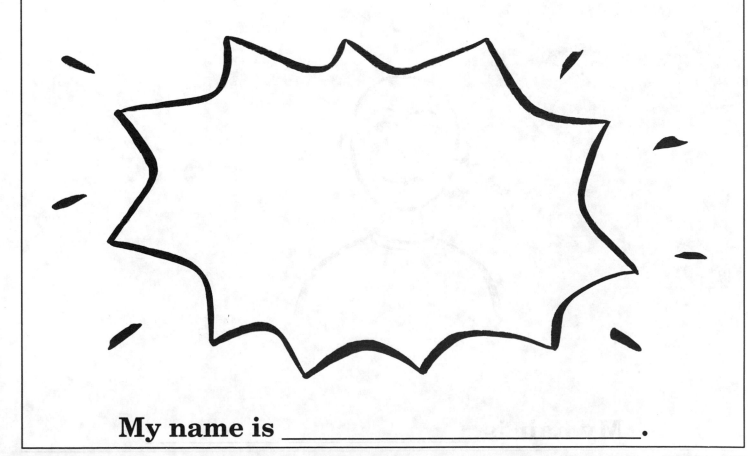

My name is _____ .

I am _____ **years old.**

My hair is _____.

My eyes are _____.

I have 2 eyes, 1 nose and many teeth.

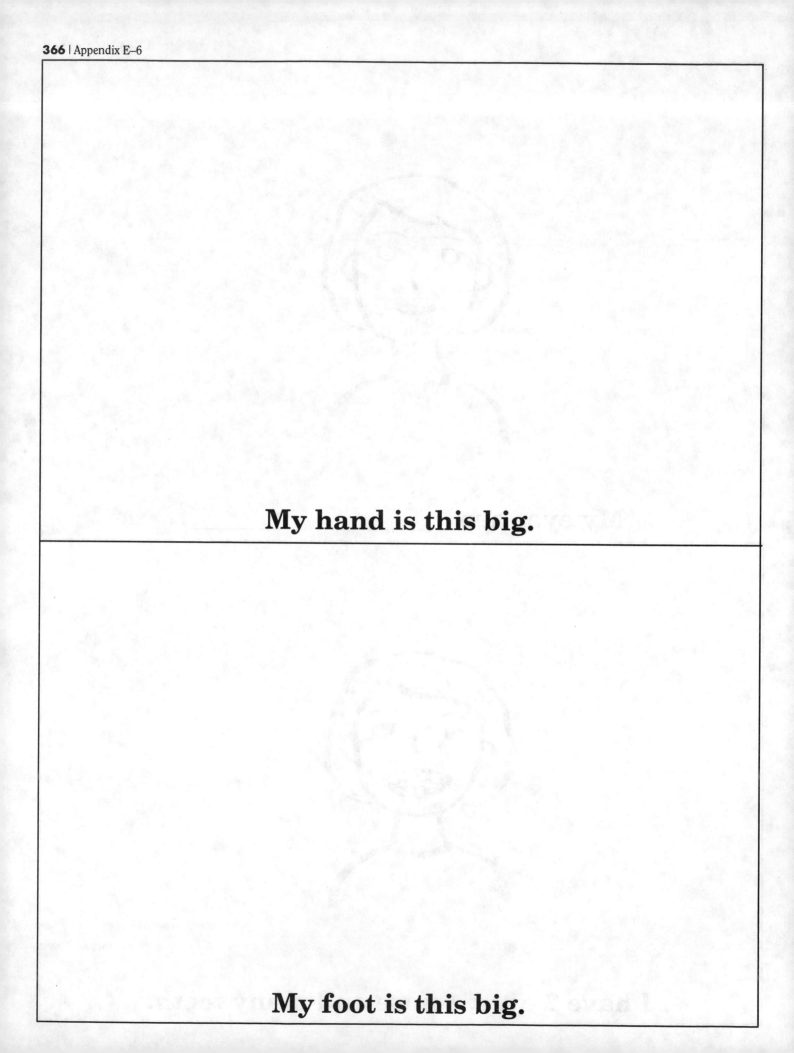

My hand is this big.

My foot is this big.

Index